*Moral Anatomy and
Moral Reasoning*

Moral Anatomy and Moral Reasoning

ROBERT V. HANNAFORD

 UNIVERSITY PRESS OF KANSAS

Published by the University Press of Kansas (Lawrence, Kansas 66049), which was or-
ganized by the Kansas Board of Regents and is operated and funded by Emporia State
University, Fort Hays State University, Kansas State University, Pittsburg State University, the University of Kansas, and Wichita State University

Library of Congress Cataloging-in-Publication Data

Hannaford, Robert V., 1929–
    Moral anatomy and moral reasoning / Robert V. Hannaford.
      p. cm.
    Includes index.
    ISBN 0-7006-0607-6
    1. Ethics, Modern—20th century. 2. Self (Philosophy)
  3. Reasoning. I. Title.
    BJ319.H276 1993
    171′.3—dc20   93-18648

British Library Cataloguing in Publication Data is available.

Printed in the United States of America
10 9 8 7 6 5 4 3 2 1

Contents

Preface

Although I have been critical of many contemporary philosophers, the ideas of this book are heavily indebted to them, and particularly to P. F. Strawson, Marcus Singer, and John Rawls.

I have benefited a great deal from discussions and comments of many readers, but I am especially indebted to my colleagues, Vance Cope-Kasten, Michael Pritchard, Laurence Thomas, and Thomas Wren.

While many portions of the book have been presented as papers, chapters 4 and 6 are based on articles printed in *The Journal of Value Inquiry* and *The International Journal of Moral and Social Studies*. I am grateful to the editors for permission to reprint this material.

Many people have been supportive, but I am especially thankful for the help and guidance of Cynthia Miller, editor-in-chief of the University Press of Kansas, and the other editors on the staff of the press.

Abbreviations

Abbot	Immanuel Kant. "Foundations of the Metaphysics of Morals." In *Critique of Practical Reason and Other Works in the Theory of Ethics*, edited by T. K. Abbot. London: Longmans, Green, 1959.
E	David Hume. *Enquiry Concerning the Principles of Morals*. Indianapolis: Hackett, 1983.
L	Thomas Hobbes. *Leviathan*, edited by M. Oakeshott. Oxford: Blackwell, 1957.
M	John Mackie. *Ethics: Inventing Right and Wrong*. London: Penguin, 1977.
MA	David Gauthier. *Morals by Agreement*. Oxford: Clarendon Press, 1986.
Matthews	Joseph Butler. *Dissertation on the Nature of Virtue*. In *Butler's Sermons and Dissertation in the Nature of Virtue*, edited by W. R. Matthews. London: Bell, 1958.
MR	Bernard Gert. *The Moral Rules*. New York: Harper and Row, 1973.
N	Thomas Nagel. *The Possibility of Altruism*. Oxford: Oxford University Press, 1970.
S	Richard Shweder. "Anthropology's Romantic Rebellion against the Enlightenment." In *Culture Theory: Essays on Mind, Self and Emotion*, edited by Richard Shweder and R. A. Levine. New York: Cambridge University Press, 1984.
TMS(S)	Adam Smith. "The Theory of the Moral Sentiments," pt. 3, chap. 1. In *Adam Smith's Moral and Political Phi-*

losophy, edited by H. Schneider. New York: Hafner, 1948.

W   Peter Winch. *Idea of a Social Science*. London: Routledge and Kegan Paul, 1958.

1 / Responsiveness and Responsibility

What motives lead us to act morally? How does our being moral relate to what we are and how we're related to each other? Pursuing the answer to the question of motives led me to an awareness of the role of our moral anatomy in moral reasoning and to a new view of moral theory. These questions will be my central concerns in this book.

I will argue that our reasonings about what is morally right proceed from our understanding of what we take to be the human response; that is, they proceed from our understanding of how persons respond, act, and are affected as moral beings. I will seek to show that in judging persons and situations, we generalize, using our conception of what we are as persons: our motives and responses, how we affect each other, and how we can reason to moral agreement. I conclude that it is imperative that those who give an account of morality be clear about these elements of our nature, since our sense of personhood determines our every move in moral reasoning.

I began these reflections through struggling with the puzzles about motives for moral action that crop up in the history of ethical theory.[1] In asking the question "How do we want to do what we ought to do or what is morally demanded?" we seem to be asking "How should we conceive of our inclinations?" and "How are they related to moral evaluation and morally responsible action?" Thinking about these motive questions led me to a different conception of the nature of the person and the different inclinations that enter into moral reasoning and responsible moral choice.

We can get at this conception of the nature of the person by speaking about the relation between responsiveness to other persons and our thinking about what is moral—about what we may do and what we may become. The title of the book is intended to point up the fact that moral reasoning and acting in a morally responsible way are dependent on our having and using a sense of our moral anatomy—that is to say, of our concerns, capacities, and attitudes.

This follows from what we mean by "morally responsible"—or from what I take it that we should mean. By acting in a morally responsible way, we should mean being willing and able to respond to others in the community in ways that are morally approved—i.e., in ways that are acceptable to the judgment of the community's members. This parallels the approach of Hume, according to which the notion of morals implies reference to "general approbation . . . [which would] render the action and conduct, even of persons the most remote, an object of applause or censure, according as they agree or disagree with that rule of right which is [thus] established."[2] That is to say, to be morally responsible we must be willing and able to reason about and make choices in ways that take account of others' interests and preferences. As responsible people, for example, we provide food and water for the victims of an urban riot or a nearby natural disaster, and when we are met by a lost child, we try to help it in finding its parents. As responsible people we respond to the demands of the situation, making choices that we believe can be shown to be acceptable to others in our community. What is morally correct must reflect the judgment of the moral community. That it must reflect the judgment of the community indicates that we, as responsible agents, are accountable to a community. Regard for a *community* of judges is central to the concept of moral responsibility.[3]

What I am talking about, then, is how we come to what Adam Smith speaks of as "the desire of being what ought to be approved of,"[4] the attitude by which we want to reason our way to acceptable, cooperative decisions. Other notions cluster around this one of moral responsibility—compassion, moral education, authority, customary practices and codes, to mention a few—but I want first to consider these in relation to reasoning to moral agreement.

First, we need to identify the particular kinds of motivation and particular kinds of reasoning involved in reaching moral agreement. I say it reflects particular kinds of motivation because to be prepared to act in ways that others could accept is to be willing to accommodate others' interests in our actions. Thus, in addition to pursuing self-interest, as responsible people we must also be prepared to consider acting in behalf of the interest of others and in behalf of the agreements we can reach with them. For example, in disposing of toxic wastes, we must consider the possible effects on others and how we can cooperate to avoid causing injury to anyone. To be prepared to accommodate others' interests means that we take an interest in others as persons and that our responses reflect concern for them. If we are prepared to act out of concern for them, we will also be prepared to uphold agreements made in support of common concerns. Thus, one of our tasks in explaining moral reasoning must be to explain and argue for the connection among these three motives: concern for self, concern for others, and interest in upholding moral agreements.

I choose "concern for others" to refer to the attitudes and feelings involved because that phrase covers the range of responses from the routine interest that is minimally required of us to the dedicated devotion that special moral relationships require. Moral responsibility requires at the least a concern for others; it requires that we be responsive (and not indifferent) to others' feelings and sufferings. By saying one is responsive to others, I mean one desires something because one thinks that the other desires or needs it. I will argue that we are called upon to be responsive in some measure to everyone we have to do with, but special others, such as friends and lovers, have a special right to demand of us sustained and attentive care—at times devotion.

I say that the notion of responsibility also reflects a particular kind of reasoning because we must reason together to reach moral agreement, and the disposition to reason together is a particular kind of mind-set. To reason with others, we must aim for ways of acting that will accommodate both our own and others' interests; our proposals must be made in the light of what others want and could claim within the demands of the situation. For example, in working out a way of disposing of a community's sewage we must be alive to the possible damage we could cause to others or their property. Others involved must be addressing the situation in a similar frame of mind. We can roughly describe the process of reasoning together by saying it requires mutual awareness, concern, and accommodation.

We need to be explicit about the mutuality: the reasoning leads us to accommodate each other because we are aware of and concerned for each other, and relationships involving special concern typically bring us to a deeper awareness of the other's situation. It also leads us to accommodate each other because our awareness and concern is reciprocal: we *see each other* as aware, concerned, and prepared. Mutual preparedness is, as Hobbes suggested, a precondition for proceeding toward moral agreement. The practical reasoning by which we direct our moral choices turns on reciprocating awareness: consciousness of oneself as *being in relationship* with others and as defining oneself in relationship with others. Our awareness of others and our relationship with them can proceed only through our reflections about our past interactions with them; our recognition of this point will lead us to see that the growth of responsibility is a gradual process in which we build on earlier reasoning and relationships.

That point will cut against the notion of coming to "an age of reason" as if it were sharply demarcated, like the time when a boy's voice changes. Although I draw heavily on John Rawls, my account will lead us to modify his theory of sequential stages of moral reasoning (along with those of Piaget and Kohlberg). According to the stage theories, one arrives at true moral reasoning and concern—if one arrives at all—only after passing through "lower" stages. By contrast, I argue that a child's awareness and concern for others are there *from the beginning* and that they must be there for children to learn the language and to learn to respond as they do.

As skill in moral reasoning is developed through the child's using these capacities successively, it's important that we *not* follow the "age of reason" or "stages of development" views of the moral person. If we did accept and follow them and (as a consequence) waited for a child to reach an "age of reason" or "mature stage" before introducing him or her to the process, we would effectively thwart the child's learning. It would be as if, in teaching the child to speak, we waited for the child to reach "the age of language" before talking to it. Thus, understanding the nature of the moral person—understanding moral anatomy—is fundamental to understanding moral reasoning and education, and these are fundamental to understanding the attainment of virtue and its relation to a life worth choosing. Even though many twentieth-century moral theorists have treated such questions as if they were alien to moral theory, these are issues that cannot be sidestepped: moral relationships turn on the psychological.

Many theorists have been reluctant to face psychological questions because they were anxious to avoid introspective speculation, many believing that these are questions that can be effectively addressed only by psychologists. As I share their concern about having solid evidential support for an account of the moral anatomy, it's important to note the kind of argument and evidence I have used in support of my account. My arguments are partly conceptual and partly empirical. A basic argument of the book centers on the following (somewhat Kantian) reflection: we see that responsible persons must engage in moral reasoning and language use; hence, by asking how the judgment and language use are possible, we can get at the question of what capacities must be involved in becoming responsible persons. Underlying these questions is the question of what conception of person we must employ in the talking and reasoning we use to develop these abilities. That is to say: What characteristics of persons are necessary for the process of talking and reasoning about people in moral situations? What must they feel? How must they be related to each other?

I'll argue that the process depends on each of us seeing others as persons like ourselves. Moral reasoning focuses on what we ought to do in a situation where we consider what others want or might want to do: it's about doing. Thus, the reasoning requires the conception of persons as agents; one of the senses in which a person is responsible is that he or she is the agent by which a change has been brought (or could have been brought) about. Responsible persons are capable of bringing about appropriate change by selecting appropriate means or instruments. As responsible agents we must describe and conceive of human action as intentional and voluntary: we must view ourselves as electing courses of action from the alternatives that are open to us.

In order to do this and see others as doing this, we must see ourselves as having control over what we do—some measure of control at least. We must also see ourselves as having control over our actions in order to accept responsibility for the action as our own. Underlying the notion of responsibility as being able and willing to respond and as being able to conceive and describe one's action lies the notion of an activity that one elects to do and has control over. Hence, if we're to be coherent, we must see persons as voluntary, intending agents, capable of controlled action.[5]

Much of my argument is based on what is required for the language use in moral reasoning: reciprocal awareness and concern for others are essential to learning and developing these processes. We must conceive of each other as persons among persons to communicate with the language; each of us must conceive of ourselves as a person among persons to arrive at generally acceptable moral judgments.[6]

Moral reasoning, with its mutually acceptable moral judgments, centers on treating each as a person among persons. Thus, it has a standard of fairness built into it. Moreover, the idea of treating people equitably is fundamental to the concept of law, a concept by which people are to be treated in the same way, in accord with a rule.

These reflections will lead us to recognize the point that the concept of oneself as a person among persons, which is required for us to think about ourselves, is also integral to the moral reasoning process and is intimately connected with norms of law and justice, which helps to account for the universality—or near universality— of these notions. It also helps to account for the fact that the Golden Rule ("Do unto others as you would have others do unto you"), or one of its variations, is a prominent feature of the world's religious and ethical traditions, a theme taken up in chapter 7. To become morally responsible we must not only be capable of responding with concern to others, we must see ourselves to be members of a community of persons with whom we can reason toward agreement in defining standards of rightness.

ASKING TOO MUCH?

It may be felt that this asks too much. On one hand, it may be granted (after more argument) that we could not share a moral language (in the way that we do) if we did not have the capacity to reason to agreement and to treat as authoritative the criteria by which community of agreement is achieved. As the ability to appreciate persons and the ability to use moral language to reason seem to be universal (or nearly so), there seems to be no doubt that almost all people have the required *capacity*. But, on the other hand (doubters may counter), even if it is a fact that we share these capacities, it also seems to be a fact that on a day-to-day basis, many people do not much care for others. Or they might observe that many do not think of themselves as members of—or responsible to—a moral community, possibly because they see themselves as cut out of the society they live in. Thus, it may be argued that to ask for concerned responsiveness and a sense of membership in a community of reasoners is to ask for more than many people are prepared to deliver. Hence, it may be said, this approach requires too much: "It kicks too many people out of our moral community."

But our approach must be consistent with, and help to account for, the facts. One of the facts is that many people do fail to take responsibility for many of their actions; those who always fail could not be considered a *part* of a moral community. A viable approach must also be consistent with the fact that we have a moral language in which honesty and justice hold a special place of honor and blame goes to those who fail to achieve them. If many people were not outside the moral community, we would not have the occasion to use the rich vocabulary that we have for expressing moral blame and describing immorality.

Many people are not, or do not see themselves to be, within a moral community (and the terms of our language indicate that we can identify them). Many do not find themselves among people who exhibit moral concern and hence, do not conceive of themselves as part of a community of concern. One of the points that emerges from my account is that our preparedness to enter into responsible, cooperative action is typically conditional on there *being* such concern or the hope of it. As we'll consider in chapter 6, those who see themselves as confronted by predatory threats find their capacity for responding with concern for others to be diminished. Moreover, they find no sense of a community of concern and perhaps no reason to hope for one. Thus, though the human capacities necessary to responsible action seem to be universal, the conditions, the healthy moral communities that are likely to elicit responsible behavior from us, are not.

It is a fact that some people do not become responsible; it is a fact that some are outside of moral communities. One of my objectives is to see what we could do to bring them into a community through changing the way they see themselves. I hope to remove some of the obstacles to that way of seeing oneself: misconceptions, misgivings, and misunderstandings that work against those conditions.

The language of this book is related to that understanding. As I've noted, I have borrowed from and extended arguments from recent studies in personal identity and action theory. To do this I have at times had to use the terminology introduced in these studies. But, in general, I have sought to avoid technical language, however useful it might be for some theoretical purposes, because I judged it to be unsuitable for my purpose: to get as clear as I can about how ordinary people come to take responsibility and enter into a community of moral reasoners. Taking responsibility and entering into such a community are activities that people must do for themselves and conceive of for themselves. If we are to get clear about how ordinary people are to reason and to conceive of themselves as responsible, I conclude that we cannot stray far from the natural language in which they do their reasoning and conceiving.

IMPLICATIONS FOR ETHICAL THEORIES
AND NORMS

In holding that in moral reasoning we use that language to generalize on the basis of mutual awareness and concern, I hold that we proceed from a plurality of inclinations and form our judgments on the basis of the (often unique) particulars of persons' situations.

Adopting my account will lead to changes in ethical theories. It will lead us to modify theories that attempt to derive all moral motives or any moral principle from a single kind of inclination (as do those of Rawls, Hobbesians, many game theorists, and many Utilitarians). It will equally lead us to modify those theories that attempt to derive all moral injunctions from a single principle (as do those of Kant and many Kantians). Nor would we be able to treat moral judgment as the work of an essentially isolated universalizer (as in John Mackie's *Ethics* and in R. M. Hare's *Moral Thinking*).

Yet, this account provides support for norms such as fairness and the concept of law. They surface when we analyze the process of moral reasoning; in analyzing it, we see a community that uses, acknowledges, and insists on such standards. We see that they are norms of a reasoning moral community and that they have their life and importance in being used by people. We shall thus need to look both at samples of moral reasoning and at the requirements packed into such reasoning.

These requirements appear in crystallized form when we look together at the terms used to express particular moral judgments that we can agree to. In looking at the usage of such terms (beginning in chapter 2), we will be looking at the way these norms work in a reasoning moral community. A sustained and wide-ranging look at a community's usage of moral terms (although it is not undertaken in this book) would give a complete portrait of how we reason using moral terms. But even with our briefer look, we will be able to describe how they function as norms.[7]

The life of the norms and the forms of reasoning is *in* their use and, as I shall try to demonstrate, we see that people apply them in simple cases with speed, confidence, and skill. When we consider some of the familiar examples in which agreement in moral reasoning is easily reached (in chapter 2), it will be clear that the community of moral reasoning and its standards of reasoning and motivation are at the center of the ordinary person's reasoning and sense of self. It will become apparent that we, in fact, use its standards as a basis for assigning blame or for evaluating excuses.

The concepts of moral anatomy and moral reasoning outlined above and developed in the book are parallel to some of the themes in recent feminist literature—specifically to the notions that a person is a being-in-relationships, one whose reasoning is informed and given point by those relationships.

But these concepts are at odds with some currently fashionable notions that are woven together into a kind of popular dogma, a dogma that is often uncritically assumed to be required by a scientific view of the world. Built into the dogma are notions about individualism, rationality, and egoistic motivation. I will argue not only that these notions are not required for a scientific view of the world, but that they are not even coherent. Those who are unimpressed with the popular dogma and its claims to be scientifically grounded may wish to skip its discussion and move directly to chapter 2. But for others it may be helpful to consider briefly here some of the weaknesses of the supposedly scientific dogma and the ways in which it is opposed to the concept of the person and moral action I hope to advance.

THE "SCIENTIFIC" DOGMA

Individualism

The concepts of person, reasoning, and motive developed in the book are opposed to the individualist belief that a person's identity, judgment, and values are, or ought to be considered to be, independent of any community. The concept of the person as one who must come to see oneself and define oneself in relation to others like one-self—as a person among persons—is radically opposed to those species of individualism that see the person as having no significant dependence on others in the community. By contrast (I argue) a language learner and a moral reasoner must conceive of him- or herself as like others, must describe him- or herself and actions by concepts and judgments on which all might agree. This leads to the point that one must judge the appropriateness of one's own and others' action by referring to common judgments and practices. The person who speaks and reasons must rely on a conception of him- or herself as bound up with others and with his or her place in the community. One cannot consistently conceive of oneself as having no dependence on the community (chapter 5).

The currently fashionable individualist stance is supported (typically) by the notion that rationality is based on cost-benefit analysis directed toward seeking one's own satisfaction. This notion gets a prominent play in arguments detailing what it is rational for an economic agent to do, arguments that take on a scientific aura because they are based on Adam Smith's supposed observation that everyone is motivated to pursue just his or her own economic advantage. The argument goes something like this: "One can fulfil one's rational social responsibility as a business person (or as any economic agent) just by seeking to maximize profits, because that's what a business person does—read Adam Smith."

Now it must be acknowledged that there are passages in *Wealth of Nations* that seem to support this construction of Smith's views. In it, he writes: "All systems . . . of restraint . . . being . . . completely taken away, the obvious and simple system of natural liberty establishes itself of its own accord. Every man, *as long as he does not violate the laws of justice*, is left perfectly free to pursue his own interest in his own way, and to bring both his industry and capital into competition. . . ."[8] Passages such as this are often construed by our individualistic contemporaries to mean that Smith believed one could do anything one pleased in business as long as there was no law specifically prohibiting it. They can quote Smith and supposedly thereby prove that that's the way a free economy must work. This lack of any kind of constraint or compunction is justified by some variation of the "invisible hand" argument, again by quoting from *Wealth of Nations'* account of what "economic man" does:

By preferring the support of domestic to that of foreign industry, he intends only his own security; and by directing that industry in such a manner as its produce may be of greatest value, he intends only his own gain, and he is in this, as in many other cases, led by an invisible hand to promote an end which was no part of his intention. Nor is it always the worse for the society that it was no part of it. By pursuing his own interest he frequently promotes that of the society more effectually than when he really intends to promote it.[9]

Such passages are interpreted as condoning, even as urging, morally unconstrained egoism as essential to a free economy; many go further (e.g., Friedrich von Hayek and Milton Friedman) to make a laissez-faire economy necessary to a politically free society.

Those who are disposed to do so may quote Smith again in an effort to show that such egoism is psychologically necessary—in passages where Smith claims that the basic source of economic activity is found in our individual "desire of bettering our condition, a desire which . . . comes with us from the womb and never leaves us 'til we go to the grave." Such passages are construed by some to mean that Smith held that all people are always self-seeking. Now it's a short move from that belief to the stance that business people have no responsibility to do anything but what they can get by with under the law; that if they seek to maximize profits, they will be bringing the greatest happiness to the greatest number through "the silent Watchmen of our Prosperity."

However, this stance is quite incompatible with Smith's views as he had expressed them in *The Theory of the Moral Sentiments*. There we find him saying: "To feel much for others and little for ourselves, . . . to restrain our selfish, and to indulge our benevolent affections, constitutes the perfection of human nature; and can *alone* produce among mankind that harmony of sentiments and passions in which consists their whole grace and propriety."[10] Such passages not only show that he did not believe in, nor did he recommend, unconstrained egoism, they also show that when he spoke of the laws of justice as the only legitimate constraint of economic liberty (in *The Wealth of Nations*), he referred to normative and not to positive law. As an economist, he intended to say that people should be given complete economic freedom to pursue their interests so long as they behaved morally. But, in Smith's view (as I note in chapter 3), for the latter task they would have to be sensitive to, and concerned for, others' needs. Smith, like his friend, David Hume, held that agreement in moral judgment is founded on our capacity to respond to others with concern. This "individualism," advocated as if it were what Smith's views would require in a moral stance, not only wholly disregards fundamental moral demands, it also contradicts Smith's expressed views of what it means to be moral.

Rationality

If "rationality" is to refer to all reasoning, the notion of rationality, as the process whereby one finds and weighs the means by which one considers only one's own interests, is incompatible with the concept of reasoning (developed in my argument) as occurring through mutual awareness, concern, and accommodation. I'll argue that moral reasoning occurs through reciprocal awareness and concern, whereas, by the notion of "rationality" currently touted, being rational consists in pursuing just one's own interests or preferences by balancing benefits to oneself against costs to oneself in a given situation. This view, in suggesting that one can regard any situation as simply and obviously *given*, is specious in another way, since (as I argue in chapter 7) any social situation involves the interplay of concerns, interpretations, and awarenesses, any of which could change from moment to moment. Any such situation is likely to be volatile, elusive, and indeterminate: that will tell against "scientific" attempts to provide fixed frameworks or formulas for the analysis of all moral situations.

Egoism

The egocentric twist to this account of rationality often rests on the confusion of the senses of *interest*. By this account, to act rationally means to act for reasons; if one acts for reasons, one must act for one's own reasons; and to act for one's own reasons is to act in pursuit of what interests one;[11] hence (so the argument goes), to act rationally is necessarily to act in one's own interest. Each of these premises gives the appearance of being true by definition. This leaves us with the impression that it is a necesssary truth that only self-interested action is rational. The proponents of this statement may acknowledge that it is true that people do sometimes act benevolently but add that this proves nothing, since people do many irrational things. Thus, by calling all potential counterexamples irrational, they seal the statement off against any act that could count as a counterexample, and thus permit it to serve all the better as dogma.

This "proof" begins unobjectionably with "to be rational is to act for reasons," but an equivocation is introduced in the following steps: (1) the conclusion makes it apparent that the argument supposes that our acting in pursuit of what interests us is equal to our acting in our self-regarding interests (where "interests" is egoistically conceived); (2) now it will not do to argue that since we act in pursuit of our own interests, that we must act in pursuit of self-regarding interests: that we always have our own interests does not mean that we are always self-interested; that we always do the regarding does not entail that we are always self-regarding. We might as well argue that since we always look through our own eyes, we must always be looking at ourselves.

Yet this fallacy dies hard. This fallacy, or something very like it, though it is not often explicitly stated, is held as dogma (often bolstered by the notions of individualism, economic freedom, and rationality just outlined), and it stands as a barrier to grasping the conceptions of person, reasoning, and motive that I hope to lay out in the book. So, I want to try to remove that barrier by reminding the reader of some reasons for rejecting the egoist-individualist fallacy.

Joseph Butler presented arguments in the eighteenth century that should have laid to rest the fallacy's "necessary truth" that in each action we pursue just our own satisfaction and that all our interests are self-regarding. I turn now to Butler because his compressed arguments not only expose the egoist fallacy but are also helpful in setting out the relation between self-interest and our other interests. Two of Butler's (many) arguments are especially noteworthy here.

One of them deals with the notions that there is a reason for the distinctions made in ordinary speech and that the "use of common forms of speech, generally understood, cannot be falsehood." What we require for ordinary speech shows the falsity of the position. For, if we were to choose, Butler notes, to describe as selfish both an act done out of friendship and an act done out of desire for revenge, we would then need to mark the difference we see and, therefore, would "want words to express the difference" between them, for "it is manifest the principle of these actions are totally different and so want different words to be distinguished by; all that they agree in is that they both proceed from and are done to gratify an inclination in a man's self. But the principle or inclination in one case is self-love, in the other hatred . . . of another."[12] Thus, if we, in following the fallacious reasoning, were to describe all acts as selfish (because all proceed from a person's interests), we would immediately need to distinguish self-regarding "selfish" acts from self-sacrificing or generous "selfish" acts, for the existence of the latter kind of acts is too obvious to be ignored.

Butler's most important argument (for our purpose) begins with critically important definitions; he distinguishes self-love, as the general desire every person has for his or her own happiness, from the "particular affections, passions, and appetites to particular objects." What self-love pursues is "our own happiness, enjoyment, satisfaction." It never seeks anything external to the person for the sake of the thing (or person). But the "particular affections are toward the things themselves." Without such affection or passion for them, he notes, we could take no pleasure in them. He adds: "that all particular appetites and passions are toward external things themselves, distinct from the pleasure arising from them, is manifested from hence—that there could not be this pleasure were it not for that prior suitableness between the object and the passion; there could be no enjoyment or delight from one thing more than another."[13]

In support of Butler's notion that we have "particular affections" which elicit from us responses to persons and things, we note that we can take delight in experiencing the objects of our passion only if we both have the capacity to care for it and do in fact care for it; we can find a friendship deeply satisfying only if we care deeply for the friend; we can enjoy a concert only if we like music; we can take deep satisfaction in getting revenge only if we feel some dislike for the person. If we use "self-love" or "selfish" to refer to our concern for our own happiness, we refer, as Butler says, to our concern about something internal, a concern that to Butler seems "inseparable from all sensible creatures who can reflect on themselves."

Butler uses his distinction to argue for the point that if we are to pursue our own happiness—if we are to achieve the object of our self-love—we must act out of our passions for particular things and persons external to ourselves. Self-love is the desire and concern for one's own happiness, says Butler; it is no more the thing itself than the desire for wealth is riches. Our happiness is derived from the *satisfaction* of the several passions and affections for persons and things external to ourselves. Self-love will often put us to work seeking satisfaction through the several passions, but unless we take delight in the objects of those passions for themselves, our work will be to no avail. If self-love would keep us concentrated on our selves, it would be self-defeating. Butler concludes, "So that if self-love wholly engrosses us, and leaves no room for any other principle, there can be absolutely no such thing at all as happiness."[14] Butler's point is that we must have a genuine regard for the person or thing itself and not just for the pleasure we plan to derive from it, if it is to be a satisfying experience.

In support of Butler's point, consider what would happen if anyone, posing as our friend, pursued that association seeking only his or her own satisfaction. The person would be frustrated in the attempt: it would not work as a friendship, and it would not be satisfying. In fact, it sometimes happens that we find ourselves with such people. When we do, we have no difficulty seeing the difference between them and one who is truly a friend. And we take care to avoid such pretenders. Loneliness and the desire for friendship may set us to work *searching* for a friend, but we will never achieve a friendship—and, as Aristotle noted, we will not have the satisfactions proper to a friendship—until there is real regard for the other person for his or her own sake. It will not come close to becoming a friendship so long as one of the parties keeps just his or her own satisfaction in mind.

Or, consider the kind of satisfaction to be had from a concert or an evening at the theater. In self-love you attend only to your own satisfaction. If you spend the evening asking yourself if you're enjoying it (as you would if you acted only out of self-love), you are bored to the point of misery. To find the concert or the play satisfying, you must love the music or care about what's happening in the drama.

It is instructive to consider the number of linguistic devices we have for expressing satisfaction that indicate either separation from our normal selves or involvement with the subject matter. We say that we "lose ourselves in it"; that we are "rapt"; or in a "reverie"; or are "ecstatic"—outside our ordinary selves. Or we say that we were engrossed in a novel or totally immersed in a piece of music. By current idiom, we say that we can't enjoy a book until we can "get into it." As Butler says, the "use of common forms of speech, generally understood, cannot be falsehood"; the expressions could never have become current if they did not mark something common to our experience.

Such considerations should lead us to set aside the notion of rationality as pursuing only our self-interest; such "rationality" would be self-defeating, not to mention immoral. They should also lead us to set aside the notion that all actions are in pursuit of our own pleasure or David Gauthier's notion that in moral reasoning we "take no interest in others' interests."[15] My act of friendship could not be an act of friendship if it were not done with my friend's well-being in mind. If, in my reasoning, I give a "gift" anticipating some future reward for myself, I will not be giving anything to another but, rather, arranging for my own well-being by making a calculated investment in my own future.

I take it that Butler shows that "every particular affection, even the love of our neighbour, is as really our own affection as self-love," and that if we are to act in the world, we must take an interest in, and become involved with, the things and persons around us. David Gauthier and Bernard Gert, current writers whose views are considered in chapter 6, seem to question whether this sentiment is as universal as the earlier writers believed it to be and question whether it is steady enough to serve as the motive for moral reasoning and choice. The philosophical arguments (taken up in chapters 2 through 7) indicate that it is universal or nearly so.

But before looking to the arguments we should look to ourselves and to those around us. One way of doing this is to consider how we feel when we encounter someone striking a child or beating up on another person, particularly if the victim is defenseless and bound to suffer. The very mention of such an encounter is apt to stir our pulse. If we did not have this feeling, if we did not have this capacity for being stirred, it would not be possible to arouse and excite us by tales of violence, however sensational. The point here is that they could not *be* sensational, however sensational we might now feel them to be, if we did not have this capacity for compassion—if we did not have that "particular passion" or regard for others. Egoistically inclined theorists sometimes suggest that we are capable of responding with care only to those with whom we are involved. But, as Hume argues, the weakness of this position can be seen by reflecting on our attraction for histories and stories about people with whom we have no personal connection. For we thrill to Socrates' defense; we are outraged by Galileo's humiliation; and we are moved to grief by the history of Anne Frank.

The connection is even more remote with fictional heroes and heroines, yet their exploits move us to laughter and tears. At the outset of a film, we may know precisely nothing about the figures involved. We come to the event because we want to be entertained and know we can be interested, perhaps engrossed, in such stories. We are introduced to the heroine, perhaps just by an image of her staring through a window on a rainy night. But the author and director know of our capacity to respond; count on it; build on it; play on it as they would on a musical instrument. Two hours later, the movie ends and we find ourselves and hundreds of strangers sobbing together in the darkness. None of us has any special relation to the heroine; all of us give only the human response.

There could be no literature or drama were we not all—or nearly all—capable of responding with concern for persons. When we look to ourselves we see that our concern for persons is as truly our own affection as is our self-love; though not as strong and persistent, it's always potentially available for a moral response.

2 / Feelings, Reasons, and Persons

We have noted that when "moral" refers, as it commonly does, to judgment acceptable to a community, the life of a moral norm must be in its function in a community, and its function in a community must be reflected in the accepted use of moral terms. Just as we find that ordinary language usage indubitably makes sense (and thus bears on issues of meaning and knowing), so the ordinary examples of moral reasoning that are commonly accepted will be expressed in common language: what is mutually acceptable must be marked out and set forth in commonly recognized terms. In being held responsible to give an account, we are required to provide an account in our commonly understood expressions about our situation. Hence, by studying that language we can get clearer about questions of acceptable standards, of the structure of moral reasoning, and of the language of judgment.

As John Austin observes, in "A Plea for Excuses," "our common stock of words embodies all the distinctions men have found worth drawing, and the connexions they have found worth marking, in the lifetimes of many generations: these surely are likely to be more numerous, more sound, since they have stood up to the long test of the survival of the fittest, and more subtle, at least in all ordinary and reasonably practical matters, than any that you and I are likely to think up in our armchairs of an afternoon." We study such usage with profit because we can thereby view the structure of interpersonal relationships. Austin explains, "When we examine what we should say when, what words we should use in what situations, we are looking again not *merely* at words (or 'meanings', whatever they may be) but also at the realities we use the words to talk about: we are using a sharpened awareness of words to sharpen our perception of . . . the phenomena.'"[1] In looking at the way the terms of moral judgment are used we are looking at the way they function in a moral situation. Our use of ordinary moral terms indicates how we, as a moral community, perceive and respond to moral situations: what we can accept; what we agree to excuse; and what we condemn. Thus, in studying the use of those terms we open up the criteria for our patterns of judgment and moral reasoning.

My emphasis here is on *ordinary* examples of reasoning. By contrast, the problems in moral reasoning that philosophers are commonly invited to attend to are *extraordinary* in their difficulty and complexity. Consider the imponderable conundrums that have been brought under philosophers' recent scrutiny: from selecting the best of the alternative strategies for nuclear disarmament and developing resource allocation policies for Third World countries to anticipating problems from doing genetic research. All of these problems are important and worthy of our best attention but our considering them probably will not clarify the way the ordinary person reasons and applies moral language. For any kind of solution to these conundrums requires erudition, long chains of inference, and speculation about choices to be made by generations yet unborn. With the best of efforts by the most capable thinkers, there is room for much difference of opinion about the solutions to these problems. Far from being the kind of case to clarify the use of norms, the study of these conundrums raises a question in some minds about the very existence of moral norms; indeed, so intrepid a reasoner as John Mackie points to the difficulty in solving such problems as a reason for adopting moral skepticism.[2] The key point here is that a community's moral language and judgment must be for the entire community, and the ordinary people who make up the bulk of the community do not employ vast erudition, extensive speculation about future motives, or long chains of inference in applying moral terms and making their ordinary moral judgments. If they did, it seems obvious that we could never have developed any moral language at all, because we could never have been clear about which of the equally reasonable alternatives another person had in mind by using a term. Even the best of reasoners would be halting and uncertain in their reasoning, and consequently, there could be no common application of terms reflecting the outcome of such reasoning.

By contrast, ordinary people's choices of moral terms and the judgments implied by them are, in ordinary situations, often swift, clear, and confident. By studying these cases we begin to see a number of points emerge about the structure of moral reasoning and the demands that it makes. By studying the use of norms in simple and ordinary situations, I think we'll bring their application in complex cases into clearer focus, and we will be able to avoid some errors in our understanding of our moral anatomy.

If we consider such ordinary examples of accepted moral reasoning, I think one current view of moral reasoning will come to seem untenable and other kinds of theory implausible: the Kantian (or neo-Kantian) notion of reasoning as purely formal, independent of any interests or feelings, seems to be defeated by such evidence; and the evidence calls into question all views that seek to explain moral motive as proceeding from a single type of impulse—egoistic, rational, or altruistic. If we look at cases of ordinary judgment and at the solutions quickly and standardly agreed upon, we will see that in moral reasoning we commonly require feelings of concern for others as well as consideration of the case from the other's perspective. These cases also help us to see that, in moral decisions in which we feel conflicting impulses, we may find that there is some justification for each of the conflicting impulses; we'll be reminded, too, that our moral action in behalf of an individual is sometimes undertaken despite a feeling of hostility toward that individual. After we've taken care to deal even-handedly with a person whom we sincerely dislike, we find it hard to believe that moral action can be explained by any single-motive account. Thus, while it seems that ordinary moral judgments often require feelings of concern, other factors seem to be at work at times, especially in those cases where we report conflicting feelings.

Along with other single-motive theories, this survey of samples of reasoning calls into question those that take all moral motive for action to proceed from a structure of moral reasoning. Despite this, Thomas Nagel's version of it raises important points about the nature of persons as moral reasoners, points which I will defend and develop in a modified form. In the course of the entire book, I will argue that feelings of concern or responsiveness to persons is fundamental to our moral anatomy and is a pre-condition for engaging in moral reasoning.

However, for the present chapter we should attend to the way in which the structure-of-reasons-account, which denies that feelings or sentiments are related to moral motive, is most directly called into question by cases where feelings of concern are required. The feelings of concern that are required may vary in intensity and duration, from that reflected in swerving to avoid a pedestrian, to trying to save a helpless, injured child, or to helping a friend through a crisis. Two points to note are that, first, some kind of caring response to an individual—and not a commitment to an abstract duty—is evidently demanded in many ordinary cases of moral reasoning and, second, this demand is reflected in our ordinary moral vocabulary.

One gets a sense of how basic to us norms of reasoning and language are by watching college students at work on ordinary moral problems. For, if one questions typical undergraduate philosophy classes about the most ordinary moral cases, one finds ready agreement among them in their responses, despite the fact that the students come from a variety of national backgrounds and claim to hold a range of philosophical positions—Nietzschean, relativist, ethical skeptic, fundamentalist, and so on. Despite the disparity between their backgrounds and their avowed moral positions, one finds swift and easy agreement among them on their descriptions and judgments of many ordinary cases. Moreover, one sees that norms of judgment are implicit in their response to these cases, so that they, as classes, express community of judgment, something quite at odds with their avowed philosophical positions. Let us consider some ordinary cases.

I sometimes ask my classes (and I ask the reader) to begin by considering such cases as that of your acquaintance, George. George has given his word that he would drive you to catch a flight, and there is no alternative transport to the plane. However, when it is time to leave for the airport, he tells you he isn't going.

He can't be serious, you say.

But he is.

We note that at this point you would register disappointment, but, as students agree, although you might be irritated, you would have no firm basis for assigning blame as yet. Suppose that George then adds that he has decided to go for a swim instead, because he finds the day's heat oppressive. Then, unless you could discover that George's discomfort had some special and grave importance, you would be annoyed: you would resent his light regard for your travel plans.

Classes do not describe their resentment as merely an emotional reaction or as social conditioning. They say one resents George's treatment because one sees that he had no urgent need to meet and therefore should have been able to meet the needs that were obvious to him and that he indeed had committed himself to meet.

Once they discover that George's discomfort has no such importance, they know what to think about George. Once they fully understand what George wanted to do and why, they are clear that his reasons were inadequate; that he had no right to consider going for a swim; that he had not regarded their interests from their perspective; and that such regard is required from one in his situation.

Some might object that our blame of George may rest on his moral failures, but perhaps not on his lack of feeling for you. Couldn't George manifest great feeling for you (in some other way) and still be open to blame because morally at fault?

How should we respond?

We may begin by noting that George's feeling of concern should be manifest in what he does morally, in his considering your interest from your perspective; responding in a moral way is a way of exercising one's care for persons. Suppose George says he's terribly sorry and knows how much this ride means to you and would like to be of help, yet continues with his plans for a swim (with no further excuse). You would not be amused. George has compounded the problem. For it is obvious from the circumstances that he could easily help if he chose to. His saying he cares in that situation shows that the reverse is true; he cares so little that he's prepared to lie to you as well. For, of course, given his commitment and your expectations, a most important way for him to show that he cared would be to do what is necessary to fulfill his obligations.

Different expressions might be used to characterize George in this situation; by descriptions such as "self-centered" and "unfeeling" you'd indicate (as classes do) that George had failed in an obligation he had to you and was to be blamed unless some valid excuse could be found.

When one asks whether there's anything George could say or do to excuse himself from making the airport run, classes are not diffident. They do not hesitate to give a number of illustrations of the *kind* of thing (and not just one specific circumstance) that would be acceptable. Nor is it the case that they can think of only one kind of excuse; they construct many kinds. They note, for example, that George would be excused if he had arranged to have someone else drive you; if he were somehow incapacitated; if his car had broken down; if his mother were dying; or if his child needed urgent medical attention. Thus they show their confident mastery of ordinary reasoning and lend support to the judgments of philosophers such as Reid, Butler, Locke, and Bradley that in everyday cases the ordinary person is a generally reliable moral judge.

Classes are equally skilled and confident in discussing and in reaching agreement on the weaknesses of unacceptable excuses and at modifying them so that they would be acceptable. Thus, they, in effect, display their skill and agreement, not just over different situations that are variations of this simple case, but over the criteria that would be acceptable.

Consider another case. Suppose you have tripped while coming down a stairway and have fallen through a glass door, breaking some bones in your legs and arms and cutting yourself badly. Bleeding profusely and unable to move, you cry out for help. Soon you find yourself in a pool of blood, and you realize that you are in an isolated spot and in mortal danger. Just then, old George steps into this godforsaken stairwell. How fortunate that he should come along! But, no: George, shaking his head, quickly leaves, saying nothing.

Assume that, through a stranger's fortunate arrival and help, you get medical attention and survive the ordeal. Afterwards, you might wonder why George had left so abruptly, but speculate that there must have been some legitimate excuse. Suppose, however, that the next time you saw George and asked him why he had not helped you in your crisis, he replied only, ''Well, you see, I had on this new suit.''

''What do you mean?'' you counter. ''Why didn't you help me? You knew I was in agony and in danger.''

''But you see,'' George answers, ''it was a brand new suit—and you were bleeding freely.''

One who has had such an experience, classes agree, has reason to be morally outraged that anyone should be so lacking in concern for one's well-being. George would be cold and unfeeling in failing to help a stranger under these circumstances; there's something brutal about his failure to help an acquaintance in such desperate need.

When one asks members of a class (with their different philosophical postures and leanings) what might have provided George with an excuse in the latter kind of case, one again finds that their understanding and agreement are not confined to a specific situation; they have no difficulty or hesitation in laying out and agreeing on a number of factors that would excuse him or in proposing others that would make him less culpable.

Someone might object that these cases mark no *moral* agreement among classes, saying: "In these cases students are responding to some imagined slight to their dignity or interests, and their responses are merely defenses of their personal interest and self-image—they're not moral judgments at all. One never hears them make an appeal to principle."

But the objection misstates the case; the students are not (and readers are not) defending their personal dignity or interests. They are responding to a *story*—they know that George isn't really their acquaintance—and they are indicating how anyone should respond in such circumstances; thus, they are speaking about what is appropriate to anyone in moral situations of the kinds described. For such generalizing, a principle is involved: our indignation is appropriate to such abuse. As Bishop Butler observes (in Sermon 8 in "Fifteen Sermons Preached at Rolls Chapel), "The indignation raised by cruelty and injustice . . . which persons unconcerned would feel, is by no means malice. No, it is resentment against vice and wickedness: it is one of the common bonds by which society is held together; a fellow-feeling, which each individual has in behalf of the whole species."

More recently, P. F. Strawson has reminded us how our moral requirements are related to a web of attitudes in the community:

> We should think of the many different kinds of relationship which we can have with other people—as sharers of a common interest; as members of the same family; as colleagues; as friends; as lovers; as chance parties to an enormous range of transactions and encounters. Then we should think in each of these connections in turn, and in others, of the kind of importance we attach to the attitudes and intentions towards us of those who stand in these relationships to us, and of the kind of *reactive* attitudes and feelings to which we ourselves are prone. In general, we demand some degree of good will or regard on the part of those who stand in these relationships to us.[3]

Strawson argues that membership brings one into a community where mutual regard is to be expected, leading one to resent those who fail to show such regard toward oneself and to be indignant toward those who fail to exhibit it toward others. In Butler's terms, that means to be resentful or indignant toward cruelty and injustice.

We can illustrate the point by noting that the same kind of responses are observed (and are appropriate) to ordinary cases in which we are not to imagine ourselves as involved. Consider a case in which your colleague, Peter, is involved. Peter is hurrying off to class one day, and, on his way, takes a shortcut through a park. There he comes across a small child who has fallen on some broken glass, has evidently broken some bones, and is bleeding profusely. She is in an isolated spot and seems to be unable to move. She is crying out in pain and in terror. Not without reason: she's apparently in real danger. However, Peter, intent on his class, brushes the child aside and presses on.

Now, unless Peter has more to excuse himself than his need to get to class, we find him to be at fault. We (like the philosophy classes who are told of such cases) can agree to a number of judgments about such cases, but "callous" and "self-absorbed" come quickly to mind.

Further points about moral reasoning emerge from class responses. Whatever diverse ethical positions students in these classes *profess*, they actually hold principles and standards of reasoning in common in their lives. They can speak swiftly and confidently because they are talking about something that lies at the center of their lives. They know that their excuses must be generally acceptable to a community, and they know that the standards by which they have proposed and assessed excuses are used by the rest of the community. They are competent and confident in giving and evaluating reasons that would pass in the community. In demonstrating their knowledge of, and agreement to, what would count as an excuse, they disclose their sense of a community of judgment exercising common criteria. In brief, such judgments and evaluation show the *point* in speaking of the "structure of moral reasoning" and "a community of moral reasoners." Moreover, in tailoring their excuses to what could be accepted, it's apparent that they take that community to have some kind of moral authority (despite the fact that such a belief is quite incompatible with their professed philosophical stances).

Further, in appealing to that reasoning in cases like George's, we (like my classes) find that our judgment of him depends on our knowing that he lacked concern for us. We are confirmed in that point and we assign blame readily when we know with how little inconvenience to himself George might have come to our aid.

Other cases might be cited to illustrate the same agreement in a fundamental mode of moral reasoning. Agreement is common, and it comes swiftly when we become aware that others have failed to regulate their actions in the light of what respect for persons requires. We can blame if we can look at failure to regulate action from the other's perspective and know how easily the person could have done otherwise. Without looking at the situation from the other's perspective, we could not know how easily George could have given up his swim or how difficult it would be for one to give up one's providing medical attention to one's child. If we did not understand or could not know how easily the other person might have given up his desire of the moment to act in our behalf, we would not be in a position to judge and should excuse ourselves from doing so. Evidently, some conception of what *a person* could feel and do is at work here, as, indeed, there must be in the notion of excuses or blame being universalizable (or judged to be generally appropriate or fitting).

There are many difficult cases where we cannot judge, but cases abound in which we have no hesitation to blame for lack of concern: where debts are ignored, promises broken, feelings willfully abused, etc. We have occasion to make such judgments continually and these are judgments that all or nearly all could manage. We could not assign blame in the confident way that we do if we did not believe that those involved would be able to see and act on their obligation in such cases; if they did not have that ability, they could not incur the obligations.

As John Austin notes in "A Plea for Excuses," we can agree to excuse someone from blame (or correctly apply the terms indicating that we have done so) only if the person to be excused has exercised the concern due to others in that situation. To reach a judgment, we must look at it from the perspective of one in that situation. Austin reminds us, for example, that we could not excuse someone for stepping on the baby's head if the best he could plead was that he had done so "inadvertently."[4] Similarly, we could add, one could not get off the hook for driving one's car into a crowd of people by remarking, "I simply didn't notice they were there." In each case, by the person's description of the situation, we see that failure to notice marks a lack of due concern.

It is apparent that the concern that is morally required in these cases is not coolly abstract or void of what we would speak of as feelings or sentiments. For such experiences are unsettling; they agitate us. If one who had committed either act was unfazed by the act he had committed, that, too, would be taken as a moral failure; if anyone remains unruffled after needlessly injuring a baby or endangering the lives of a number of people, we worry about his moral health.

Note that ordinary language is shot through with terms by which we may assign blame for exhibiting a lack of feeling or concern for others: "negligent," "careless," "inattentive," "uninterested," "inconsiderate," "reckless," "self-centered," "ruthless," and so many more. The point of emphasizing their number is to indicate that this is no small or inconsiderable part of our moral life.

It might be thought that these terms of condemnation do not necessarily connote a lack of feeling, but merely a lack of legitimate focus on the legitimate interests of others. That would be true of some uses of "negligent," "self-centered," and "inattentive," for example. But it would not be true of all uses, and there are many terms of condemnation that carry only the sense of a lack of feeling. "Ruthless" is an epithet by which we condemn, and we can do so because it carries the sense of mercilessness, of lacking compassion for the misery of another. To describe others as "uncaring," "unfeeling, " "heartless," or "lacking in compassion" is to blame *because* of the lack of feeling and not because of their failure to focus properly.

Some may object that we cannot put much argumentative weight on the existence of such terms because we may misapply them and we may err in making some moral judgments. True, we may err, and we may misapply. But it must also be acknowledged that the words could not be part of our common language if people generally did not know how to apply them in common and publicly acceptable ways; the notion of misapplying such terms could make no sense if there were no standard criteria for applying them.

When we note that such terms reflect blame for lack of concern, that there are so many such terms, and that they loom so large in our moral life, we may be tempted to say that all that is ever morally required is that we act with feeling or concern for others. By this move moral theorists' puzzles about moral motivation would be settled simply by saying that responsiveness to others provides the motive for moral action. In recent years feminist writers have focused on the moral value and importance of compassionate, altruistic responses. Some indeed have held that responding with compassion is all that is morally required, contrasting their views with those described in the Kantian universalizing that is said to be a feature of "masculine" ethical theory.

Thomas Nagel provides a contemporary example of Kantian formalism, though Nagel, of course, holds that a *kind* of altruism is necessary to moral reasoning. In *The Possibility of Altruism*, he argues for a kind of altruism that *follows* from what he calls "the structure of moral reasoning," but it is an altruism that is said to be independent of any sentiment, feeling, compassion, or inclination. Nagel holds that altruism is "a requirement of rational action," and something that "may not be in our power to renounce."[5] He uses the term to refer not just to self-sacrificing behavior but to any action done for the benefit of another. It is "any behavior motivated merely by the belief that someone else will benefit or avoid harm by it" (N:16). But Nagel "is opposed to any demand that the claims of ethics appeal to our interests: either self-interest or the interest we happen to take in other things and persons" (N:3).

Nagel's statement of his position is puzzling, reminding us of the Kantian problem of moral motivation. In Nagel's case we, as moral agents, are to act in behalf of others' interests, but not because we have any interest or feeling for things or persons ourselves. He defends the thesis that "one has a direct reason to promote the interests of others—a reason which does not depend on intermediate factors such as one's own interests or one's antecedent sentiments of sympathy and benevolence" (N:15–16). Nagel takes the rational requirement of conduct to be the "pure altruism" that comes from seeing oneself as a person among persons, for thus another person's interests have a direct influence on one's own actions: "simply because in itself the interest of the former provides the latter with a reason to act" (N:79–80).

The interests of others provide us with a reason to act though *not* because we have an interest in others? Our sentiments or feelings for others are not involved? Nagel addresses this puzzle through his conception of seeing ourselves as persons among persons. One of his most important arguments, a profoundly important one that is reminiscent of arguments by Strawson and others, is that one must conceive of oneself as a person among persons if one is to be able to articulate a conception of oneself. The language that one uses to describe oneself and one's actions must be used in the same sense when applied to oneself as others mean when they apply it to themselves: "one must mean what they mean" (N:107) by the term (if one is to be able to commmunicate and avoid solipsism). If I am to describe an action of mine, I must have a sense of "persons" who are agents like me in aiming to bring things about in order to achieve their goals. Our being able to take the position of the other as a person, to know what one would feel as a person in that situation (despite differences in taste and background) are basic to the reasoning process in which we praise or blame another for his or her response (a process which we indeed employed in blaming George).

Nagel takes a critical and, I believe, a necessary step in saying that "meaning what they mean" must extend to the motivational content of moral judgments: we will not mean what they mean by a moral judgment unless we have the same motivation accompanying our own judgment. This indicates that we must be able to see how others see the situation that is judged and know what they could accept as morally permissible motives. The structure of reasoning that is involved in moral judgments is in universalizing; in universalizing we treat each as a person among persons. Altruistic motives (for Nagel) will be those where our action is influenced by the interests of other persons; for Nagel that influence can't be feeling, sentiment, or other emotion: the motive must come from the structure of practical reasoning which, for him, is pure universalizing.

Although the cases we've cited appeal to general acceptability and thus show that universalizing judgments go into the use of a moral vocabulary, they also show some other things about the structure of moral reasoning. Nagel (and other neo-Kantians) can make no sense of the nature of moral reasoning apart from what counts as moral reasoning in a moral community. Yet, when we examined samples of that reasoning to see what motives are accepted or involved, we found that reasoners commonly look for—demand—the influence of feelings and sentiment in moral decisions. They look for indications that the agent cared; that he or she wanted to benefit, or to avoid harming, another.

In the case of our supposed acquaintance, George (who refused to take us to the airport, lied to us, and refused to help us when we were in desperate need), the blame centered on the fact that he showed no feeling for us, a charge all the graver because he was an acquaintance. As an acquaintance, he would ordinarily be clear about our interests and needs and, hence, more subject to blame for failure to respond to our needs.

Concern is required quite apart from the special obligations he

would have as an acquaintance, however, as is apparent from our ordinary moral vocabulary. We are judged to be morally remiss any
time we can be correctly described as cruel, unfeeling, or heartless.
As we've seen, terms that assign blame for lack of concern make up
an important part of our moral vocabulary. Moreover, we note how
the *degree* of blame increases with the degree of the lack of concern
when we move from "she's uninterested" to "she's ruthless." The
condemnation attaches to lack of feeling and does not apply only to
cases where one has a special connection with the others involved.

It's also significant that we are not morally blamed for purely logical or factual mistakes in our reasoning. In blaming, we might say,
"That was a brutal or an insensitive act," but not "There must have
been some error in his reasoning" or "She must be guilty of some inconsistency." A logical mistake, a misdescription, or a failure to focus on others' legitimate interests is not taken to be morally significant unless it is to be read as a symptom of failure to exercise due
concern for persons.

This is the language of a community of moral reasoners. Its *members* make the demands for a structure of moral reasoning. One cannot invoke the structure of moral reasoning and then describe it in a
way that is at odds with the members' demands and attitudes. Note
the point that is critically important for Nagel's argument: "one
must be able to mean" by one's moral language what the community of users and reasoners means. If we accept that point, we cannot
accept Nagel's claim that moral reasoning involves "no appeal to
our interests" or feelings. Philosophy classes and readers, though
drawn from a range of ethnic, economic, and religious backgrounds,
can't be assumed to represent a universal pattern of moral reasoning;
but, in working out mutually acceptable solutions to moral problems they do constitute a community of reasoners and one whose
conclusions provide a counterexample to the no-feeling hypothesis.
Moreover, the number of terms, in English and other languages, condemning those lacking in feeling suggest that the demand to include
it in a structure of moral reasoning is universal.

While Homeric heroes and the warrior ethos of different societies
have commended "hardness" and "manliness," they did so with the
understanding that respect and honor was due to a courageous oppo-
nent in battle. Even Nietzsche, who professed to admire the noble-
men's ability to "indulge spurts of violent rage" when outside their
own community, found that these are men who, amongst them-

selves ''find so many new ways of manifesting consideration, delicacy, loyalty, pride and friendship.''[6] It is, of course, amongst themselves where what they consider to be their moral impulses are to be read. Hence, we are led to reject any account of moral reasoning that holds morality never makes an ''appeal to our interests'' or feelings. In subsequent chapters we shall explore evidence which indicates that it always does .

Can we describe moral actions as simply and directly motivated by concern or care for those who immediately benefit from our actions? If we look at the reasoning displayed in ordinary cases, there seem to be at least two additional motives at work. When we reflect on the standard responses to examples involving George, we find that the judgment of blame does center on his lack of concern. However, we also noted that we are brought to consider what excuses would be *generally* acceptable and in so doing recognized a community whose agreement held some authority for each individual member. Whereas each responsible agent shares in its judgments, the judgment is made in the light of what would commonly be regarded as acceptable or required. Acceptable moral judgments typically proceed from some deference for those who judge them to be acceptable; the motive here is not compassion or a concern to help individuals but a respect for, and a willingness to abide by, commonly held criteria and attitudes of judgments.

Since criteria are accepted as generally applicable, they apply to oneself and define what one could find acceptable in one's own behavior. One's seeing oneself as a person among persons requires that one apply generally acceptable criteria to one's behavior if it is to remain acceptable. We see such motives at work in statements such as ''We couldn't live with ourselves if we failed him.'' Evidently our wanting to be able to ''live with ourselves'' is part of our motive for upholding norms; we aim to maintain our self-respect, a motive distinct from the concern for others and distinct from respect for the authority of the community. We pursue self-respect through responding with concern and out of deference for a community's criteria of judgment, but we aim to satisfy self-concern as well.

In acting on those motives, we may also feel hostility toward an individual for moral reasons, yet judge that he or she must be treated with deference. Suppose that after all you've been through with George, you are required to write a letter commenting on his professional competence. You may have had some difficulty being civil toward him and perhaps will have more difficulty now in resisting the temptation to get revenge. Your feelings of hostility are not without reason: he's been described as cold, insensitive, brutal, and a liar into the bargain; you would be foolhardy if you were not wary of such a character. Yet, you recognize your obligation; you, as a responsible individual, would be concerned that your letter give an accurate account of his professional competence, adding, "Any self-respecting person would do the same."

This illustrates the point that many impulses may be at work in moral decisions: concern for self, respect for a community and its standards of judgment, concern for persons affected, and repulsion by those who disregard or threaten its standards. It also illustrates the point that the stringent claims of duty may proceed from our own not very mystifying inclinations (a point we shall take up in chapter 3).

In reaching such a decision, we note that duty's stringent claims oblige us to set aside our particular feelings for George when we make judgments about him. Similarly, in cases where we have a special fondness for a person, we may have to set aside such feelings in order to act fairly; if we must mediate between our child and other children, our special feelings make it difficult for us to respond fairly. This is reflected in the fact that the law would disqualify one as a judge if one had any special attachment to the individuals involved in the case. Thus, it is clear that moral judgment cannot be simply an expression of our special feelings for the persons involved; if judgments are to be fair or impartial, they must be more than that. This point helps to explain why formalists suppose that moral action is sentiment-free: in order to be impartial one must treat each as a person among persons. In their view that means free of any feelings or sentiments.

Our look at cases of ordinary moral reasoning shows that it is not free of feeling. Despite this, we should be grateful to Nagel for helping to open up the issue by saying that altruism is a requirement of rational action, and it is not in our power to renounce it. It is part of that web of mutual regard, noted by Strawson and Butler, by which we are members of a community of moral reasoners. However, these conclusions would be challenged by Kant and John Mackie, among others. Therefore, in the next chapter we must turn to their objections and the bearing that they have on the question of objectivity in moral judgments. In working with this issue, we will get assistance from David Hume as well as from those neglected masters, Joseph Butler and Adam Smith.

3 / Mutual Responses and Objectivity

In reviewing the examples of ordinary reasoning we saw that our reasoning turned repeatedly on what George and Peter must have known about the other person's feelings and fears. We were able to agree in our judgments because we employed a common conception of what any person would feel and want in particular situations, a conception we expected George to use in reaching his decisions to act. That is to say, our moral reasoning was made possible and was considered to be objective because we, as informed and concerned persons, referred to our common understanding of human nature.

However, Kant, John Mackie, and others would deny the claims of such reasoning: Kant because of its reliance on a conception of human nature and Mackie because of its claim to objectivity. Both philosophers would base their denials on their beliefs about moral motivation; both believe that one could not account for constraining moral obligation as the expression of natural human inclinations. Kant believes the norm behind such obligation is the work of a purely rational being; Mackie believes we must deny the objectivity of value judgments that could support such a constraining obligation.

But I shall argue that the claims for our examples of reasoning are unaffected by Kant and Mackie's objections since (1) neither man is able to make his case consistently, and since a conception of human nature is indispensable to forming a basis for value judgments; moreover, (2) a kind of objectivity for value judgments can be found in our sampling and in moral discussions and, indeed, objectivity is basic to our use of moral language; and finally, (3) the motivation premise supporting both Kant and Mackie's positions—that one cannot explain one's feeling of constraining obligation as a case of natural inclination—is also called into question by the success of features of

Joseph Butler, David Hume, and Adam Smith's (pre-Kantian) naturalistic explanations of our judgment and motivation.

HUMAN NATURE AND THE BASIS
FOR OBJECTIVE JUDGMENTS

We would do well to begin with Kant's objections, for there we find the fundamental epistemological issue raised sharply. He cautioned against a view of reasoning that considered the essential moral person by studying or reflecting on the "particular attributes of human nature,"[1] because, he argued, the moment we attempt to base our moral principle on human nature, it will lose its unconditional categorical quality. Recognizing his approach as revolutionary, he nonetheless insisted on it because "the universality with which (moral laws) should hold for all rational beings . . . is lost when their foundation is taken from the *particular constitution of human nature*, or the accidental circumstances in which it is placed [Kant's emphasis] (*Abbot*:61). In this Kant seems to go against what D. W. Hamlyn has expressed concerning what should be a point of consensus among contemporary philosophers—namely that "human beings are biological entities embedded in a public world, and it is only relative to such a framework that questions of what is and what is not intelligible can even be raised. Such questions cannot be answered by reference to such things as data provided by the senses or 'inner processes'."[2] It seems that Kant attempted to base his criteria on the mysterious inner processes of noumenal being. In effect, he insisted that we approach our moral judgments as if we were not biological entities, were not involved with other natural processes, and did not need to direct our lives in relation to such a framework. Rather, he sought to develop principles valid for "all rational beings" whose nature was to be found outside the phenomenal world. A moral principle that is assumed to lay unconditional claims on us, he wrote, cannot be derived from a study of human feelings, for they could not provide us with "an objective principle on which we should be *enjoined* to act, even though all our propensions, inclinations, and natural dispositions were opposed to it [Kant's emphasis] (*Abbot*:43). Unconditional moral law could only be the work of autonomous beings; he seeks "autonomy, that property by which will is law unto itself, independent of the property of objects of volition" (*Abbot*:59).

But there are serious problems for Kant's theory—or at least for this version of it.

If one could find some of Kant's purely rational beings—unencumbered by human dependencies, desires, and capacities for feeling pain, grief, and compassion—one might find beings for whom the only necessary moral test was consistency. But, so long as such beings disregarded our nonrational desires and capacities (following Kant's instructions), one would also find beings who were wholly incompetent to judge the moral performance of beings whose rationality is linked with a number of drives and passions (as well as with a web of social relationships). Purely rational beings who considered only purely rational nature would not have *access* to the information by which to understand, judge, and guide human life. They could not *speak* about what provides the nonrational, but indispensable, conditions for human action. They would be incompetent to judge human action because they would have no way of appreciating the ease or difficulty with which humans could, for example, face pain or deprivation.

Moreover, whatever norm such beings developed would be incapable of giving us judgments about what would harm, kill, or extend human life. It follows that if one actually followed Kant's injunction about disregarding the merely contingent aspects of human nature in forming criteria for judgment, the criteria would be useless. In short, valid moral judgment must be human judgment, a judgment in and of human involvements.

Now it may be said that such criticism is unfair; that Kant intended only that we formulate the law as rational *human* beings; and that he elsewhere advocated the study of human psychology. But such a defense would contravene Kant's explicit charge in these passages that the moral law be considered for purely rational beings; it would also contradict his doctrine that the essential moral person was a purely rational being. *As* an essential moral person, setting aside all information about human needs and inclinations when one chose one's criteria for the law, one would not have the right to take such specific conditions into consideration in developing one's judgments. One's imperatives would not be unconditional—could not be categorical—if one did.

A tenable guide for human action cannot really *be* unconditional: it must somehow come to terms with natural conditions, since it is only through them that humans can act, exercising such limited control as we can. Because intentional action must be based on desires, a choiceworthy life (for continuing human action) must give us reasons for ordering and deciding between desires to be fulfilled. A plan for such a life can only be developed by those who study the particular conditions and inclinations so that they can see that the fulfillment of some desires are indispensable and must serve as a basis for enjoining us not to act on others.

Now, of course, when Kant begins to use his "purely rational" test for unconditional judgments (the categorical imperative) to exclude impermissible wants and maxims for action, he insists that our maxims be those that are consistent with fulfilling the familiar contingent wants and capacities of nature-bound humans—and not those of purely rational beings. It turns out that maxims must be consistent with the fulfillment of desires drawn from Kant's particular understanding of our nature, arbitrarily chosen and elevated to a commanding role: to develop our talents, to receive help when needed, and so on.[3] Kant thus violates his injunction against basing criteria for moral reasoning on the particular attributes and wants of human nature.

He could not have avoided doing so. If, following the second formulation of the categorical imperative, one tries to universalize with a view to treating all persons with respect, one must act in a way that will avoid harm to persons. A primary reason for an act being impermissible must be that someone would be harmed or injured thereby, and "injury" must be understood in relation to human capacities to function in ways important to the person. Without reference to such contingent, natural capacities, one could have no objective ground for one's universalizing; without referring to them we could have no basis for setting limits to permissible action. Thus, it cannot be a fault in ordinary reasoning that it reached its decisions through referring to such capacities.

John Mackie also feels that the objective moral values that could justify our feelings of obligation would have to be found outside of nature; they would have to be found as non-natural qualities by some non-natural means. Mackie holds that "objectivity . . . (is) engrained in our language and thought" both of which presuppose that their value judgments are objective, but he claims that such assumptions are "not meaningless but false."[4] They are false because there are no objective values to be found. Thus, he finds that our whole moral way of speaking and thinking is in error: finally, for him, "it is this that makes the name 'moral scepticism' appropriate" (M:35).

He finds such judgments in error because they lack what he calls "objective value," and he believes whatever exhibited objective value would have to do so by virtue of a "queer" and "non-natural" quality. Natural qualities and a naturalistic analysis are thought to be eliminated, for "on a naturalistic analysis, moral judgments . . . are wholly relative to the desires or possible satisfactions of the person or persons whose actions are to be guided, but moral judgments seem to say more than this. This view leaves out the categorical quality of moral requirements" (M:33). Obligations and objective moral values are thought to have authority over us, authority which we feel constrained to follow. Mackie, like Kant, assumes that the desire to uphold a moral principle (which could sustain a "categorical quality") could not proceed from our natural concerns. We have already seen the incoherence of pursuing a moral principle that is "categorical" in the sense of being unconditional: principles have to be applied to the conditions of human life and, hence, cannot be independent of those conditions.

Because he insists on their categorical quality, Mackie is led to deny the possibility of any objective value. Further, it leads him to ask us to look for objectivity among "queer" and "non-natural" qualities, "utterly different from anything else in the universe" (M:38). Moreover, if we could know such qualities, it would have to be by some "special faculty of moral perception or intuition, utterly different from our ordinary ways of knowing anything else" (M:38).

Moreover, he asks us to look for a kind of "objective value" that is conceptually odd. For it must both validate and justify our concerns and yet be valued independently of all human concerns. Mackie writes that the importance of the notion of objective value was that it "backs up and validates some of the subjective concern which people have" (M:22). But in explaining what an objective value must be, he writes: "An objective good would be sought by anyone who was acquainted with it, not because of any contingent fact that this person, or every person, is so constituted that he desires this end but just because the end has to-be-pursuedness somehow built into it" (M:40). It would be valued (objectively) and *would support* our interests and concerns but would not be valued *because* it sustains our concerns? If it sustains our standard concerns, why is it that it cannot be known by standard means? If it sustains natural concerns, why is it that it must be known by mysterious non-natural means? This notion of objective value is alleged to be the one assumed in ordinary natural judgment and moral language.

But ordinary moral language and judgments do not deal in nonnatural qualities or depend on non-natural means. As we saw, we use ordinary means to identify specific human interests that are or would be violated by acts which are, consequently, prohibited: such acts are said, for example, to harm, injure, frustrate, or cripple. There is nothing mysterious about the mode of knowing or the qualities on which such judgments are based: they are based on respecting human wants and needs within the context of familiar institutions and practices.

Why does Mackie exclude such natural concerns as a basis for objective judgment? Because he, like Kant, felt that natural desires and qualities could not explain—could not lead us to—a principle that would enjoin us to act, constraining other desires with its authority. So, as we feel enjoined by a moral authority, he holds that we must assume it to be of some non-natural quality or relation. Kant concluded that such a value must exist in the noumenal world; Mackie concluded that it was nonexistent. A fundamental mistake of both men seems to be the belief that in order for a principle to have *constraining authority* it must be regarded as *categorical or unconditional*. This leads Kant to look for the purely rational will in a noumenal world and leads Mackie to pursue qualities outside of nature.

Given that we are unable to find such qualities, Mackie is left with the task of explaining how this most fundamental and ubiquitous mode of thinking and talking—moral language and reasoning— is in error. But when he turns to explain this general error in our moral reasoning, he does not address our *actual* reasoning about our natural capacities nor does he discuss the role that criticism and inquiry can play in moral thinking. Rather, he describes each individual judging as if he or she were socially isolated and passive with respect to the moral world.

A primary difficulty with both Kant and Mackie's account of moral reasoning is that they do not take account of the way in which moral judgment and obligation proceed from—turn on—our perception of our relationship with the person(s) affected. Both Kant and Mackie treat judgments about obligation as if they could be rendered by a person in isolation. The whole task of judgment for Kant is a logical one: it consists of deciding whether one's maxim (intention or plan of action) could be consistently applied universally: no need to attend to relationships, possibilities, or mutual perceptions. There is no need to imagine or canvass alternative lines of attack in cooperation with others. He gives no attention to what alternative moves might be entertained or to how others might respond to them as a consequence of their plans. Yet, patently, these are the elements that must go into moral decisions, if they are to be justified. Similarly, Mackie wants to understand the authoritativeness of moral claims by *isolating* them from the social relations in which they are embedded. He wants to isolate and expose moral claims which are alleged to be obscured because they are "presented along with relations to desires and feelings, reasoning about the means to desired ends, interpersonal demands . . . the psychological constituents of meanness and so on. There is nothing queer about any of these" (*M*:42). Mackie wants to see a moral claim of obligatoriness in itself and "for this purpose it needs to be isolated and exposed as it is" (*M*: 42).

But, of course, obligatoriness *is* in its relationships. Obligations don't exist and can't be known in isolation from the social relations in which they appear. On this point we might extend Hamlyn's thesis about intelligibility to state: "Human beings are biological entities embedded in a [social] world and it is only relative to such a framework that questions of what is and is not [obligatory] can even be [intelligibly] raised." The moment one begins to isolate a moral claim from the personal and social relations that give it point, one moves into the unintelligible. The oddity of the isolating technique is apparent in Mackie's questioning: "What is the connection between the natural fact that an action is a piece of deliberate cruelty— say, causing pain just for fun—and the moral fact that it is wrong? It cannot be an entailment, a logical or semantic necessity. Yet it is not merely that the two features occur together. The wrongness must somehow be 'consequential' or 'supervenient'; it is wrong because it is a piece of deliberate cruelty. But just what *in the world* is signified by this 'because'?" [Mackie's emphasis] (*M*:41). By isolating the description from the story which would validate it, he deprives us of any means of saying what in the world enabled us to say it was wrong. By emphasizing that we are then to look *in the world* for it, he suggests that we might be able to extract human concern from inanimate matter.

His question was rhetorical. He assumes we will be powerless to find any basis for moral judgment there. Note, however, that Mackie found it to be a "natural fact" that it was "a piece of deliberate cruelty" and then set us to work looking for the moral fact of its wrongness. But, in describing an act as a piece of deliberate cruelty, one already has a moral judgment. By common usage, its wrongness *would* be entailed by its being a case of deliberate cruelty, though one would ordinarily not have occasion to draw the inference, "It's wrong," because that would already be understood.

Here Mackie's denial of the objectivity of value judgments gets what plausibility it has by his excluding the role of all human interests: if one were unable to take human interests into account one could not judge any act to be wrong. The case is parallel to our findings concerning Kant's purely rational beings who suffer and respond to no human pain and needs. Under those conditions, anything would be permissible. That seems to be reason enough to abandon those conditions.

As Mackie finds that the moral quality is not *in* the object, he holds that the judgment of its wrongness can lay no claim to objectivity. His solution is to "replace the moral quality with some sort of subjective response which could be causally related to the natural features . . . [of the situation]" (*M*:41).

Mackie allows that our feelings and affections lead us to have moral responses to actions, but these reactions are in us, rather than in the things. (Nothing is said about the possibility of the value being found in the *relationship between* us and the actions.) If we took away our feelings and capacities, we would find no wrongness in the action itself. Since it is a subjective response and neither in the world nor in objects, he concludes that it can have no objectivity. Taking the subjectivist view, he finds that "the supposedly objective values will be based in fact on attitudes which the person has who takes himself to be recognizing and responding to those values. If we admit what Hume calls the mind's 'propensity to spread itself on external objects', we can understand the supposed objectivity of moral qualities as arising from what we can call the projection or objectification of moral attitudes. This would be analogous to the 'pathetic fallacy', the tendency to read our feelings into objects" (*M*:42). Although Hume considered that in warranted moral judgments our moral response ('propensity') was based on objective features of our relationships in a situation, Mackie holds that the objectivity of moral judgments is illusory: we have feelings or attitudes caused by the "natural features" of the situation; these we fallaciously project onto the objective world: "How much simpler and more comprehensible the situation would be if we could replace the moral quality with some sort of subjective response which could be causally related to the detection of the natural features on which the supposed quality is said to be consequential" (M:41).

His explanation of the "error" leaves some problems in its wake. The first problem is that while Mackie denied that any value judgments could be objective, he went on to argue for the superiority of some value judgments over others, often following familiar kinds of argument. There could be no objective value, he wrote, yet he went on to outline features of the good life—a practice in which he must assume he knows what would *be*, and not merely seem, good. A second problem is that by adopting the 'pathetic fallacy' explanation, Mackie must conclude that all moral constraints are similarly fallacious. Why then should one who accepted this explanation take obligations seriously? Though Mackie wrote that objective values would validate one's purposes, he claimed that denying objective values would not affect one's purpose or direction: "The lack of objective values is not a good reason for abandoning subjective concern or for ceasing to want anything" (M:34). However, if one believed that all moral judgments were fallacious, that would seem to be a good reason for abandoning concern about fulfilling them. What could be a better reason?

Simon Blackburn adopts the same "moral-sentiments-as-effects" theme (supposedly from Hume) and describes himself as a "projectivist," because, like Mackie, he takes value judgments to be "projections upon the world of a sentiment which we feel."[5] Despite acknowledging that "a properly working morality" has an "objective 'feel,'"[6] he opposes any suggestion that our subjective moral responses could be defended as objective.

Blackburn also assumes that to claim objectivity for value judgments is to imply that values are perceived to be in things; he holds that in claiming to make objective judgments we imply we have "a mysterious ability to spot the immutable fitnesses of things.'"[7] He opposes any talk of our perceiving objective moral properties, for he holds that in cases of well-founded perceptions of objective properties, one can support one's statements about the perceptions by counterfactuals: in support of one's statement that something was square, one can say, "If it hadn't been the case that the thing was square, I wouldn't have believed it was." But, says Blackburn, "The important point is that talking of moral perception by itself provides no theory whatsoever of such conditionals. It provides only a misleading sense of security that somewhere there is such a theory. The theory is not causal, as in the case of shape, nor can it be a matter of conformity with a community, for that just misplaces moral reality which is not created by community consensus . . . So what is it? It just doesn't exist."[8]

However, Blackburn's case of perceiving a shape to be square is not a case of a merely *causal* relationship, for it (like moral judgments) requires that one be selective and interpretive about what one sees: one must have attended to the shape; one must have known what it meant for something to look like a square; one must have taken account of one's perspective, and so on in order for one to have seen the shape as square.

Moreover, contrary to Blackburn's claim, counterfactual reasoning is commonly used in moral judgments and could always be used. We often explicitly invoke it. In the case of the examples of the last chapter we might have said, "If George had been disabled, we could not have blamed him for not taking us to the airport." Or, remember the case of Kant's purely rational beings: If humans could feel no pain, we would have to describe and blame people differently than we now do. When Blackburn says that "the important point is that *talking of moral perception by itself* provides no theory whatsoever of such conditionals," one could agree. But the important point is that we do use counterfactuals in our judgments and do not invoke "moral perception by itself" in doing so; and, as the above cases indicate, we can provide theory in support of such conditionals.

Moreover, Hume argues for the objectivity of moral conclusions and does so as an outgrowth of his treatise on human nature. In the *Treatise* and the second *Enquiry*, he repeatedly employs counterfactual reasoning to show how moral conclusions are dictated by our condition, our feelings, and capacities. For example, when arguing for the utility of justice in the *Enquiry*, he writes: "Reverse, in any considerable circumstance, the condition of men: Produce extreme abundance or extreme necessity: Implant in the human breast perfect moderation and humanity, or perfect rapaciousness and malice: By rendering justice useless you thereby totally destroy its essence, and suspend its obligation upon mankind."[9]

Counterfactually speaking and in the general spirit of Hume, we can say that if we were not creatures tied to a particular objective set of conditions and capacities in nature, we would not have a basis for making the evaluative judgments that we do. Because we can specify how our judgments are grounded in natural relationships, we can use counterfactuals about the natural relationships to characterize the moral relationship.

If we did not believe them to be objective, we would find it hard to believe that they had any obligatory force. One wonders, of course, what account the projectivist could give for respecting the constraining feelings of obligation that were at the center of Kant and Mackie's arguments. If one believed one's judgments were fallacious projections, why feel constrained by them? As an explanation for why we have such feelings of constraint, Simon Blackburn says that it is because one "has been brought up in a certain way and a consequence of this upbringing is that he looks upon certain courses of action with horror." As a product of such training "he will only be able to keep his self-respect" by living up to his feelings of obligations.[10]

That, however, will leave no feelings of obligation (and no problem of self-respect) for the projectivist who has come to understand that all such training is the product of *unwarranted* projection. The projectivist must finally conclude that all feelings of constraint are the direct or indirect result of fallacious projection; their mentors may have been sincere, but as projectivists, they must know that the mentors were misguided. So, judgments of obligation, being erroneous, are irrelevant to projectivists' maintaining their self-respect. Moreover, without the notion of objective moral judgments, they seem to be in danger of losing the concept of self-respect.

OBJECTIVITY IN REASONING AND
LANGUAGE

Since Mackie and Blackburn are looking for objectivity of judgment and find that disagreement of judgment is evidence for the denial of objectivity, it seems that we are in need of clarification of what we could or should mean by "objectivity" (whether of scientific or moral judgments). And it appears that our account must pay particular attention to whether or not feelings or sentiments could play a role in any judgment that could be called objective. Moral judgments (and moral motives) appear to be connected with our approving and disapproving passions and sentiments.

There is a tension in Mackie's treatment of the relation between our passions or sentiments and reasoning; he at times treats sentiments as purely passive, yet at other times each treats them as reason-directed. We've seen Mackie speaking of sentiments as the subjective effects of the objects of the natural world, known through introspection and not from any kind of reasoning; as such it seems they could hardly be a reliable source of judgment. If we were merely the passive receivers of such sentiments or feelings, could we in holding them be said to exercise judgment at all? We are aware that Hume held that the sentiments which were worthy of our moral attention were those calmer passions at which we arrive through reason—reason was not to be the slave of all passions nor were passions and sentiments to be known only through introspection. Similarly, Mackie found that moral reformers may approve or disapprove of a practice "for moral reasons and often for moral reasons that we would endorse" (*M*:36). Here, once again, Mackie seems to have found something objectively *in* the world about how one should react.

To clarify the notion of objectivity in our moral reasoning and language, it seems we need to address a number of questions: (1) What conception of objectivity are we dealing with? (2) What conception of emotion or sentiment is required for sentiments as they are incorporated in moral judgments? (3) Is this view of them compatible with any kind of objectivity of moral judgments?

Objectivity Supported by Evidence and Critical Discussion

A judgment can legitimately be said to be objective if it is supportable by evidence. A proposition is objective in this sense if it is experience-based; it refers to what is a matter of "fact" in the sense that its characterization can be supported by evidence available through observation. Implied in this description is the point that such propositions would be open to refutation by evidence and rational criticism too. This conception does not require that there be no subjective or interpretive elements. It claims a proposition to be objective if it is supported by common evidence and rational criticism.

This conception presupposes the possibility of disagreement and the appropriateness of disagreement leading to discussion and inquiry. Both parties to a moral disagreement could be mistaken (as could those disagreeing on a scientific issue). But, as G. E. Moore observed, the fact that moral disagreement leads to both debate and factual inquiry is intelligible only on the assumption that the judgments could have an objective basis in fact; moral disagreement assumes that those facts could be illuminated through discussion and inquiry. Disagreement and discussion would be unintelligible if moral responses were *caused* by the events around us. Consider how absurd discussion and disagreement would be for cases of responses that are caused. If the plant that feels silky to you causes welts to be raised on my skin, I do not say that I disagree with your response, nor do I try to persuade you that you have made a mistake. Yet moral disagreement invites and is sometimes resolved by discussion and inquiry; this is intelligible only if judgments can be objectively based.

Emotions about What? What Conception of Emotions?

Emotions are *about* something. Events provide the occasion for our sentiments of disapproval, but evidently they do not cause the sentiments—contrary to what Mackie and Blackburn (at times) have said: for the significance of events is open to discussion, redescription, and reinterpretation. For the past twenty-odd years philosophers have been pointing out the cognitive element in emotional responses. That there are cognitive elements entails that our emotional responses and responses of sentiment are open to criticism and discussion. This means that there are conditions to be satisfied for one to claim that one's shame, indignation, or resentment is an appropriate response. These are conditions that are in general open to public observation and, thus, one may judge the appropriateness of a response. Accordingly, the projectivist's ground—that sentiments are passively acquired and purely subjective—seems to have been chipped away by all those studies of the emotions.

Some have pointed to hysteria and other responses as instances of our emotional life that do seem to be caused by the events around us. But these are exceptional cases and they will not save the projectivist's position. The sentiments that Hume saw as guiding action were those in which we exercised reflective control. Mackie's account of passive emotions is another feature of his doctrine of the 'passive knower of moral qualities'. But it scarcely strengthens it for, as John McDowell remarks, it does not enable us to make sense of the multitude of other emotions such as that of fear: "We make sense of fear by seeing it as a response to objects that *merit* such a response, or as the intelligibly defective product of a propensity toward responses that would be intelligible in that way. For an object to merit fear just is for it to be fearful. So explanations of fear that manifest our capacity to understand ourselves in this region of our lives will simply not cohere with the claim that reality contains nothing in the way of fearfulness."[11]

As the literature on emotions reminds us, we commonly acknowledge the role of such reflection in our emotional life by the cognitive qualities we incorporate into our description of emotional responses. We say, for example, not only "the situation was fearful" but also that "his anger was inappropriate" and "she overreacted." These and other common locutions mark off our agreement that there are objective features of a situation that can provide or deny warrant for our emotional responses and responses of moral sentiments.

Reflective Responses: Objectivity of Judgment

The moral censure implicit in such terms as "inappropriate" and "overreacted" indicate that we are expected to exercise control over our emotions. That we have a moral requirement to do so is perhaps more explicit in expressions like "justifiable resentment" and "unwarranted hostility." Such evaluative language, used in describing our responses, cannot be arbitrarily applied or applied without objective reference. It is hard to see how Mackie could square this point with his claim that we are in error in thinking any moral judgments objective. The evaluative expressions describing our emotional responses must be applied in accord with the requirements of usage; if one does not follow such requirements, there will be objective bases for criticism and revision of one's remarks—as MacDowell makes clear in his remarks about the use of "fear."

We cannot make sense of our language behavior unless we treat it as related to that public context which is open to all to observe. We identify a person's intent through the context. As Donald Davidson has argued, in developing his 'principle of charity,' "if we are intelligibly to attribute attitudes and beliefs, or usefully to describe motions as behaviour, then we are committed to finding, in the pattern of behaviour, belief and desire, a large degree of rationality and consistency.''[12] In order to interpret another's actions we must take them to be intentional and, in general, rationally expressive of their preferences in the light of the context of their action as they see it. Without such an assumption, Davidson argues, we could not make sense of anyone's behavior. As Wittgenstein remarks, reasons to act must be "embedded in . . . [a] situation, in human customs and institutions.''[13] The same applies to reasons to use terms of language: if we are to understand language use, users must have reasons to use the terms that are connected with the situation through its customs and institutions. To communicate we must employ common criteria in applying terms. What could it mean to learn to use a term except learning to apply it by its commonly accepted criteria? Thus, in agreeing on the appropriateness of applying an evaluative term in a situation, we must agree *because* of the objective features of the moral situation that make it appropriate.

This point is perhaps obscured by the fact that the criteria for applying terms of moral judgment are more intricately connected with context than are most descriptive terms. Indeed, the description of action—what one passes judgment on—requires that we go beyond description of physical movement to take in the intention of the agent. To grasp the intention of the agent—what he or she aims to bring about—we must often put the action into its context of social practices, as when we describe someone as breaking a contract or stealing property.

Finally, we cannot reach a judgment or apply an appropriate term until we place the intended action in its relation to the intentions and expectations of others involved in the practice. To describe George as inconsiderate and dishonest or Peter as callous (as we did in the last chapter) we must tell a story, laying out a sequence that would give reasons for the judgment. And Mackie would have to do the same in order to support his description of an act as a piece of deliberate cruelty.

This contrasts with what we need to do to apply descriptive terms such as "red" or "rough." Whereas the latter terms are related to a context (what is called "red" must be capable of being seen as such by a normal observer under conditions approaching that of ordinary daylight), the context for sensory quality terms is a constant one and drawn from the usual context of sense experience. One's response to color, for example, is relatively constant and straightforward; it could be described as a purely causal relationship. Accordingly, it seems misleading to liken the "qualities" that figure in moral judgment to the secondary qualities of color, taste, and texture. Moral response is *dis*analogous to a response to color, for the latter requires no special preparation and no understanding of a story or context, whereas a moral response can only be the work of a concerned person who understands the moral situation.

Given that the audience is concerned and understands the story, we often reach agreement on the terms of judgment that can be applied. We have a basis for discussing the kind of consideration that would be relevant to its application. We can ask, for example, What were the practices involved? What were others' expectations? and so on. Thus, we have conditions which we can investigate and discuss in considering the appropriateness of a term or judgment.

Given audience concern and understanding, we elicit an evaluative response. Audiences normally feel attracted to or repelled by characters presented in a story; the dramatic power of literature and the theater depends on it. As the story unfolds and our grasp of the situation deepens, we feel our emotional and moral responses develop. This point comes out clearly when Joseph Butler reminds us that "The sight of a man in misery raises our compassion towards him; and if his misery be inflicted on him by another, our indignation against the author of it."[14] As we gain an understanding that another willfully inflicts this misery, we feel ourselves becoming indignant toward the victim's attacker. However, Butler notes, "when we are informed that the sufferer is a villain and is punished only for his treachery or cruelty; our compassion exceedingly lessens, and in many instances our indignation wholly subsides" (*Matthews*:249–50). Thus, Butler gets us to authenticate his point that the appropriate response shifts *as we enlarge our perception* of the intentions of the agents in the situation.

Because terms of judgment are typically so context-dependent, we often find that our judgmental term refers to the fact that the act in question fails to meet what the context requires. As Butler has it, "hence arises a proper application of the epithets, *incongruous, unsuitable, disproportionate, unfit* to actions which our moral faculty determines to be vicious" [Butler's emphasis] (*Matthews*:251). Often the term to be applied more explicitly describes the specific practice being violated: witness "theft," "promise-breaking," "looting," and many more. When one wants to know whether one can apply any of these, one knows where to look. The application of the global terms of approval or disapproval—good, bad, right, wrong—are typically derived after the context-dependent judgment is secured.

Patently, mistakes can be made in the application of terms, but as Susan Hurley observes,[15] one cannot even be in a position to make a mistake except as one who judges, working within a system, within a language game—a game we can play only by using the same objective criteria. Similarly, there will be borderline cases where we will disagree on the appropriateness of a judgment, but, once again, we can only have borders around areas that are *not* on the borders. As our discussion of debates on disagreement indicated, disagreement and discussion are intelligible only if we could have a means of objectively resolving them.

Contrary to Mackie (*Matthews*:247), the situation would not become "simpler and more comprehensible if we could replace moral quality with some response causally related" to a situation: such a causal explanation would make it completely alien to our moral judgments in which our response requires that we investigate and inquire—and do so out of our concern and interest.

In looking at cases judged by ordinary reasoners, we saw that for them the rightness of any move is grounded in what they found to be the specific conditions of action and their relation to what we are, to what we feel and care for. Thus—contrary to what Mackie's title suggests ("Inventing Right and Wrong")—moral reasoners do not suppose that they arbitrarily invent what they take to be right or wrong; rather they suppose that they discover the particular features that could be said to make it right or wrong, and do so through discussion and inquiry into human relationships and feelings. They identify the limits *within which* permissible responses lie. The inquiry does not yield moral facts or moral truths that exist independently of any reference to human interest (as the Kantian view and Mackie's "isolation test" would require). The corollary to Hamlyn's thesis once again applies: to make sense of our moral life, we must explain it in relation to human concerns in the natural world.

The moral judgments reasoners develop (often described as true or false) are based on an understanding of the situation and of the feelings of those involved; thus, they are objective in the sense that they are grounded in what we are and how we can relate to each other in our situation as we commonly perceive it. For such judgments, we note, reasoners did not require a single uniform response to any situation: alternative moves were permitted, but the alternatives were approved or condemned on the basis of objective criteria. For them, judgments were universalizable but did not require uniformity; were based on feeling, but not purely subjective; were grounded in our interests and concerns but not arbitrarily inventive.

Butler, Smith, and Hume on Motivation and Judgment

When Kant posed his motive problem, Joseph Butler and Adam Smith had, like Hume, already explored the role of feelings in objective moral language and judgment. Their reflections suggest a solution to what was to become both Kant's and Mackie's motivation problem: How can one's own interests and concerns provide a motive for constraining other concerns? How does one explain the fact that the community makes claims on one?

Butler, Smith, and Hume were confident that sentiments such as sympathy and concern for others, as well as reason, were involved in moral judgments. Butler, for example, was uncertain whether one should speak of our faculty of moral judgment as a ''sentiment of the understanding'' or a ''perception of the heart'' but he thought it must include elements of both.[16] To him it seemed clear that ''reason alone, whatever anyone may wish is not in reality a sufficient motive for virtue in such a creature as man; but this reason joined with those affections which God has impressed in his heart'' (*Matthews*:248–49). Butler (unlike Hume in Book 3, Part 1, of the *Treatise*) left no doubt that both reason and the affections are required. Reason ''joined with those affections'' provide a motive that would constrain us in fulfilling our other inclinations.

How is it to be joined with natural desires and affections? How do we combine the two in forming judgments (which we then feel obliged to fulfil)? Part of the answer comes in Butler's point that we judge actions and motives—and not consequences: ''Acting, conduct, behaviour abstracted from all regard to what is in fact and event the consequence of it, is . . . the natural object of moral discernment . . . Intention of such and such consequences, indeed, is always included; for it is part of the action itself'' (*Matthews*:251). One judges an agent as aiming to bring about good or ill consequences; thus, judgment centers on motive, on attitudes toward other persons. Such judgment is possible because we take in the social context and mutual intentions; as Butler showed earlier, we may, by increasing our understanding, move from compassion to indignation toward one figure and from indignation toward sympathy for another. One's judgment and one's description proceeds, employing something like Davidson's principle of charity, taking note of actors' particular situations and capacities. We see this as Butler notes, "For everyone has a different sense of harm done by an idiot, madman or child, and by one of mature understanding; though the action of both, including the intention, which is part of the action, be the same. . . . Now this difference must arise from somewhat discerned in the nature or capacities of one, which renders the action vicious."[17]

Because it is these features of one's action and situation that "renders the action vicious," they also determine how the agent judges his or her *own* action and determine what "one could say" of an action: they are the features that make moral judgment and language possible. "One"—that is, an informed and concerned one—reaches judgment of motives by considering what a person in such a situation with such capacities could do. Agreement in judgment of motive is possible because we can proceed from and make use of a common understanding of people's abilities and needs as well as their commitments within a situation.

Self-judgment assesses motives, and, in Butler's view, moral self-judgment is authoritative over other inclinations and motives. It is authoritative in the sense that its authority is acknowledged, not in the sense that it always turns out to be dominant. How or why should it come to be conceived as having such authority? Or, put in terms of Mackie's and the projectivists' question: How does it come to constrain our other inclinations? Perhaps we should abandon the projectivists' causal model and ask: Why do we come to defer to the voice of our self-judgment in constraining our other inclinations?

Adam Smith's explanation seems helpful. Butler had taken it that our "several affections" included regard for others, so that by nature we are "fitted for society." Adam Smith also found evidence that our natural motives led to moral constraint: "Nature, when she formed man for society, endowed him with an original desire to please, and an original aversion to offending his brethren. She taught him to feel pleasure in their favorable, and pain in their unfavorable regard . . . Nature . . . has endowed him, not only with a desire of being approved of, but with a desire of being what ought to be approved of" (*TMS(S)*:138).

Smith says we first learn moral judgment through observing others': "It is placed in the countenance and behavior of those he lives with, which always mark when they enter into and when they disapprove of his sentiments; and it is here that he first views the propriety and impropriety of his own passions" (ibid.). Observing that mankind "approve of some of them, and are disgusted by others," he becomes "elevated in the one case, and cast down in the other" since he longs for the others' approval: "his desires and aversions, his joys and sorrows, will now often become the cause of new desires and aversions, new joys and sorrows; they will now, therefore, interest him deeply, and often call upon his most attentive consideration" (*TMS(S)*:138, 139). Thus we are led to "examine our own passions and conduct and consider how these must appear to them by considering how they would appear to us if in their situation"(*TMS(S)*:140). We learn to judge ourselves because we see how others judge us, and as we have a powerful desire for their approval, we adopt their standard as authoritative over our own behavior.

He describes the process by which we judge ourselves:

When I endeavour to examine my own conduct, when I endeavour to pass sentence upon it, and either to approve or condemn it, it is evident that, in all such cases, I divide myself, as it were, into two persons: and that I, the examiner and judge, represent a different character from that other I, the person whose conduct is judged of. The first is the spectator whose sentiments with regard to my own conduct I endeavour to enter into, by placing myself in his situation and by considering how it would appear to me from that particular point of view" (ibid.).

Butler tells us a story about others to get us to authenticate *that* impartial spectators would agree in their responses about *others*; Smith explains it in relation to *self*-judgment. Moral reasoning and the standard of rightness can be defined by referring to the process of considering what sentiments (of approval or disapproval) an action would elicit in concerned judges. Note that, whereas the standard requires attention to consequences, it is impartiality and *not* the utility standard that fulfills it. It is not judgment that is to be reached by simply counting or guessing at the total amount of happiness in an act's consequences. It is not a judgment that one could reach in isolation from one's involvements and responses to others. Our native concern for others leads us to value what others could accept: this leads us to judge by the criterion of mutual acceptability. It is a judgment that centers on the mutual responsiveness of persons. We come to judge ourselves and others by the impartial standard by which we perceive others to judge in a mutually responsive community.

The community makes moral claims on one from the beginning, and it is through responding to these claims that one comes to make impartial judgments of oneself, organizing one's activities around them. Smith holds that what would or should be generally acceptable becomes what would be acceptable to oneself and what is required for self-respect—"that inward tranquility and self-satisfaction" (ibid., 141). We apply the impartial-spectator standard in aiming for self-respect, a quest originally founded in our admiring regard for others and our awareness of the standard by which they are judged to be admirable; moral rectitude and self-respect come to be desired for their own sake. "Man naturally desires . . . not only praise, but praiseworthiness, or to be that thing which, though it be praised by nobody, is, however, the natural and proper object of praise" (*TMS(S)*: pt 3, chap. 2).

Hume (Butler's admirer and Smith's friend) offered parallel reasoning. In the *Enquiry*, he argues that like the terms of moral language, "the notion of morals implies some sentiment common to all mankind, which recommends the same object to general approbation and makes every man, or most men, agree in the same opinion or decision concerning it"(*E*:75). When one uses moral language, he "expresses sentiments, in which he expects all his audience are to concur with him. He must, therefore, depart from his private and particular situation, and chuse a point of view common to him with others: He must move some universal principle of the human frame, and touch a string, to which all mankind have an accord and symphony" (ibid., 85). For Hume, one must choose an impartial point of view to speak coherently about oneself and avoid contradictions in one's own view of the matter: " 'twere impossible we cou'd ever make use of language, or communicate our sentiments to one another, did we not correct the momentary appearances of things."[18] Thus we come to the "calm determination of our passions" by which we are able to oppose our passions under the guidance of reason.

Our assessment is to be based on the facts of the situation. "In moral deliberations, we must be acquainted, beforehand, with all the objects, and all their relations to each other; and from a comparison of the whole, fix our choice or approbation. . . . All the circumstances of the case are supposed to be laid before us, ere we can fix any sentence of blame or approbation. If any material circumstance be yet unknown or doubtful, we must first employ our enquiry or intellectual faculties to assure us of it; and must suspend for a time all moral decision or sentiment" (*E*:77). Thus, on Hume's account, we do not passively receive sentiments of moral approval or blame; nor do we project a character on events that can not be warranted through cooperative inquiry. By coming to agreement on the character of the moral situation and by responding with a sentiment common to all humanity, we can achieve the impartial judgment reflected in our agreement with others.

Kant had argued that "the universality with which (moral laws) should hold for all rational beings . . . is lost when their foundation is taken from the *particular constitution of human nature*, or the accidental circumstances in which it is placed" (*Abbot*:61). Yet the judgments described by Smith and Hume are universal and are "taken from the particular constitution of human nature" and the circumstances in which it is placed.

Kant had reckoned it would be futile to study our feelings and desires to determine "an objective principle on which we should be *enjoined* to act" (*Abbot*:43) in ways that would override our desires and feelings. But there is overriding injunctive power in such judgments; they can constrain our other impulses and desires. They do so because *we recognize what is mutually acceptable as having moral authority*. We recognize that the procedure of looking for what can be universalized defines the procedure for moral judgment and hence defines what commands moral respect.

We feel constrained to act in accord with what impartial judgment of the community requires because we take its judgment to be authoritative. Although Hume is famous for his remark that reason must be the slave of the passions, he finally held that "reason requires . . . impartial conduct" and reason provides "a calm determination of the passions."[19] Coherent and appropriate moral sentiments and passions must be impartial and generally acceptable. It is their impartiality and universalizability that commands our moral respect and gives them their legitimate constraining power.

In this Hume, like Smith, seems to have offered a plausible explanation of why we adopt commonly accepted standards of judgment as authoritative and why we should be willing to redirect our other inclinations in order to meet moral obligations and uphold moral law. If we have a natural regard for others and a natural desire that they have a regard for us, we have a natural desire for mutual approval. Mutual approval of mutual relationships is the judgment of the community. If moral virtue is understood as being what is generally acceptable, we can take what is worthy of others' approval— what is universalizable—as a morally authoritative standard.

Given that members of our community make moral demands on our motives; that those demands are taken to be the authority for moral judgment; and that members are perceived to judge and approve actions on an impartial basis, we have reason to adopt their standard of impartial judgment as authoritative and to organize our activities around it.

Butler, Smith, and Hume's accounts would not require that we go outside of nature for the justification of a moral standard nor for the explanation of motives for respecting moral norms and constraining other inclinations. If we take "moral judgment" as referring to judgment acceptable to members of the community, it seems that our view of what a concerned, impartial spectator would demand should exercise moral authority over our lives. To take as one's own standard what an impartial spectator would accept is a way of insisting that one find one's standard by considering what kind of action should be regarded as generally acceptable. So, this sense of moral judgment seems to give a plausible explanation for our moral motives while it takes account of the specific conditions and consequences of action: by this account, moral objectivity is not to be found *in* non-social *things* (contrary to Mackie), and it implies nothing about any "immutable fitnesses of things" (contrary to Blackburn).

Yet, this account meets Kant's morally important requirement that we be impartial in our judgments; it also explains how we acquire our respect for the moral law. Kant writes, in *The Grounding for the Metaphysics of Morals, (The Doctrine of Virtue)*: "The moral law interests us because it is valid for us as men, since it has sprung from our will as intelligence and hence from our proper self" (*Abbot*:43). It is valid because it is the rational product of a community of moral judges: this gives it its authority and right of command.

While the account of the impartial spectator's judgments would seem to explain both how judgments can be the expression of our sentiments and can be articulated on objective ground, it also makes intelligible the role of disagreement and discussion. Moreover, the account of these judgments seems to reflect what we saw going on in ordinary cases of moral reasoning, especially as this involved a role for the concept of our moral anatomy. Reasoning turned on seeing oneself as a person to be understood and treated like others. Part of that requirement is that one understand what persons could do and how and why they would judge.

To further confirm these views we need to see how they square with other current philosophical and empirical studies of moral reasoning, action, and language use. It will be especially useful to look at studies of such activities in young children—a matter to which we will turn in the next chapter.

Before we do so, it may be helpful to summarize the principal points we have argued for in this chapter. We began by arguing, against Kant and Mackie, that moral judgments cannot be unconditional and hence can be based on our sentiments, our understanding of human nature, and the facts of the moral situation. Further, since in judging we evaluate decisions about human actions, our judgments must be based on these factors: the moral life can only be intelligible if we do not attempt to judge unconditionally, if we consider and judge people as biological entities who are involved in a web of social relationships.

Against Simon Blackburn, I argued that although moral judgments are based on our emotive response to a situation they are not *caused* by the situation; they are not the projection of our passive reactions: moral judgments are reflective responses and are open to support and correction by inquiry and discussion. As the responses of informed and concerned agents they can be said to be objective, and this is reflected in our objective criteria for the application for the terms of moral judgment. Moreover, the projectivist position (of Blackburn) must end in denying the validity of our fundamental moral notions such as obligation and self-respect.

In the final section, I appealed to the work of Butler, Smith, and Hume as showing how our moral motive to constrain by a universal standard is grounded in our feelings and reason. Our concern for others leads us to take what is mutually approvable as the authoritative standard for judging our obligations to others and for our moral judgment of ourselves.

4 / Moral Reasoning and Action in Young Children

Through sampling everyday moral reasoning and the use of ordinary moral language, we have seen that responsiveness or concern for others is one of the natural motives that enter into the acceptable moral reasoning and action of a responsible person; we've also seen evidence that such reasoning and action proceeds from self-concern and a respect for the reasoning of a community. Because we saw that we could discuss, inquire into, and agree on moral judgments, we confirmed the idea that they could be objective and impartial. If we agree that we judge impartially by assessing the motives of the agent, the drive for self-respect becomes a quest for action in accord with acceptable motives. But these notions need further support. How do they tie onto our cognitive life generally? Just how do we come to be able to make such judgments? How and when do these motives become inter-related? How does our moral anatomy develop?

Thus, we need to focus on the way in which very young children come to reason, speak, and act morally. For that we'd do well to look first at recent philosophical discussions of the conditions of moral responsibility and then at some empirical studies of child development. Drawing on these points and on elements from our samplings of reasoning and usage, we can trace out the ways in which they support each other and provide a sketch of the moral anatomy. This sketch will give us reason to modify the views of moral development posed by Piaget, Rawls, and Kohlberg. It will lead to a rejection of the egoist philosophical positions as these have been defined by Bernard Williams's and Robert Nozick's presentations of egoist views (in chapter 5) and will provide grist for many of the arguments of subsequent chapters.

A SKETCH OF THE MORAL ANATOMY

Four recent philosophical accounts of aspects of moral responsibility, if they are taken together, suggest some of the qualities of consciousness necessary to functioning as a morally responsible person. We shall find that they confirm many of the ideas of Butler, Smith, and Hume. If we look at these together, along with accounts of reasoning and usage, they provide what may be called "a sketch of the moral anatomy," elements fundamental to being a moral person. Though the four accounts joined together were not always so interrelated, we will see that the four cohere with each other and with other philosophical and empirical accounts. Of the four, one concerns how moral reasoning requires that an individual be able to give an account of his or her actions. A second concerns our acquisition of moral language by which we can describe our actions. A third deals with language for ascribing motives, while a fourth treats the kinds of reasoning acceptable in moral judgments. Although they were first presented as individually necessary, they will be seen to contribute to a joint account that is further supported by evidence from empirical studies and ordinary moral reasoning.

Being Accountable

The first line of argument holds that a necessary condition of becoming a responsible person is that one be able to give an account of one's actions: to become a responsible person one must be able to answer questions about one's actions and give reasons why one acts as one does. For this one must be able to see one's actions as falling under a description that is current in one's community. Daniel Dennett, in quoting an argument by G. E. M. Anscombe, makes a philosophical point on which many agree when he writes: "If I am to be held responsible for an action (a bit of behavior of mine under a particular description), I must have been aware of that action under that description."[1] I must be able to see both what others include under a description and see my actions as falling under that description. To fulfill this requirement, I must be informed about the nature and quality of my actions: I must know how to describe what I am doing.

Some might object that to claim that this feature must be universal for all societies is unwarranted now and must be so in the future;

that we could not support such a claim without checking all possible societies, and that could never be done. But the objection is surely ill founded, for if we are speaking of judging someone to be at fault in his or her voluntary actions, we are necessarily speaking of actions of which the person is aware: it will not count as an action of the person if the person does not aim to bring about a set of consequences in their person or in the world around them. And in aiming to bring about a set of consequences one must be aware of what one is aiming for. In acting, a person must aim to bring about some consequences, and the proper description of the action is determined by one's understanding of the circumstances in which one acts. One cannot speak of a voluntary act without speaking of what consequences a person aims to bring about, a notion that is logically tied to the person's understanding of the circumstances of the act. It would not make sense to blame people for actions if they did not know what they were doing. There is no need for some kind of wait-and-see empirical check to see whether this is universally a part of holding people responsible for their actions: so long as people make moral judgments, they will judge actions in which people seek to bring about some consequences.

Acquiring Moral Language

Moreover, this point ties onto arguments developed by Grice and Strawson (among others) which show that using language requires that one be able to ascribe to oneself the same kind of intention that one ascribes to others: "One can ascribe states of consciousness to oneself only if one can ascribe them to others. One can ascribe them to others only if one can identify other subjects of experience. And one cannot identify others if one can identify them only as subjects of experience, possessors of states of consciousness."[2]

There must be some objectively identifiable criteria for the term to be intelligible for people generally, if I am to communicate about my intentions or subjective states. As Smith, Hume, and Davidson noted, I must describe my own purpose and situation in a language that I can apply to others. I must, in the language of Strawson's *Individuals*, see the connection between the criteria for the first and third person application of a term. Hence, in acquiring the ability to apply personal predicates and descriptions to my behavior, I always put into use my ability to identify others' intentions and determine that they are like my own. It follows that as I come to use self-descriptive language I must be able to reason about other's intentions. To learn to use any language by which we can describe human action, I must, in some measure, conceive of myself as a person among persons, one with motives and intentions like others', one whose "first person criteria" correlate with the "third person criteria" I apply to others.

As the "in some measure" suggests, this ability to conceive of ourselves and other persons must be a matter of degree—it does not come to us all at once or in equal amounts—and this gives us one of the reasons why we are held responsible in various degrees, degrees that change as we can acquire a clearer conception of ourselves and others through acquiring a language.

In learning the language a child must be interested in, and attentive to, persons around it, for it is from those persons that the child must acquire a sense of the terms by which it can describe its own feelings and situation.

The Language of Motives

The third line of argument, advanced by R. S. Peters, in *Reason and Compassion*, and Thomas Nagel, in *The Possibility of Altruism* (considered in chapter 2), can be linked with the above two. It holds that some of the mental predicates one must learn to use are terms by which we ascribe motives and give moral reasons—terms which, again, must have the same meaning for others as for ourselves: in order to describe myself as penitent, remorseful, or impartial, I must know how those terms are to be tied onto others' intentions and actions. To learn them, I must be able to read others' intentions, see others as like myself, and compare their intentions, motives, and moves with my own. A child must master this language to describe its actions and to give reasons for them. To master fully the language of reasons it must be able to compare its own reasons with others' reasons. To apply correctly the moral language related to acceptable, other-regarding motives for action, it must know what it is to have such motives itself.

Acceptable Reasoning

Thus, the first three points tie onto the fourth in that one must be able to compare reasons and know what counts as a good reason to be able to evaluate one's own or others' reasons. If reasons are to be taken seriously as reasons, others must see them as relevant to the conclusion reached and as proceeding from morally acceptable motives. As Smith and Hume indicated, if I can be described as acting responsibly, my reasons must be acceptable to impartial judges generally.

If I am to be able to understand my actions and know what I am undertaking, I must be able to describe my actions in generally intelligible terms. But a central feature of my understanding what I do is my understanding whether the action is permissible in my society; I have an incomplete understanding of its real effect on myself or others until I see it as acceptable or not by my society's evaluation. To acquire and use correctly moral terms that pronounce actions to be permissible or not, I must become practiced at the role of impartial spectator. Until I master that language, I cannot describe or clarify purposes or plans of action for myself.

It follows that if I become a person who projects plans of action (as I must), I must (to some degree, again) have mastered the moral language within its matrix of acceptable reasons and permissible actions. I do not understand the language of reasons until I learn how they would apply to my own and others' actions. I must see how they and the reasons supporting them will bear on, and will be perceived to affect, others as well as myself. Thus, once again, I must conceive of myself as a person among persons, and in conceiving of myself as a person among persons, I must be able to focus alternately on my own and on others' interests and purposes and, where the occasion demanded, to act out of concern for the interests of others.

But, once again zealous empiricists may object that we cannot know that this quest for reasons is indeed universal, adding that it is, after all, common enough in our own culture for people to be dim about their reasons for acting and even to be unable to give reasons to support their decisions. True enough. But that does not mean that we do not hold that people should have reasons and reasons that we judge to be relevant. If someone fails to give a reason for, say, hitting another person or gives as a reason "Because his eyes are blue," we do not take kindly to that. The action must be seen to be suited to the situation, and the reason must be seen to cut to the relevant features of the situation, in order for reasons to be judged adequate.

It may be said that just because we give reasons and judge whether they are adequate in our own moral life, it does not follow that other cultures must engage in reason giving and assessing in their moral life. It may be felt that only members of a culture predisposed to rational method would so judge and that the view I have argued for is only a symptom of my cultural bias.

But the concept of blaming seems to be a part of every human culture and the concept of blaming involves the giving of reasons (though not necessarily so describing it). If we can speak of blaming someone, we are speaking of it being appropriate that people generally judge them to have acted wrongly; that means that they have acted wrongly in some identifiable particular. Whoever blames must identify the particular feature that makes the act wrong, and whoever identifies the particular will thereby have given a reason in support of the judgment; whoever cannot identify the specific feature of the action that makes it wrong could not be said to have made a clear or reliable judgment of the case. Reasons, to be reasons, must be such that their relevance could be made clear to people generally,[3] and so, reasons must be treated as relevant or not to the conclusion reached by the members of the community. Hence, our reasons for blaming must take the relevant particular into account; we can't speak of acceptable moral judgments for any culture without implying the existence of reasons in support of the judgments.

If someone objects that it may be that not all possible societies will employ moral judgments, one can't argue against the possibility of such nonmoral creatures, but one would be dealing with creatures who lack fundamental dimensions of life as we have experienced it: they would lack the experience of guilt, blame, self-respect, resentment, and much besides that is tied to these. These are activities that seem to be fundamental to living in society. Could it be called a society if its members did not cooperate? If they cooperated must they not act in mutually approved ways? How could they be mutually approvable if they did not make judgments of approval? To make judgments according to what is mutually approvable is to make moral judgments. Making moral judgments seems to be inseparable from living in human society. Moreover, if empirical support is wanted, comparative anthropologists have maintained that moral judgment and the giving of moral reasons are features of every culture.[4] Carolyn Pope Edwards holds: "Moral values, or standards, constitute one of the most important aspects of social knowledge for children in any society. Standards are defined as conceptions of the 'good,' 'right,' or 'obligatory' that influence choice in human action.''[5]

If an observer of another culture reported that it lacked all moral concepts, we might question what conception of "moral" the observer was using in arriving at this conclusion. It would be as if the observer reported that members of this culture did not see and feel the world as you and I do. We could not know how to speak of such creatures' experiences. We could not know how to understand their reasons or their view of the world. As Martin Hollis and others have argued,[6] our ability to translate and give an account of another culture depends on our assuming that they experience and think in ways parallel to our own.

Thus making moral judgments seems to be essential to being human.

In any event, for those of us who make moral judgments, giving and assessing moral reasons is one of the essential features of our moral anatomy.

GOOD REASONS AND FEELING CONCERN

As Butler and Smith argued, coming to agreement on others' moral reasons involves agreement to accept or reject their motives as well as agreement in reading their intentions. Nagel spells out how those whose motives we accept as responsible are those who exhibit some concern for others; this is similar to Herbert Fingarette's description of responsibility as a "specific kind of care." A parallel point is made by theorists such as Rodger Beehler, who notes the connection between caring and prescriptive moral language: "Just as in the case of colour discrimination there is a public criterion of 'red' which we can appeal to by virtue of the fact that we agree in what we see, so too, in the case of moral discrimination, there's a moral concept (and specific criteria) of 'decency' to which we can appeal by virtue of the fact (and to the extent) that we agree in caring about one another.''[7] By this line of argument, caring is a central factor in moral reasoning: minimally our reasons must indicate that we have not neglected to consider others for our reasons to be acceptable to them. For Nagel, one's moral reasons must be comparable to others': in them "the same motivational content of one's ethical judgments must be present . . . One must be able to mean by it what they mean when they make the same assertion."⁸ We must be able to know how others see a situation and what kind of motives they could accept. Packed into this move is a recognition of what it means to be a person, a recognition that must inform the process of communicating about and judging actions.

Thus, on the one hand the notion of good reasons implies the notion of a community of moral reasoners whose agreement gives at least a prima facie sanction of one's judgment. On the other hand, the notion of good reasons implies the notion of acceptable motives, of acting out of deference or concern for others' desires and intentions. One's motives in acting will not, as a rule, be acceptable to others if one shows no concern for how one's acts undermine others' interests.

We find these notions illustrated in our case studies involving George (in chapter 2). Class members evaluated reasons and excuses in relation to whether they would be acceptable, and thus, there was always tacit deference to a community of acceptors and refusers of reasons. Class members blamed George for his lack of concern and portioned their blame according to the degree of his unconcern, a point confirmed by terms from ordinary usage.

A person who takes his or her identity from a society responds to its moral demands as these are reflected in its moral terms. One's choosing that identity is an expression of regard for its members as well as an acknowledgment of the community's claim to moral authority. In doing so, one achieves self-respect, "that inward tranquility and self-satisfaction" of which Smith wrote, by satisfying the demands of the impartial spectator. In doing so, one must choose acts that are generally acceptable—that is, acts which show regard for others and acknowledge the claim of community judgment against one's other inclinations. And so, this aspect of Smith and Hume's solution to Kantians' and projectivists' problem of moral motivation is confirmed.

One might object, acknowledging that in learning how to apply moral terms, we would learn the criteria for the acceptability of actions and inclinations as these are held in our community. The objector could agree that learning how to communicate would involve learning of others and their intentions. But, the objector might continue, this does not require that we postulate that the person must have the right kind of concern for the others: one could be concerned to know about the intentions and desires of another, but none of that means that one must have a concern *for* the other, as an end in itself.

In reply, we must note that to know what it means to have the right kind of concern in specific situations, one must have felt the concerns *oneself*; one must know the first and third person criteria for the application of the terms: to be terms descriptive of persons they must apply to all alike. One must have felt the concern that is required for the various terms that must be used to describe acceptable behavior to learn how to apply the terms correctly. That does not mean that one is always feeling such concern or is always acting on it. It does mean that such feelings of concern *for* others are part of one's moral anatomy and that they have been put to use in grasping the sense of the moral terms that indicate what is morally acceptable.

Some might object to saying that acceptable motives are those reflecting concern for others on the ground that we have no warrant for saying that others will have any concern for themselves and, hence, need make no demands on others' motives. They might support their stance by saying that it seems to be a fact that some people have no care for their own lives whereas others are listless and numb to any kind of abuse: if people can be suicidal or catatonic, can we say that people generally require that we take their interests into account in making our moral decisions? Could we know that all people from all cultures have such self-concern?

In response, we must note that ordinarily we are aware that people do have concerns for themselves. It may be granted that suicides and catatonics show that not everyone has such concerns, but anyone who is to function responsibly as a member of the community (of any culture) must have such concern. For they must meet obligations, control their actions, and be able to give an account of them; in all societies, they must aim to meet obligations and control their actions with understanding. Those who have such aims cannot be without interests; to them it cannot be a matter of indifference whether their interests are taken into account in others' reasons.

Our having concern for others and seeing ourselves as persons among persons must be, in some degree, with us from the beginning and be part of the process by which we become morally responsible. Without being concerned about, and attentive to, others' interests we could not learn the language by which we describe our situation. Without the language, we could not effectively conceive of ourselves or offer reasons in support of our choices to others: we could never learn to reason without the concepts acquired in our community. Thus, in a language-using and reason-giving community—in a human community—mutual awareness and concern (in varying degrees) must pervade these moral relationships.

EMPIRICAL STUDIES OF CHILDREN
AND THE MORAL ANATOMY

We find evidence that reciprocating awareness and interest in others is found in infants and is put to work in their earliest learning of social relationships. The presence of this awareness and interest is vividly suggested in this description by the father of a newborn:

> Thirty minutes after her birth, my daughter was already taking my measure. She lay in my lap, startlingly alert, scanning me as I scanned her, our gazes moving about each other's bodies, limbs, faces, eyes, returning, then locking. The same thing happened, I soon noticed, as she lay cradled in my wife's embrace, this locking of gaze into gaze. And it was only gradually that the wondrous mystery of that exchange began to impress me—for even an hour ago my daughter's eyes had been sheathed in undifferentiated obscurity, and now what captured their attention? Other sets of *eyes* . . . Of all the possible objects of attention, what is so naturally compelling about two dark pools of returned attention?[9]

Part of our fun in baby watching comes from seeing its delight and excitement grow with the appearance of its mother, perhaps beginning to cackle and to pedal its feet in the air, as she engages its eyes, and then in seeing the delight with which it imitates her moves in little games. Part of our fun comes in witnessing their communication and in seeing the baby's demonstration of its awareness of its mother and its delight in her. Our philosophical interest is drawn to its concern for her and its lively interest in others, but it is especially drawn to the baby's delight in entering into little games with its mother and others. For, to play a game you have to recognize what the other person is up to, what kind of rule is to be followed.

Some may feel that appeal to such observation must be inconclusive because one can't be sure that we are all reflecting on the same
kind of mother-child interchange. I'm inclined to think that all readers will be able to call to mind interchanges that involve the same
kind of communication and play. But if there is doubt on that score,
we can consider one of the filmed studies of mothers playing with
and caring for their babies. In one such extensive study, the mother-
child relationship was filmed during the first twenty weeks of the infants' lives. From studying the films, the authors report that from
the first "the mother takes on facial expressions, motions and postures indicative of emotion, as though she and he were communicating . . . Most mothers, in sum, are unwilling or unable to deal with
neonatal behaviors as though they are meaningless."[10]

The study continues, describing how the mother's treatment initi-
ates a reciprocal caring relationship with the infant through which it
learns to play, and, hence, communicate. The authors report that the
mother treats her time with the infant as a time for communicating,
adjusting the complexity of her behavior to fit the infant's stage of
development. She presents behavior as a model for the infant. She
imitates his activity, enlarging upon it and he delightedly enters into
the play. Thus, the infant "becomes aware of his action, visualizing
her imitation of it and reproduces it for himself again. As he does so,
he has the opportunity to add on to it . . . (in part) by modelling his
behavior to match the enlarged version."[11] After observing mothers
with their newborns over a twenty-week period, the authors concluded that both mother and child were learning rules for their interaction, rules "which were constantly being altered by each."[12]

In these accounts we notice at once that the child's capacity for
seeing what its mother is doing and responding to it requires that the
child see her intent and reciprocate, knowing that she will see its intent and respond to it: reciprocity and each's taking the view of the
other is essential to the play. Theirs is a kind of game in which the
mother does this, the infant does that, then the mother does another
thing (in accord with a pattern), or it might be a case of imitation
where if the mother does this, then the infant does this also. In either case, there is a kind of rule generation involved in the communication: the infant knows how to take the mother's intention,
knows what she has in mind for it, and knows that she will also
know how to take what it does. So the infant must have an aware-

ness of its behavior as falling under what it takes to be intended for it.

Thus, at the age of four weeks (when we can definitely say that such play begins) we find, in primitive form, what looks like the abilities that are described as necessary to moral personhood in the philosophical literature—down to and including the beginnings of self-consciousness. The infant's self-consciousness is not consciousness of behavior as falling under a verbal description that is known to the infant, but it is consciousness that it uses in its game and on which it builds in subsequent learning.

Not only do the studies show the child's ability to read intentions, the same group of filmed studies exhibit the infant's *interest* in others, noted, in part, in its use of some bits of vocalizing to bring about action, to bring about a repetition of the game. It is also reflected in the youngster's shift in mood and attitude in response to the moods and concerns of those around it.

The child's attitudes and responsiveness reflect those of its caretaker(s). Another investigator reports "the mother who hears these episodes of non-crying vocalizations, even though busy, often cannot resist the appeal, and comes to the infant to enter the game."[13] In such play, which continues through the first year of the child's life, both the use of rules and communication appear. "The young child reproduces parts of what the model is doing, and then puts the components together in new combinations. The young are able to play with the components."[14] Moreover, the interest in the other partner to the play was a consuming interest for both parties to it. Investigators report that in looking at films of four-week-old infants at play, they "could look at any segment of the infant's body shown on the film and detect whether he was watching an object or interacting with his mother—so different was his attention, vocalizing, smiling and motor behavior with the inanimate stimulus as opposed to [the child's response when with] the mother."[15]

Thus, we find in primitive form, not only the kind of ability to gain insight into another's desires and intentions that is required for moral reasoning (contrary to Piaget and Rawls), but we also seem to find, in addition to the reading of intention, an indication of the presence of concern for others that enters into moral motivation, according to our account of the moral anatomy. Such concern does not seem to be alien to tiny infants: the infant searches for its mother and registers delight on finding her. This appears at a time when we could not speak (as supporters of egoism are wont to do) of the infant calculating as to what would serve its future interests. Moreover, the concern is an important factor in the game in which it begins to develop its capacities. The games begin because of the interest the infant first takes in others and the interest is apparently heightened because of the games. In those interchanges—which are marked by the child's continual interest and responsiveness to the moods and concerns of its caretaker—we see its first exercise of capacities that will be required for it to *develop* rational competence.

Thus, we cannot explain the child's interest as flowing *from* its rational calculation of self-interest. We cannot accept the view expressed by some Freudians, that the infant comes to be concerned *about* the caretaker—and not feel concern *for* her—and takes this interest because it recognizes that it is completely dependent on her. At this stage, the child is in no position to grasp the notion of dependence or to calculate the beneficial consequences of its taking an interest in another. Rather, we must say that the interest, the responsiveness, and concern for others seem just to be there, in us from the beginning, waiting to be channeled into the many determinate kinds of concern and respect for others that figure in moral action and reasoning.

Mother-child interchanges such as those described earlier mark peaks of cognitive performance for an infant under six months old. But the child builds on that beginning. Other studies, made of children from six months to one year old, show that during that period the child is more likely to become involved in activities turning on such reciprocity and mutuality. If given a caring environment during this time, the child will be likely to be working out what a number of investigators describe as a secure attachment. This attachment is characterized by the child's preference for its caretaker, shown by its heightened interest directed toward her (or him) and by the frequency with which it takes care to establish eye contact with her (or him). It's also characterized by its initiating relationship with the caregiver and by what investigators describe as trust. For them, there is no single set of discrete bits of behavior that can be individually counted to be taken as evidence of a child having formed an attachment with its caregiver, investigators such as Ainsworth insist.

Rather, the child's behavior forms a system, including the following features:[16] (1) the securely attached child of twelve months will take its caregiver as a secure base for explorations, from whom it readily separates for forays into the unknown; (2) it shows signs of enjoyment at sharing its play with its caregiver, turning to her (him) to establish eye-contact and smile; (3) it is generally friendly toward strangers when its parent is present though it becomes wary when strangers approach too closely; (4) typically, it is easily comforted by its caregiver when it is distressed; and (5) when it is separated from its caregiver, it is active in seeking contact with her (or him) and in seeking interaction with the caregiver on their reunion.

Our interest here is drawn to the point that while the child moves toward limited autonomy and independent satisfaction in its activities, responsiveness toward others develops: it is eager to share its pleasures with its mother, and if separated from her, it is quick to rejoin her (even though it has been observed to enjoy its play in isolation). In developing this kind of relationship, the child shows that the insight into others' intentions and the concern for their wishes that could be detected in its play as a young infant are now taken up and incorporated into its self-directed exploration and play: it reads its mother's approval and disapproval; it enjoys her presence and (within limits) that of others; and it is eager to share its satisfactions with its caregiver and willing to share some with others.

Ainsworth, who has pioneered much of the work in this area, holds that individual differences in the quality of attachment derive from differences in the quality of the care given. Other investigators agree: they hold that it is not the mere presence of the mother but her psychic responsiveness that is required in order for the infant to develop confidence about its relation to the caregiver and to its environment. They consider psychic availability to be indicated by the promptness, consistency, and care with which the mother responds to the child's growing autonomy.[17] Ainsworth asserts that one could predict what the quality of the attachment will be from observing the quality of the care given: consistent, prompt, sensitive care leads to secure attachment, to the child's development of its own sense of control of its actions, and to its forming a pattern of relationship with others.

The studies agree that the patterns of behavior found in the securely attached child are relatively stable, and, of these, the patterns for forming personal relationships are of particular interest for us. The securely attached child who at eighteen months is appreciative of and alive to its parents' presence, who is eager to share its satisfactions with them, will be interested in others and responsive to them—unlike the child who has failed to form a secure attachment. The same child is likely to show similar signs of secure attachment in follow-up studies (which were done on many of the same children in successive six-month intervals). Of the follow-up studies, investigators report that the securely attached children show both pleasure at meeting with new acquaintances as well as an ability to enjoy cooperative activity with them.[18] They reason that the skill and capacities for cooperation for each period grow out of the interest and insights developed during the preceding periods.

Our philosophical interest in attachment is drawn to the point that the child can only become attached through an already present responsiveness and ability to read others' intentions. It is as a result of the attachment that it moves through limited autonomy and becomes more responsive to others.

A number of observers of child development support these conclusions and suggest that the child's relation to other members of its family is crucial to that development. Martin Hoffman is among those who have called attention to toddlers' ability to take an interest in, and to interpret, others' intentions. He noted that very young children are able to learn about social rules through conversations about others' feelings conducted among members of their family.[19]

Judy Dunn reports that children in their second year grow in their ability to anticipate others' feelings, to understand others' intentions, and to understand and communicate about social rules. She observes that such "children . . . take part in conversations about others' feelings in the second year; they play and show interest in the cause of such feelings." Although they are not yet able to make judgments about Kohlbergian hypothetical dilemmas, she writes that . . . they are very close to being able to assign responsibility for family transgressions, to make choices about whom to support in family disagreements and to use this understanding."[20] Their understanding of the simplest of moral relations and rules is not always acted upon. As Dunn observes, it is indicated as much by their knowingly breaking the rules to tease or demand attention as it is by their willing compliance.

Moreover, the child's preparedness to comply and act out of concern for others seems not to be a matter of fixed phases or stages but rather to be related to the concern exhibited by other members of their family. Dunn notes that as parents were more intensely concerned in discussing the importance of not hurting others, urging children to consider how others would feel if mistreated, children were more likely subsequently to be sympathetically aroused and helpful in responding to others' distress. Then, too, she finds that toddlers with close affectionate relations with their siblings show an earlier development of the ability to consider the position of the other, to act as conciliator, and to cooperate with others. Thus, it appears that the family's existence as a micro-community of mutual concern and its concern for others is important to the child's gaining a sense of community. The family's discussion with the child of the importance of such concern is instrumental in introducing the child to a sense of its membership in the larger moral community.

Observations of children's actual behavior provide the most persuasive evidence of the young child's ability to grasp another's situation and act out of concern for the other. Lawrence Blum offers a few examples:

[Example 1]
Sarah, twelve months, is sitting with Clara, fifteen months, on Clara's mother's lap. The girls have grown up together and are very close. Clara is holding a plastic cup which she drops on the floor, cries, and points to. Sarah climbs out of Clara's mother's lap, gets the cup, and gives it to Clara.

[Example 2]
Michael, fifteen months, is struggling with his friend Paul over a toy. Paul starts to cry. Michael appears concerned and lets go of the toy so Paul has it. But Paul continues to cry. Michael pauses, then gives his own teddy bear to Paul. Paul continues crying. Michael pauses again, runs to the next room, gets Paul's security blanket, and gives it to him. Paul stops crying.

[Example 3: Number six in Blum's list—and my favorite.]
Sarah, three, gives Clara, three, her own Donald Duck hat (to keep "forever"), saying that she has done so because Clara has (recently but not in the moment) lost her (Boston) Celtics cap.[21]

As Blum remarks, these examples indicate not only the child's grasp of what is causing the other's distress but a concern to remove the condition. Although the children were presumably in the presence of adults, each intitiated the solution independently. The oldest child in these examples, Sarah, is three. Observers note that by the time the child is five, it is involved in relatively independent relationships with other five-year-olds.[22]

WORKING OUT SOLUTIONS

I want to remind the reader of the moral significance of some of the things that we, as nonprofessional observers, observe five-year-olds doing. We see them engage in a good bit of struggle and strife over toys and favored positions at play, but we also see them work out moral solutions to problems arising in their play situations. In doing that, I submit, they often respond to parents' moral expectations and exhibit the capacities for principled moral reasoning and responsible action. Consider a pair of five-year-old boys at play with a truck and a miniature racecourse. Each prefers the truck and the other knows it—neither has made a secret of his wishes. One of them may appeal to his mother to resolve their dispute, but she—perhaps, like the mothers in these studies, unimpressed (or unfamiliar) with Piaget—may say that they will have to work it out for themselves. When she does so, they become aware of another set of intentions and expectations—hers—within which they are to work. Many things might happen, but one of the things that often happens is that they seek to satisfy both children's desires and the mother's expectations, doing so by taking turns with the truck. In working out this solution, they were not mechanically following a rule: they came (as children often do) to a mutually satisfactory conclusion out of mutual concern. Although each was obviously driven in part by self-concern, I say they came to their solution out of mutual concern because if they had not had some concern for each other, they could have walked away from the play entirely. In reaching their agreement they came to regulate their actions out of deference to the desires of others in their situations.

Here we see an early form of taking responsibility: they acted out of moral concern. Their solution could be universalized for those in that kind of situation; it could not be improved upon by someone using some "higher" or "more principled" form of moral reasoning. They had taken into account the relevant moral considerations and they acted on moral motives.

It might be objected that the boys would not be able to explain the final authority for such judgments, nor would they have presumed to have offered their judgments as universalizable. And that is true. But many of them would see it as the right thing to do and would be able to give good reasons why—reasons like: "This way no one's left out," or "Now each can have a turn."

Moreover, the five-year-olds who say, as they will, "He doesn't know how to share," are making moral judgments, and they know it. Whereas the children have not mastered the use of these concepts for all occasions, they are using them correctly in making judgments that reflect moral reasoning and that cut to the issue of fairness. And when they act by such reasoning by electing to share (or take turns, or cooperate), we need to say that they can and sometimes do act responsibly. We might say that *within the limits of situations they can understand*, they accept responsibility: they reason and act morally. It comes easily and naturally.

Moreover, by comments such as those cited, they show that they take some pride in their own moral behavior, and they see their behavior as moral, as falling under descriptions of what could be accepted. When they use expressions referring to their "sharing" and "not leaving any one out," we see that a sense of their person is connected with their activities.

Clearly, the motive of concern for their self-respect, reflecting their acknowledgment of what is approved, is at work along with their concern for their own interests and concern for the interests of those with whom they cooperate. We see the same acknowledgment and sense of their person when they feel resentment at being excluded from an activity: they see it as an affront—a morally objectionable affront—to their person; others *should* take their interests into account.

As children enter into more complex practices and social relationships, they extend the limits of the situations they can understand. As they do so, they must be able to govern themselves responsibly for those practices to function. Organizing a classroom would be unthinkable if no child in it could voluntarily act to share, to defer its gratification or to cooperate. There could be no organizational rules, since the notion of rules presupposes an ability to apply them cooperatively. The rules of a classroom do not provide a child with its first understanding of the concepts of fairness or cooperation (as some suggest); rather, rules will set up new routines and expectations within which a child must use and perhaps extend its already available concept of fairness. The child must be prepared in some measure to treat others respectfully as persons and to do it within the framework of, for example, a class. The classroom provides a more complex setting within which to practice what must already have been acquired in some measure before the child entered it.

With such practice at reading intentions related to new situations and at reasoning about them, children become better at it, as parents will note. If children of eight or nine come to their parents to ask them to resolve a dispute involving sharing with each other, their parents are likely to register some impatience and tell them that they have to work such things out for themselves. Again, we note the expectation that they can and should have resolved it for themselves—and again the common phrase, "work it out for yourselves." The phrase carries the note of mutual adjustment, of taking the relevant intentions and considerations into account.

It should be observed that parents who give this instruction to their children are imparting a central conception of what it means to be moral. It is implicit in the instructions that approval will attach to just those solutions that are "worked out," that is, to those worked out together, or to those that all affected by the action could agree to. Thus, children develop skill in the practice of fairness in society because, as Adam Smith observed, they recognize it as expected, and the expectation marks what is seen to be moral: what could be generally approved. Children might be less likely to arrive at such conclusions or such skill without the expectation of their parents, but they commonly meet the expectations and extend the approach to new situations. They commonly accept responsibility for working out solutions in specific engagements.

USING MORAL LANGUAGE AND HAVING A
SENSE OF SELF

A preparedness to act in accord with fair treatment begins to emerge for some of the child's activities, and this preparedness is furthered and made apparent by further learning of moral language. By using that language a child is able to express agreement with others in describing behavior in a way that carries approval or blame. In doing so, the child gives a new dimension to its relation with its peers. Together they will have a new regard for those with whom they can come into agreement in resolving issues of responsibility. Their agreement marks a mutually recognized level of competence and concern, a recognition made explicit in such assertions as "he doesn't know how to take turns.'' In taking up the language, the child comes to share and to acknowledge sharing—a way of looking at acts and of judging them. By doing so, the child enters a community and becomes more likely to see itself as a member.

Children's judgments of those who fail to exercise moral concern shows that recognizing that others follow moral principle comes to be a basis for indignation and hostility as well as for bestowing affection and forming attachments with others. They come to develop moral attitudes because of their concern for others and their sense that others are persons like themselves; once the attitudes are developed, they affect the quality of children's concern for others as well as the terms on which they can find self-respect.

Thus, they come to take their place and responsibilities in the world through reading each others' intentions, caring about them, and reasoning and speaking about them. This is a gradual process that begins in infancy. Reciprocal intending and caring for others is central to the process whereby one *becomes* a person, whereby one becomes able to reason about one's world. For, to be accepted as a responsible and cooperative member of the community, one's reasons for acting must have been acceptable; to have acted on acceptable reasons is to have acted out of concern. Moreover, for one to reason about and describe what would be permitted to one and what would be open for one to choose to do, one must have reasoned about such intentions. Therefore, moral reasoning and concern for others must have entered into our consciousness along with an understanding of moral terms and our early cooperating activities.

Since a child's thinking develops around thinking about action, the thought that is required for acting in the world must come early in our development: it will not do to say—as many have—that we will have to learn to reach such moral judgments *after* we have reached the age of reason. We will have to begin with some moral judgments in order to make much of a start toward the 'age of reason.'

PIAGET AND RAWLS

Piaget and Rawls are two influential writers on the development of moral reasoning who have placed in question both a very young child's ability to identify another's intentions and its ability to reason from another's point of view.[23]

Whereas Piaget sometimes offered observations that could be made only if the children were reading intentions, he has been taken as the authoritative source for the notions that very young children are incapable of reading others' intentions.

Piaget found that these weaknesses were related to children's supposed lack of concern for others. In discussing his observations of the speech of Swiss preschool children, he asserted that the young child does not attempt to place himself at the point of view of his hearer, for the young child's egoism is "complete and unconscious." In formulating a theory of how an infant formed a concept of reality, he argued (in contrast to what the above-cited filmed studies show) that for an infant, there is no difference between another person and the rest of the world.[24] Hence, the young child is said to be unable to reason about another's point of view, and Piaget characterizes the first stage of moral development as the egocentric.

Piaget's account is systematic and empirically based, but there are reasons for seriously questioning it (in addition to the philosophical arguments and empirical evidence already cited). Some of the reasons come from Piaget himself: he acknowledges, for example, that infants often take a keen interest in other persons. Indeed, it seems to be beyond question that a child must take an interest in others for it to learn from them. Moreover, a number of empirical studies with children call Piaget's findings into doubt. Many who have attempted to replicate his study found that young subjects exhibited neither complete egocentricity nor crippling inability to form insights into another's point of view. Some have suggested that we can explain this anomaly by remembering that Piaget based his conclusions on his questioning of young children. They suggest that his child subjects may have been unable to deal with his questions because of the terms he used in asking them. Recent investigators have found that when sufficient care was taken to make the questions clear to children, children of the same age as those questioned by Piaget exhibited a lively concern for others and an ability to reason from others' point of view.[25] The investigators surmise that Piaget might have reached his conclusion from using situations or terms unfamiliar to the children with the result that they were bewildered and appeared to Piaget to exhibit indifference to the points raised. From such a bewildered response, Piaget might have concluded that the children were radically egocentric (quite unlike the children current investigators have observed).

The ability to recognize others' intentions and think about them is an ability that the child must have in order to begin its moral learning from adults: as the philosophical argument concerning language learning shows in detail, the child must grasp what adults intend to say and do, even if only to follow their instructions. These propositions seem to be accepted and used even by those who formally deny them. It is instructive to see what happens to a major theory when a philosopher attempts to work with a contrary hypothesis. John Rawls's *A Theory of Justice* is a case in point. He holds that infants and young children misread or neglect to read the intentions of others, and as a consequence, he finds that a child's moral reasoning and sense of justice must develop first through the stages where it accepts authority and social associations before it comes to principled morality: he holds that the morality of authority and association are stages (stages reminiscent of Piaget's) through which the child must pass because it is *not yet able* to reason about others' intentions.

However, we are immediately puzzled by his description of the first stage of morality. He writes: "When the parent's love of the child is recognized by him on the basis of their *evident intentions* the child is assured of his worth as a person. He is made aware that he is appreciated for his own sake. In due course, the child comes to trust his parents and have confidence in his surroundings."[26] One is struck by the fact that we must make use of the child's capacity to read intentions to say that he feels loved, that he can trust his parents (in what they will intend) and feel that he has a secure place in the world. All these crucial items are tied to his ability to read the intentions of his parents, and it is from this reading that he comes to accept their authority.

It is thus with some surprise that one reads in his account of the morality of association that "motives and intentions are largely neglected by children in their appraisal of actions. The child has not yet mastered . . . the art of discerning others' intentions and feelings so that an awareness of these things cannot inform his interpretation of their behavior . . . It is no surprise then that these elements, so important from the final point of view, are left out of account at the earliest stage."[27] We should agree that the young child has not *mastered* the art of discerning others' intentions. Hence, one must agree with Rawls that young children are heavily dependent on the judgment of authorities and on associates during those formative years. But some awareness of others' intentions *must* inform children's interpretation of others' behavior, so it cannot be treated as a stage of development that excludes such awareness. (Without it they could not have come to love and trust parents and accept their moral authority.) But it is not just that Rawls's own work implies that they can read intentions. Investigators report that children as young as three years old take motive for acting as the *key* factor in making their moral evaluations.[28] This is not surprising in the light of what the philosophical arguments show: that concern about motives and intentions has to be at the center of the process by which the child learns to use the language for describing what it and others may do.

Moreover, Rawls must himself depend on children's ability to read intentions and reason about them in describing his 'morality of association.' He writes of children entering into the association morality: "Since the arrangements of the association are recognized to be just (and in the more complex roles the principles of justice are understood . . .). We may suppose that [friendship and mutual trust] have been generated by participation in the association."[29] One wants to repeat that intention is logically tied to the notion of 'trust': trust is placed in what others intend. Rawls's subsequent statement confirms the point: "Thus once a person's capacity for fellow feeling has been realized by his acquiring attachments . . . then as his associates with *evident intention* live up to their duties and obligations he develops friendly feelings toward them, together with feelings of trust."[30] Thus a reading of intentions and reasoning about them enters at each stage of the developmental process Rawls outlines: finding a secure attachment; finding friends whom one can trust; agreeing to do one's part because one can see that others do theirs. What this shows is not only that Rawls is inconsistent but also that *anyone* who attempted to deny this capacity in children would run into similar trouble. We could never account for a child's learning to understand and appreciate others' (intentional) actions without making use of the notion that the child could grasp others' intentions. The inconsistency would always appear when we deal with what we cannot avoid in dealing with normal children: one's love of parents, one's friendship and trust, and one's seeing how others intend to act.

Thus one sees the importance of Frederick Olafson's remark that "reciprocity governs the relationship of one consciousness to another" and his insistence that this reciprocity is "something more than an appendage to an already fully constituted self."[31] Rather, it is a fundamental dimension of the self and the social practices into which it must enter in order to develop. It will not do to offer an account of moral development in which mutual awareness, concern for others, reciprocity, and the reading of intentions come late in the process, for the process could not get under way without it. These are elements of our moral anatomy by which we *become* persons.

The philosophical arguments and the psychological evidence indicate that a child comes to apprehend moral meaning through observing and using moral language in action. It is a process that can take place only through the child's entering into the relationships of mutual concern in the moral community. We cannot look beyond the concerns of persons in a community for an account of the process. P. F. Strawson, in speaking of this web of mutual regard, remarked that "the existence of the general framework of attitudes itself is something we are given with the fact of human society."[32]

ARGUMENT SUMMARY

Of the motives that enter into moral reasoning and action, chapters 2 and 3 focused on the importance of concern for other persons, concern about their moral opinions, and respect for the moral judgment of the community. In the sampling of moral reasoning in chapter 2, we saw that judgments were made on the basis of what the person could do; that lack of concern for each person was taken to be a basis for moral condemnation; and that the standard used for a moral excuse was that an act be generally acceptable. In the sampling of ordinary moral terms, we saw that the required concern was understood to involve feelings: "unfeeling," "uncaring," "cold," and "lacking in compassion" are among our expressions of moral condemnation. This led us to say , in considering Nagel's point (that altruistic concerns must be a part of one's motives in moral reasoning and action), that the motives that we look for (and must have felt ourselves) in applying moral terms, must include feelings or sentiments for others. Thus the "structure of moral reasoning" could not be independent of our feelings for others.

This led us to deny—in chapter 3—Kant's claim that moral reasoning must be independent of our inclinations or reference to what humans could do. Our showing that judgment must be grounded in the understanding of the persons and the situation of action enabled us to indicate (against Mackie, Blackburn, and projectivists) how judgments could be objective. Our showing how judgments were made out of our concern for persons and our desire for their good opinion of us (and, hence, what was mutually approvable by them) enabled us to show how feelings of concern for, and desire for the respect of, others could provide the basis for respect for moral law as well as the motive to act morally. Feelings for others were seen to be required in the examples of moral reasoning and by the terms of our moral language. They were seen to result in our constraining our desires out of respect for law, for what could be universalized.

Chapter 4 sought to show how such feelings were integral to the development of our moral anatomy—how they are integral to the process by which we become moral persons. A critical point in the argument goes back to the point that we have a rich vocabulary of moral terms which require that we act out of concern for others. We took that point, together with the point (from Thomas Nagel, R. S. Peters, P. F. Strawson, and P. Grice) that, in correctly using moral terms, we must employ the same meaning and that the same meaning includes our grasp of the motive. It follows that to learn to use the altruistic terms of language one must have felt those other-regarding motives oneself. It follows that very young children, who learn to use these terms forcefully, must—contrary to Piaget and Rawls—have had such feelings; they must be able to read others' intentions; and they must be able to take the point of view of the other. The argument indicates that those elements of our moral anatomy are contributors to our development during the first two (language-learning) years of our life. Psychological observations support these claims: we see infants exhibiting an awareness of, and interest in, other persons and their intentions along with a desire to comply with their wishes; we see them responding to others' changing moods with concern; we see them responding to others' distress with help; and we see them coming to use the moral language that requires such concern. Finally, by the time children are five we see important beginnings: they begin to take responsibility for solving conflicts; they begin to recognize and apply the standard of what is mutually approvable; and they begin to identify themselves as members of the community that upholds it.

5 / Philosophical Egoism: Denial of the Self

The point in speaking of philosophical egoism as a denial of the self (as the chapter title does) is the same one suggested by Thomas Nagel's remark that altruism "may not be in our power to renounce,"—namely, that egoists, in attempting to renounce all interests except selfish interests, are renouncing what is fundamental to their moral anatomy. We have seen evidence from a variety of sources to indicate that persons who can describe their moral situation and reason about their choices are thereby shown to have felt, and acted on, concern for others. That seems to make philosophical egoism untenable.

However, some familiar facts have helped to make it seem like a live option. It is a plain and familiar fact that at almost any moment one can choose to ignore everyone else and become wholly self-absorbed. It is equally familiar that at any moment one can understand the point of a moral judgment showing one's obligation to another, yet choose not to act on it, choosing instead to look out for one's own interests. These are abilities that are also important to our moral anatomy. And these make egoism seem to be a possible choice at almost any moment.

And it is an option *for a moment*. But, unless egoists could provide a novel explanation for acquiring moral language, it is not a coherent position for one who is to be a person who can plan for the future.

Bernard Williams has argued that the egoist position is a philosophical choice that is secure against critics such as Nagel and R. S. Peters who seek to undermine egoism by alluding to what's entailed in moral reasoning. Williams writes: "It [universalizing moral reasoning] provides no argument for one who is to be an exception [to moral reasoning]. . . . it gets no internal hold on his position." Wil-

liams uses the strict definition of egoist as "one who rejects, is uninterested in, or resists moral considerations . . . and is concerned ex-
clusively with his own interests"[1]—Williams's "his" casts the
egoist as a male, and I shall follow his lead. Williams wants us to
consider a person who never responds to others and their moral
claims: if the person shows any interest in them we are to conclude
that it is feigned; that the egoist is thereby attempting to use others
for what the egoist takes to be his own interests. It is this exclusive-
ness that supposedly provides Williams and others with a basis for
rejecting the arguments from the nature of moral reasoning.

To the arguments that the egoist "could not do and be what he
does and is unless others were otherwise than he is," Williams
counters that this, if true, is irrelevant "since the egoist can agree to
it without disturbance. . . . The only means of bringing the external
argument to bear on him is by some such consideration as that if
everyone were like him he could not exist—that is to say via an
imagined universalization. But an imagined universalization will
merely be of no interest to him."[2] Williams's point is that the altruist argument seems to assume that one cares what would happen if
people generally followed one's example: if one had no such interests, the altruist's argument would collapse, Williams supposes.

However, the point that both we and Williams need to be clear
about is that the egoist could not be and do what he is and does unless his motives had been other than he claims. If he had not had
some altruistic interests, he could not have become a person, as considerable argument and evidence have indicated. The egoist position
will be of no interest to us unless it can tell us what we are to use instead of universalized judgments in planning and describing our
acts. It is not a question of the egoist's decision to shirk duties at a
particular moment; it is rather a question of whether he has developed the capacity to make moral judgments and use moral language.
We are dealing not with an external argument, but rather with the
fundamental features of the egoist's moral anatomy. Responsiveness
to other persons is integral to his having become a person himself.
The egoist cannot choose to have been an exception to fundamental
modes of self-description and moral reasoning, yet project plans of
how he intends to act in society. This reasoning is integral to the process by which his choices can be made.

The egoist can only have planned his moves with the understanding and knowledge of what are taken to be acceptable claims and de-

List of your checkouts:

Library name: Main HCC Library

Author: Lykken, David Thoreson.
Title: The antisocial personalities
Call number: RC555.L95 1995
Item ID: 38533000608964
Date charged: 3/10/2016,13:03
Date due: 4/7/2016,23:59

Author: Hannaford, Robert V., 1929-
Title: Moral anatomy and moral reasoning
Call number: BJ319.H276 1993
Item ID: 38533000434957
Date charged: 3/10/2016,13:03
Date due: 4/7/2016,23:59

****ATTENTION****
Overdue notice will be emailed
to your HCC email account.
If you don't use that account
regularly, please set it up
to forward email with the
subject "HCC Library Notice"
to your preferred email
account.
Have a great day!

mands, even if the plans were for acts that were immoral or criminal. No matter what moral stance he adopts at the moment, if he is able to see his life and describe it as it is,[3] he must hold before himself descriptions of actions and projected actions that are impregnated with references to moral claims and demands. These are references that would be meaningless to him apart from his mastery of moral reasoning and moral language.

All our evidence indicates that he could not have acquired the vocabulary apart from his awareness and attention to others around him. To use the language for description, he must "mean what others mean" by terms such as "compassionate," "remorseful," "cruel," "inconsiderate" and the rest. He must understand and have experienced such motives and understand how concern enters, or does not enter, into acts describable by these terms if he is to be able to correctly describe moral moves.[4]

If the egoist is to be taken seriously, we need to hear how his position can take account of other moments when he might want to work out plans dealing with other people. It is unhelpful to be told that the egoist is uninterested in universalizing judgments; that will be a stand that can be taken only for a moment: his moral language can be correctly used only if he can say under what *general* conditions one could apply each expression. In understanding what one could say morally about a situation, or when one could apply an expression, one must make use of universalizing reasoning. If the egoist is not to use such reasoning, we need to hear how he could come by a moral language. Without such a language, how will the egoist be able to function as a person? What will he say and do about people like George? What can he do about reasons and excuses? What or who will determine whether they are good or bad ones? How can he describe his situation without an understanding of the moral import of the moves he contemplates? How can he plan for future action?

It will not do to use the egoist in an argument against the role of concern in moral reasoning (as Williams and Robert Nozick[5] have done) unless the egoist stance is a tenable position that can give its own account of fundamental modes of our functioning as persons: reasoning, self-description, and planning. If the egoist stance is to be plausible, it must go beyond the determination of whether his claim of an isolated moment is self-consistent.[6] It must give us an account of the concrete cases and vocabulary of ordinary moral reasoning, with its requirement for mutual concern and its appeal to acceptable standards. To summarize the connection:

Self-development entails self-description;
self-description entails the description of projected actions';
description of one's projected actions entails understanding of the language of moral motives;
understanding of the language of moral motives entails that one have experienced acceptable other-regarding motives in one-self.
It follows, then, that self-development entails the denial of egoism and egoism entails the denial of self-development.

With that, the possibility of a philosophical defense of strict egoism fails.

In point of fact, the strict egoist's claim of even an isolated moment is of doubtful consistency. In making the claim, he seems to manifest some interest in what his audience's view of him is. If he cares for nothing outside himself, why does he talk (or write) at all? This consideration makes a coherent defense of the position impossible. For the more he attempts to defend and explain his position showing its relation to a range of activities, the more we should be inclined to think that he values our opinion and those activities that he tries to account for in the world. Similarly, his claim to present a *tenable* position betrays a regard for a position that other people could credit, and a regard for norms of reasoning and evidence that would be acceptable to others. As he makes his claim, he disavows the characteristics of personhood that are required for making the claim. Indeed, any expression or defense of his position betrays the fact that he values what others might have to say and thus contradicts his claim.

One must echo Nagel's claim: responsiveness and concern for others seem to be requirements of rational action, something that it is not really in our power to renounce. In the act of denying its existence, we exhibit its presence.

This perhaps accounts for the fact that, instead of defending a strict egoist claim, philosophers have proposed models of rational moral and political thinking as "essentially egoistic" or of persons as taking almost no interest in those with whom they must interact. These are themes which we must address in chapter 6.

6 / Gauthier, Gert, Hobbes, and Hobbesians

Instead of the strict egoism considered by Williams and Nozick, contemporary philosophers have been more inclined to follow Hobbes in claiming that moral and political reasoning is *essentially* egoistic. Hobbesians seek to justify morality by showing that we can reason together to agree on its constraints as necessary for our individual fulfilments. They attempt to justify what they call morality by what they call reason by an appeal to what everyone has to be concerned with: what is necessary for the fulfilment of the individual's interests. They seek to make morality palatable, or at least acceptable, to everyone, even the most egocentric. In the words of one contemporary Hobbesian, David Gauthier, they provide a "worst case scenario" for its justification. Hobbesians, such as Gauthier and Bernard Gert, acknowledge that we commonly have concerns for other persons and that such concern is involved in our providing support for moral norms. However, they hold that such concern for others is not required for the reasoning by which we reach justification and agreement on moral principles.

But it seems that what Hobbes and Hobbesians justify—constraints on action among equals—falls far short of what we ordinarily include under "morality"; and what they call reasoning—guiding action to achieve individual fulfilment—would not result in the justification of, or agreement on, moral principles. (So their view of reason would justify neither their moral constraints nor what we ordinarily call morality.) Moreover, these contemporaries acknowledge what can be seen in Hobbes—namely, that the constraints would not be complied with, so long as one appealed only to those "rational" egocentric motives. They propose to have us contract from the egocentric motives, but they must depend on our having altruistic motives to comply with its constraints. Thus, it turns out that the Hobbesian motive for complying with moral principles must be nonrational, on their own account of "rational." Therefore, though the work of egocentric reasoning may be thought appealing, it doesn't do the job. That is to say, it will not show how we are brought to agreement about how we will live together.

Let Hobbesians be granted the point that we justify by showing that judgments and moral reasons are acceptable to reasonable people; it is a notion, as we have maintained, that is fundamental to our ordinary moral reasoning. That said, we must then argue that we can not reach moral agreement, that is, agreement on how we are to live together, unless we get beyond the Hobbesian notion of reasoning people as self-absorbed, cost-benefit calculators. We must also get beyond the Hobbesian split personality—split between the egocentric motives supposedly used in rationally proposing principles and the altruistic motives required to secure compliance with them.

What is necessary to an understanding of how we reason to agreement on moral action and political obligation is a different conception of reasoning, of mind, and of self. The conception must note that reciprocating awareness and concern for others play a fundamental role in reasoning to such agreement.

I suggest that we look to Hobbes himself for insight into that conception—to his presentation of moral reasoning, not his theory of it. For, although Hobbes's theory offers the cost-benefit-calculator conception, his presentation of examples of moral reasoning shows a much richer conception of moral reasoning at work. Despite the fact that Hobbes is there concerned to show how equals bargain about mutual constraints, the moves he shows us and the motives they entail could be extended so as to apply to moral judgments about relations between *unequals*. Thus, by the motives he actually employs, one would have no reason for confining one's moral concern to members of a community of moral bargainers or reasoners.

In arguing that concern for others is an element of many of those moves, I will not always specify the various attitudes of concern—respect, compassion, trust, sympathy, and deference—that are among those involved. Although a great deal is to be learned by looking at, and describing these attitudes individually[1] my aim for the present is to show how they involve concern for others, considered broadly, and thereby provide a counterexample for the Hobbesian thesis.

JUSTIFICATION AND COERCION

One of these counterexamples seems to be found in the very concept of justifying. Hobbesians, in attempting to justify moral rules by agreement in reasoning, appeal to a community whose rational agreements *define the conditions* of moral legitimacy—an agreement which, if the justification is accepted, must command our own *moral* allegiance. Thus, the egocentric rational support the agreements invoke would only make sense within the setting of a moral community whose members' judgments the individual respects. The supporting and justifying reasons each of us offers must be addressed to, and validated by, the authority of the community of moral reasoners, as, indeed, we found to be true of the judgments in the cases of ordinary moral reasoning (concerning our acquaintance, George, in chapter 2) and as we noted in considering the source of our respect for moral obligations in chapters 3 and 4. Can we take that stand and say that moral reasoning does not commit us to a measure of mutual concern and respect? Does it not presuppose a shared identity (of common membership) and mutual trust?

That justification is a problematic notion for Hobbes is suggested when Hobbes resorts to force to secure compliance with the moral agreements. For surely ready compliance would be the mark of successful justification and genuine moral agreement. Hobbes, of course, tries to use force to "make good that propriety" for which bargainers covenanted: "Before the names of just and unjust can have place there must be some coercive power to compel men equally to the performance of their covenants by the terror of some punishment greater than the benefit they expect by the breach of their covenant, and to make good that propriety which by their mutual covenant men acquire in recompense of the universal right they abandon."[2]

Having argued that a concern for justice and for other persons does not occur in the State of Nature, and that "just" and "unjust" have no application apart from the covenant, Hobbes concludes that one must punish covenant breakers to create a motive for compliance. In such enforcing, the sovereign would lead one to seek the same thing one is said to seek in making the original covenant: "nothing else but the security of a man's person in his life" (*L*:87). Here the conception of reasoning offered is, of course, that of a cost-benefit calculator, looking strictly to his or her own advantage.

COERCION VERSUS VOLUNTARY
COMPLIANCE

The problem raised, of course, is that in using coercion, Hobbes reminds us that, for amoral egoists, compliance would often be (as in the case of desire-frustrating constraints) *against our will* and against "reason." Could coercion change that? Could coercion give us desires or reasons to: (1) believe in the moral validity of the law, or (2) care about what the law seeks to protect—others' liberties?

If one enforced desire-frustrating constraints, simple concern for one's person would provide one with a motive not to get caught at covenant breaking, but since, by Hobbes's account, justice and propriety have no claim of their own, this provides no motive for covenant *keeping* if one is sure that one will not get caught. If it is true that "nothing can be unjust" without an enforcing power and "where no covenant had preceded . . . no action can be unjust" (*L*:94), why should covenant breaking be regarded as unjust? No covenant has preceded our making of the covenant. What could it be that would make us believe covenant-breaking to be wrong? What moral reason has one for avoiding it? If Hobbes's answer (coercion) provided the only motive, one would have a motive for being clever in crime, but none for being moral or just. For, if we did not believe in the propriety of our agreements without enforcement, enforcement would add nothing to make us believe in it. The enforcer's actions would be arbitrary abuse; they might terrify one but would not make one feel guilty and would provide no motive for voluntary compliance.

Clearly, the use of force would not alter our other potential motive for voluntarily complying with constraints on our fulfillment—namely, having concern for those whose freedom is protected by the constraint. Fear for our own security can not, by itself, bring us to have interest in, or compassion for, others.

Therefore, Hobbes's enforcement, or physical abuse, cannot create respect for law or regard for persons. Only by respecting one or both of these would a Hobbesian covenanter be voluntarily compliant; respect for persons is essential to the motives for compliance with laws by, and for, persons. Unless a large percent of the population voluntarily complies, enforcement would be impossible. So, in order for Hobbes to expect a stable society with enforceable law, he must rely on covenanters acting from altruistic motives.

For Hobbes, the presence of a covenant is indicated by compliance with its demands: men must "perform covenants made" (*L*:93). In this "consisteth the fountain and original of justice" and without their willingness to perform, we have, not a genuine covenant, "but empty words" (*L*:93).

As noted above, Hobbes seeks to induce this compliance or performance of covenants by force of punishment (and thus he would complete the community). But, if one reasons as an amoral, self-interested calculator, one has no motive to comply. In fact, the Hobbesian account puts one in the position of Hobbes's fool who "hath said in his heart there is no justice." The fool holds that "every man's contentment being committed to his own care, there could be no reason, why every man might not do what he thought conduced thereunto: and therefore also to make, or not make; keep or not keep covenants, was not against reason, when it conduced to one's benefit" (*L*:94). The fool wonders whether injustice may not at times "stand with that reason, which dictateth to every man his own good" (*L*:95). If it should serve one's interests to break the covenant on occasion, why would it not be rational to break it?

Hobbes answers the fool that a covenant breaker "cannot be received into any society, that unite themselves for peace and defence, but by the errour of them that receive him; nor when he is received be retained in it" (*L*:96). Thus Hobbes says that the fool will be led to see the danger of his mistaken judgment: unless members make an error, the fool would be excluded from the advantages he would get from the united society. The fool would have no (theoretically recognized) motive to deplore the loss of the pleasure of their company; his motive must be that he could not "reasonably reckon" upon such a policy as "the means to his own security" (*L*:96).

But Hobbes gives the fool no reason for valuing action in accord with justice for itself or for his own self-respect; instead he gives him a threat. And thus, compliance becomes a necessary evil in his eyes; the threat would prove no more effective in changing motivation than enforcement did. For, of course, the fool knew that as long as lawbreakers are punished, it would not pay to get caught at covenant breaking. But where one would not get caught, why not break the covenant? Similarly, in cases where one could count on "the errour of them that receive him," Hobbesian rationality would *require* covenant breaking, if it served one's own purposes. The Hobbesian view of the isolated, unconcerned calculator excludes mutual respect and respect for shared moral reasoning, without which justice would have no appeal. So long as the fool reasons as a Hobbesian man, his argument—and his essentially criminal attitudes—triumph. Once again, we see that if Hobbes is to have a stable society, he must tacitly rely on his citizens to act out of respect and concern for one another.

This problem of how we could create a stable society—of how we could elicit the uncoerced preparedness of unconcerned people to respect others and their rights—becomes a key problem for Bernard Gert and David Gauthier. Both, like Hobbes, seek first to provide such motives from selfish interest, then both finally acknowledge that concern for others is critically important for compliance with moral constraints. But despite the fact that both explicitly acknowledge that voluntary compliance depends on our having nonegoistic concerns, both seek to ground moral principles on self-interested reasoning. Thus, they, too, offer motives for proposing principles that differ from the motives that are required for compliance. The motives to which each of them finally appeals, in explaining how one becomes a person, turn out to be inaccessible to their contracting "reasoners." Gert struggles to bring them together, in his "advocacy" of concern for all, as does Gauthier, in proposing his "disposition" to comply. Both strategies would make it impossible for one to integrate one's reasoning. To see that this is so, we will need to review briefly their accounts.

GERT AND ADVOCACY

Gert's concept of reason is central to *The Moral Rules*, whose task is to "justify moral rules in the philosophical sense, i.e., to show that they are required by reason."[3] Whereas Gert holds that reason permits that we take an interest in other people, reason is "essentially egoistic" and requires that one avoid suffering harm oneself. Thus, as in Hobbes, one's motive in moral reasoning is to avoid harm to oneself (*MR*:40–41).

If we seek the rules which are necessary for avoiding harm to ourselves, Gert believes that all would agree to the necessity of the following rules:

1. Don't kill.
2. Don't cause pain.

3. Don't disable.
4. Don't deprive of freedom or opportunity.
5. Don't deprive of pleasure.
6. Don't deceive.
7. Keep your promises.
8. Don't cheat.
9. Obey the law.
10. Do your duty (*MR*:125).

Ignoring some of the problems one might face in attempting to apply these rules simultaneously, one notes that Gert, like Hobbes, prohibits causing evil: "Moral rules demand only that one avoid causing evil," something one can do "by doing nothing" (*MR*:69, 73).

We note that Gert's morality also falls short of what ordinary morality requires; by ordinary morality one is often morally required to do more than avoid causing evil. One is frequently called upon to prevent it, given that the evil is grave; that it is easily within one's power to prevent it; and that no one else is available to do so. If, for example, we do not throw the switch that prevents a child from being electrocuted, we will hear about our moral failure. To fail to prevent evil in such circumstances is to disclose one's lack of concern for those about to suffer and for that lack one receives moral censure.[4]

Lack of concern is also the root of the central problem of Gert's book: how to get people to uphold other-respecting rules from purely self-regarding motives. Gert notes that the egocentric stance "does not seem to be the attitude we think should be taken toward the moral rules" (*MR*:88) since, if people held this attitude, rules could not function as rules. Like Hobbes's fool, those with such an unconcerned attitude would all try to be "easy riders," people who benefitted from, but did not support, moral rules.

Gert sees this, not as an insuperable difficulty with his notion of reason, but as a problem to be resolved within its application; he proposes to eliminate it by his strategy of public advocacy. Facing the same problem Hobbes did in securing compliance, Gert says that one must advocate that rules be obeyed by all, including oneself; to get the rules obeyed by all one must "advocate the attitude of one who had an equal concern for all mankind" (*MR*:88). "Rationally" we want the rules for egoistic reasons, but to secure agreement on them Gert must publicly advocate nonegoistic attitudes.

Can one rely on such selfish motives to bring one to become unselfish in one's attitudes? Gert says that one can advocate that others adopt the necessary attitude, "when and only when one . . . believes [one] could accept the attitude being advocated" (*MR*:89). Thus, one must believe that everyone has this (nonrational) capacity for concern and believe that the attitude must be held, if we are to bring everyone to comply with moral constraints. Gert holds that the attitude of concern to be publicly advocated (for everyone including oneself) may not be held by the advocator in fact: "There may be a conflict between what one publicly advocates and the attitudes one actually holds—i.e., that one is prepared to act on . . . Public advocacy need not be sincere" (*MR*:89). Still, one would be required by reason to advocate it, for by refusing to do so, one would increase one's chances of suffering at the hands of the rules' violators. Thus, Gert acknowledges the "possibility of hypocrisy."

But for those who had no such altruistic attitude, hypocrisy would be more than a possibility: Gert finds that it would be required by reason. To avoid hypocrisy, such a person would have to refuse to advocate publicly (*MR*:93). Since, according to Gert, one "has no reason for not advocating it," reason requires advocacy in all cases.

To the extent that advocacy is not a pose, it will not be based on Gert's egocentric use of "reason." If advocacy is based purely on Gert's Hobbesian rationality, the advocacy must be a pose. But, then, if one "justifies" by what's required by "reason," one will be justifying moral rules by the use of deception. And "Don't deceive" and "Don't cheat" are two of the rules Gert is seeking to justify.

We note that the Hobbesian conception of reason is again at the heart of both the problem of securing compliance and the contradiction resulting from his attempt to bring about compliance. Gert's "reason" excludes motives judged to be both universally available and required for compliance: one who uses "reason" is obliged to offer rule-violating, deceptive advocacy.

In a later comment, Gert acknowledged that Hobbesian reason could not be invoked to guide our actions: "Public reason determines what morality is, but concern for others, not reason, determines if one acts morally" (*MR*:xix).

But this is to introduce the problem of a divided self. This is to say that our rational motives for proposing moral laws differ from our motives for compliance with them, a move necessary for Hobbes and also taken up by Gauthier, but one which raises serious questions about how we reach agreement and how we could become integrated as individuals.

GAUTHIER AND FORMING DISPOSITIONS

In *Morals by Agreement*, David Gauthier also struggles with the same Hobbesian problem. The book, often profoundly illuminating, attempts, like Hobbes's and Gert's, to show how self-interested reasoning would lead one to accept and comply with moral constraints on one's actions, supposedly showing how morality can be "generated from non-moral principles of rational choice."[5]

Gauthier (like Gert in his later acknowledgement) holds that the concerns from, and by which, one reasons to moral agreement differ from those required for our compliance with such agreements. For Gauthier, morality is a set of "rational, impartial constraints on the pursuit of individual interest" (*MA*:6), and so, the notion of "rational" also becomes central to his book. He finds that a person acts "rationally if and only if she seeks her greatest interest or benefit"; "the rational person . . . seeks the greatest satisfaction of her interests" (*MA*:7).

Defending Hume's dictum that "reason is, and ought to be, the slave of the passions," Gauthier takes it that our desires and volitions must provide the motives for moral action (*MA*:21). But he holds that we are not to appeal to desires and "particular" (*MA*:103) and "contingent" affections related to others. Such affections are termed "tuistic," and moral reasoners, as such, are taken to be "non-tuistic," that is, unconcerned about others: "the non-tuist is one who takes no interest in the interests of those with whom he interacts" (*MA*:311). Non-tuistic concerns are said to be involved when we appeal "directly to reason." Thus, we are to suppose that what is *directly* involved in rational action is non-tuistic; non-tuistic interests, by contrast with the "particular" and "contingent" interests we may take in others, are seen as essential and necessary to the person. The Hobbesian account is acknowledged to be inaccurate in detail, but is held to be true to the essential person: it "enables us to demonstrate the rationality of impartial constraints on the pursuit of individual interests to persons who may take no interest in others' interests" (*MA*:17).

Gauthier holds that morality arises as equally rational (non-tuistic) people can agree on the constraints that would be mutually advantageous; in bargaining with others, each seeks to gain as much as possible while conceding as little as possible. What equally rational, non-tuistic people can accept under these principles captures the idea of fairness and so serves as the basis of justice and morality (*MA*:14). As morality is held to arise from agreements conferring mutual advantages among equally rational bargainers, Gauthier would deny any moral status to relationships outside the bargaining context (*MA*:16). As we'll note, that seems to leave out a lot of what we ordinarily call moral relationships. However, assuming that morality is comprised solely of such bargained agreements, he takes his problem to be found in showing that it would be non-tuistically rational to comply with them. As in Hobbes and Gert, the would-be easy rider can see the advantages in having others adopt the constraints.

On this issue, Hobbes's easy riding fool won out and Gert was driven to self-contradiction and to advocating deception. Gauthier seeks to circumvent the problem by showing that it is tuistically rational to adopt a *disposition to comply* with the agreements. His argument in support of this strategy is that only by being seen as having such an honest disposition will one be admitted into advantageous cooperative ventures. One would not be admitted unless others could see one as compliant. Gauthier emphasizes that this must be more than a motive to *seem* to comply, for deception here is not really possible (*MA*:174). Our motives are more or less transparent, and so, "only the person truly disposed to honesty and justice may expect fully to realize their benefits, for only such a person may rationally be admitted to those mutually beneficial arrangements . . . that rest on honesty and justice, on voluntary compliance" (*MA*:182). Thus, Gauthier answers Adeimantus's question ("Why isn't it better to seem just than to be just?"): In order to seem just, one must *be* just. Therefore, to avoid exclusion from advantageous cooperative activity, we must choose to be honest—that is, form the disposition to be honest. For Gauthier, "in making that choice . . . [we] would be expressing . . . [our] nature not only as rational beings, but as moral beings" (*MA*:184).

However, illuminating as the argument is, it merely leads us to try to be honest (or just) in order to reap the advantages of doing so. The problem here parallels that found in Hobbes's attempt to use coercion. As Laurence Thomas notes,[6] coercive forces would be behind our adopting the strategy; it would not be a case of our giving "un-coerced support for the norms," which was said by Gauthier to be necessary for the effectiveness of the norms (*MA*:179). Our interest in complying is an instrumental strategy and not an expression of our desires—not, one would say, an expression of our moral beings. As Thomas observes, by Gauthier's advocacy, being honest and being just must be viewed as necessary evils,[7] since they do not satisfy deeply felt desires.

One might add that if we sought to be honest simply to win advantages for ourselves, it's doubtful we would be or do all that is required by genuine candor and openness. The strategy may seem advantageous, but that will not bring real compliance, unless one involves interests of the self in others' interests.

Compliance and Concern

Indeed, Gauthier, agrees that we must get beyond morality-as-a-necessary-evil. For, as noted above, although he takes non-tuistic reasoning to be the proper determiner of the content of morality, he takes it that it is our *affective* concerns for others that lead us to comply: "And so we may now suppose that persons have . . . an affective capacity for morality, not so that we may show certain moral constraints to be justified, but rather so that, for persons with such a capacity, moral constraints do not constitute a necessary evil, and are not willingly circumvented" (*MA*:329). He claims that moral affections arise as "an appropriate extension of his concern for others in the context of valued participatory activities . . . [one would] then consider those activities appropriately valued in so far as they were morally constrained" (*MA*:339).

But this does not square with Gauthier's position. In telling us how we could reason to moral constraints, he had told us our moral allegiance must be won without appealing to "our feelings for others" (*MA*:17). If so, it cannot be that one's affective capacity for morality is to be an "extension of his concern for others." Yet here he finds that one's having the affective capacity is the mark of one's having moral allegiance, and it is necessary for compliance, by Gauthier's account.

Gauthier indicates elsewhere that although concern for others is outside the moral contractor's reason, such concern—going beyond the mutual unconcern of the "economic man"—is essential if we are to be morally compliant. He writes that if morality played "only the role of necessary evil or of convenient deception that it plays for the economic man, then we should expect that awareness of its role would undermine his moral affections" (*MA*:33). Thus, concern is required for Gauthier, as it is for Hobbes and Gert, if we are to comply with constraints. If we know that tuistic concerns are necessary for a stable, lawful society, can we accept Gauthier's stance that we can ignore such concerns in reaching the principles for a just society?

Reasoning with Concern

It will be helpful to consider this together with his statement of the goal of contractarianism: to show that it is "advantageous for each person to comply with constraints that it would be rational for all to agree to, provided others may be expected to be generally compliant."[8] From this we would have to say that no one could be expected to be compliant (on Hobbes's, Gert's, or Gauthier's account) unless he or she can believe that people are motivated by concern for other persons.

It follows that, *from the beginning*, Gauthier's contractarian argument must assume (as Hobbes and Gert must assume) that others have mutual concern. Contractarian reasoning requires that everyone (or nearly everyone) be compliant; he acknowledges that others would not be compliant if they were merely non-tuistic economic men. By his reckoning, then, mutual concern is a pre-condition for *reaching* moral agreement: reasoning to agreement depends on willing compliance and willing compliance depends on mutual concern.

Gauthier sees no need for tuistic reasoning in justifying and sees no problem for the content of morality. For, in response to a critic's comment that the content of morality cannot be independent of our affections, he replied, "This is no objection to my theory, since the particular moral constraints that will be justified will be determined by particular preferences persons have, and these, of course, will be influenced by their affective capacities. My theory concerns the justificatory structure for morality, and is open with respect to determinate content."[9] But it cannot be open. For the non-tuistic reasoning to be used in justification would not permit appeal to (and hence could not be "influenced by") one's affective capacities. Since it cannot, the resulting morality cannot be open with respect to content.

Persons reasoning *qua* mutually unconcerned would have no basis for making proposals that would fulfill their *tuistic* interests. For one to make proposals that would promote sharing or trust would be considered irrational. It would be irrational to give any kind of priority to such associations, even though they turn out to be critically important for compliance and, hence, for the content of one's moral agreements.

Reasoning about such concerns is also critically important in achieving our own fulfillment and integration. If one is to fulfill one's interests in an integrated way, that will mean one *must* take those tuistic interests into consideration before making one's choices. It would follow that one could not achieve integration or maximize the fulfillment of one's interests if one reasoned as one of Gauthier's non-tuists; as a non-tuist, one could not even consider the fulfillment of tuistic concerns as relevant.

This brings us back to the questions raised by Glaucon and Adeimantus in *The Republic*, where the notion of a purely instrumental social contract is raised in one of its earliest forms. In asking, "Why isn't it better to seem just than to be just?" they take no note of the point that one of the things that honesty and justice are better for is the mutual trust and communication with others whom you value for their own sakes. Openness and integrity permit communication and trust; one cannot seem just without being just (usually at least); one cannot be admitted into open communication and interchange without the trust that comes of honesty and justice. Since we have seen that our interest in others is a precondition for moral reasoning, we see that it must be a natural as opposed to a derived or purely instrumental interest. Openness before others and respect for them are its natural expressions, and thus, honesty and justice are fulfillments of that natural interest. To aim to merely seem honest and just is to thwart that interest by basing one's actions on purely egocentric attitudes. Honesty and justice cannot be taken as merely instrumental goods: they fulfill a fundamental interest that we must consider in the reasoning that goes into reaching moral agreement.

HOBBESIAN VIEW TENABLE AS A MODEL

Some have held that to criticize Hobbes's and Hobbesians' accounts on the ground of their inaccuracy to literal fact is to miss their importance as hypothetical models. Such defenders say: The models justify morality and political life without appealing to uncertain altruistic motives. Thus it is held that they may simplify but that they deal with what is essential to the person. Using them, we can found explanation on what we know to be a real motive, self-interest, one that economists can link to a scientific account of value.

In response, I should first remind the defender that what is said to be justified—constraints among equals—is not equivalent to what we ordinarily mean by morality; that it does not explain or justify how we could come to obligations toward unequals and obligations to act positively to prevent evils.

We should also note that our market preferences, studied by economists, often reflect tuistic interests (I can save or spend for others), and market preferences often do not reflect our strongest non-tuistic interests (such as the desire for self-respect or desire for fame). There is thus no special connection between ego-centered interests and economic explanation; thus, they have no claim to being more scientifically confirmed and, therefore, more real or more essential (even if one could agree that being scientifically confirmed made it more real).

Next, we should make it clear that (while idealized models may at times be useful) Hobbesian inaccuracies do matter. It is because of them that their accounts do not work *as models*. Their "essential" motive and account of the "rational" can not, by themselves, explain how we could achieve personal integration, reason together to agreement, justify, or actually uphold moral law. It turns out that the motives that were excluded as nonessential, or merely contingent, are in fact necessary to these processes. In treating only self-interested pursuits as being rational, the model draws our attention *away* from what we must attend to, in order to understand moral reasoning or justification.

CLUES FROM HOBBES'S MORAL REASONING

To understand such reasoning, we would do well to look at Hobbes's own use of moral reasoning in the justification of the Laws, together with the assumptions that he must draw on to make it plausible. By looking at the attitudes and beliefs that must exist in order for his account to make sense, we can find suggestions for expanding the model. We have already noted one: that the concept of justification can be used only if we are to hold shared reasoning to have some authority and if we have some respect for the reasoners. Some of the other relevant features include: that we are reciprocally aware of each other's intentions; that we proceed from shared hope, trust, mutual respect, and concern; and that in reasoning, our attitudes and conclusions are tentative and conditional on such sharing. Empathy and reciprocal awareness of one another's desires and intentions—our knowing what others know and our knowing that they know that we know—is integral to our understanding their desire for power, our own condition of risk, and our seeking peace. We do not reason as completely separate and isolated beings; we reason, again, as beings *in* relationship.

We begin to see the other relevant features emerge when Hobbes makes his first move toward the covenant; for that, he says, we must have some hope: "Every man ought to endeavour peace, as far as he has hope of attaining it" (*L*:85). "He" must have some hope of attaining peace, though he knows he is at risk. Can he trust those around him? Would they act with good will toward him? Of course, one of Hobbes's men-in-the-State-of-Nature could never know what it meant to trust someone. He could not have learned to—would not have started to—trust people whom he knew to have no regard for him. In order to hope for such a relationship to emerge one would have to be aware of the existence of such good will. One's making peace must begin with felt kinship, reasons for trusting, and, hence, respecting others.

The need to expand the model becomes more apparent in Hobbes's illuminating account of the covenant's transfer of rights (in the Second Law). In his account we note that the Second Law builds on our having hope, some sense that others are similarly inclined and are to be trusted. Given that, we can mutually propose *"that a man be willing, when others are so too, as far forth, as for peace, and defense of himself he shall think it necessary, to lay down this right to all things, and be contented with so much liberty against other men as he would allow other against himself"* [Emphasis in original] (*L*:85).

We see that one's willingness is *conditional* on others' willingness: it would not make sense to propose it unless one was aware that others were willing to restrict their liberties and respect the liberties of their fellow citizens. Hence, one must have some awareness of others' intentions as well as of the kind of moral proposal that they would find acceptable; for one must believe a proposal to be morally acceptable to them in order for one to believe that by it one could reach agreement on it.

We see also that the laying down of one's liberty is conditional: one gives up one's freedom as necessary for peace and self-defense. One appropriately reserves an area of freedom to oneself out of self-concern, but one can decide how much freedom is possible only by referring to what is necessary for peace—that is, by referring to how one's exercise of freedom will be *seen by others* to be an unacceptable or war-making interference.

Note that others must find the laying down *morally* acceptable. The description of the State-of-Nature as without moral concepts cannot be taken literally, for each covenanter must know that others could agree to the transfer. And the agreement must have moral force if it is to be taken seriously; otherwise, as noted above, it would be pointless to invoke the agreement as providing moral reasons. Packed into the covenant, as we saw before, is the idea that we, as members of a community, validate our individually applied moral principles by reaching agreement as to their appropriateness.

We should also note that our reaching agreement indicates that we can know what others would find acceptable because we can put ourselves in the other's place ("be content with so much liberty . . . as we would allow"). Our validating moral reasoning consists in— our moral knowledge is derived from—putting ourselves in the other's place and deciding whether we should allow such treatment against us. Not only must each have the willingness and know that mutual willingness and agreement establish moral legitimacy, but each must also recognize that the *method* of moral reasoning consists in taking others' places to see what one could[10] accept there, given everyone's natural desire to act freely.

We should recall that our shared willingness to lay down those liberties (required by the Second Law) entails that we *begin* our reasoning with concern for others. Concern is not derived from reasoning and so may be applied—as it may be in ordinary moral relations—to equal and unequal alike and to our felt obligations to prevent evil. Thus, if we credit Hobbes's account, the model must be expanded so as to admit of: respect for the authority of community reasoning; belief in a method of moral reasoning as using reversibility; and our acting out of mutual respect and concern.

The elements of this expanded model of the conception of mind and self that is required to achieve a contractarian agreement are also found in our sketch of the moral anatomy necessary to ordinary moral reasoning (as drawn from our sampling and from the philosophical literature) and necessary for the motivation to uphold constraining obligation. This is not to say that ordinary reasoning is thereby shown to be contractarian, but rather that these are elements necessary to reasoning to moral agreement. The implications of these elements for ordinary moral reasoning will be further developed in chapter 7.

The suggested expansion of the model notes what critics of Hobbes have observed: that in order to move out of the State of Nature and into a covenanted community, people must be changed in nature. Some have suggested that the change is like a transformation by grace. I suggest that it would be helpful to think of this as a reordering of the elements of our nature that we *bring into view*. To speak of "transformation by grace" is an apt metaphor to capture the extent to which we seem to be totally changed when we move out of a threatening, predatory world and into a civilized society. We bring different capacities of ourselves to view—trust, respect, concern—on perceiving that we have reason to do so.

Moreover, if we find ourselves in a situation (like the State of Nature) where we can trust no one and are in danger of death, we may well behave as the model would indicate and feel neither compassion nor concern for our would-be killers. In such a situation, egoistic responses are morally excused, if not expected, within a moral community. We are reminded once again of Butler's account of the way in which appropriate moral response is dependent on the situation and varies in relation to the treatment of persons within a situation.

The tentative and conditional quality of Hobbes's moral reasoning should remind us that our "transformation" comes gradually and that the gradations of our response may be justified by our perception of the changes in the attitudes and intentions of those around us. Our having the capacities for mutual trust, respect, and concern does not entail that they are always felt or acted upon to the same degree.

7 / The Golden Rule: Motive and Method in Moral Reasoning

Hobbes refers to his negative statement of the Golden Rule, offered as a variation of the Second Law, as "that law of all mankind." We might regard this remark as merely his attempt to curry favor with his seventeenth-century Christian readers, but we saw that his actual reasoning in deriving the Laws repeatedly achieved moral agreement on principles by taking the place of the other (in the manner enjoined by the Golden Rule). On reflection it seemed that the reasoning for reaching agreement in principle must extend to that used to reach agreement in individual judgments: How could one achieve agreement in moral attitudes with others except by entering into the situation from which their attitudes are formed?

Moreover, our own sketch of the moral anatomy suggests that some such process as the Golden Rule invokes must be at work in our making responsible judgments and in our giving of moral reasons and descriptions. Indeed, our sketch points to a method of moral reasoning combining elements of the Rule, and it suggests answers to some of the objections raised against the Rule and the ethics of good reasons.

Further, the Rule is ubiquitous in its various versions, and each of them claims universality for its method. Consider:

> Therefore all things whatsoever ye would that men should do to you do ye even so to them: for this is the law and the prophets. (Matthew 7:12)

> What is hateful to yourself, do not to your fellow man. That is the whole of the Torah and the rest is but commentary. (Rabbi Hillel)

Do naught to others which, if done to thee, would cause thee
pain: this is the sum of duty. (Mahabharata 5:15)

These and other versions[1] of the Golden Rule figure prominently in
all the world's major ethical and religious traditions. The importance of the point lies in the number of people and the variety of cultural conditions from which these versions emerged. They appeared
at widely separated places, in pre-Christian times, and sometimes
without any religious connection. Considering the diversity of the
texts and the secular nature of some, one could not approach them
as a kind of supernatural revelation. They can be traced to no single
historical source or social movement. These facts lead one to wonder
whether some common elements of them might reflect something
fundamental to all moral reasoning—as, indeed, each of them claims
to do.

In fact, whatever was fundamental would have to be some common subset of their elements, considering the differences between
them.[2] Yet they are all alike in requiring each of us to consider our
actions from the perspective of those affected and to respond with
some degree of concern to avoid harming each other. They all bring
us to conceive of moral reasoning as involving mutual, reciprocating
awareness rather than as cost-benefit calculating or as applying a formula, as proceeding from reflection about each other's situation
rather than as the isolated calculating of an essentially separate individual.

I am not making a claim in behalf of any of the comprehensive religious viewpoints represented by the world religions that invoke
some version of the Golden Rule. In showing that their point of consensus has support independent of them all, I do not intend to claim
that any of the comprehensive world views or global systems of
value is valid in its entirety, or that any of them has a relatively
stronger claim to truth as a comprehensive view as a consequence of
the validity of its point of consensus.

If we may speak of these common elements as "the Rule," the
fact that versions of the Rule occur in writings that sometimes express intolerant, chauvinistic, or authoritarian attitudes may give us
pause. That may seem to argue against its being universal. But we
can't reject it on these grounds, since we can't demand that we be
able to agree completely with texts before we can take any part of
them seriously. But we are left wondering why we have just these

common parts that we should take seriously. Why should these elements appear universally?

I want to try for an answer to these questions by drawing on the account of the moral person we have developed and using that account to argue that the Rule captures an essential pattern or method of moral reasoning between individuals. By "moral reasoning" here, as elsewhere in this study, I mean the reasoning connected with what is commonly called moral behavior and reasoning in actual communities: the kind of reasoning and judgment by which a community can agree to approve or condemn actions.

THE SKETCH, THE RULE, AND
ANSWERS TO SHAW, KANT, AND PARFIT

In developing the sketch from the philosophical literature, we saw that responsible persons in any society must be able to describe their individual moral situations and actions. This leads us to the heart of the matter for, as we saw,[3] in describing our moral situation (in any society) we must employ a language whose terms can be applied to others as well as ourselves and whose terms reflect some common moral judgments. Our most fundamental means of conceiving of ourselves, our language, brings us to conceive of ourselves as a person among persons, with common attitudes and purposes. The point, very briefly, is this: the terms of this moral language must be applied in accord with generally accepted criteria, one of which is that their use must be supported by generally acceptable reasons; a reason that is generally acceptable must be acceptable by those affected by the action, and so we must take into account, and show concern for, the interests and purposes of those affected. Therefore, bringing together the arguments of the philosophical literature, we saw that to act in morally approved ways, we must act toward others in ways that persons in their positions could accept. In order to do so, we must enter into the situation of the other and act out of respect for what a person in that situation requires.

The concern for others required by the philosophical literature was seen to be with us from earliest infancy (chapter 4) and integral to the process by which we acquire a language and thereby become persons who could project actions in society (chapter 5).

Our look at cases of ordinary moral reasoning—George's exploits considered in chapter 2—gave reason to believe that our showing lack of concern for others is morally condemned. Moreover, it was apparent from looking at our own ordinary moral vocabulary that lack of concern is cause for blame: a rich variety of expressions from "lacking in compassion" and "inconsiderate " to "reckless" and "unfeeling" are used to affix such moral blame.

Thus, our reciprocating concern, seeing ourselves as like others, reading others' intentions, and ordering our behavior in accord with their perceived wishes are evidently capacities by which we direct our earliest behavior and are central to the development of the moral person. To the degree that we behave acceptably and responsibly in the community, we must have imaginatively put ourselves in the position of those who are to be affected by our actions and have acted in ways that would seem appropriate if we were informed and concerned persons in their situation.

This demand to put ourselves in others' position and consider what would be acceptable to them (or appropriate to their needs) is a norm that is extended to our conversation as well, though we might not want to characterize this as a moral application. That the norm is exercised is apparent, as Grice demonstrates in his study of informal rules of inference.[4] He shows that we expect, and we draw inferences on the expectation, that others' conversational responses will be appropriate to one's evident purposes in initiating the conversation. Suppose that we ask an acquaintance, Lester, how we could get in touch with his friend, Martha, and he replied only, "She's somewhere in the West," when he knew her address and phone number in Sacramento. If we were known to have a legitimate reason for asking for the information, we'd judge Lester's reply to be deceptive (once we discovered that he had the information), for he failed to provide it and by his answer suggested that he did not have the information he knew we wanted. If people fail to meet these Gricean Rules when a cooperative response would create no problem for them, we judge them to be remiss in their reply. This illustrates the point that the moral anatomy underlying the Rule is not only with us from the beginning but is exercised in cooperative interchanges throughout our lives. It may seem a little high-flown to speak of the Rule as a method of moral reasoning. It is, at any rate, an approach to moral reasoning which requires that one be alive to and concerned about the changing needs and desires of persons in one's situation and that one base one's decision on that awareness and concern.

We note that various versions of the Rule specify the motive that is to inform duty and law in claiming that the Rule is the sum of duty or the sum of law. When one considers the role of "Love thy neighbor as thyself" in the Jewish tradition and the importance Jesus assigns to it in the Gospels,[5] Jesus' rule to do unto others as you would have others do unto you must be seen as requiring that one be sensitive to others' concerns and to their situation. When he treats the Rule as the sum of the law and the prophets and as flowing from concern for one's neighbor, it is clear that he also intends that the motive of concern be applied universally, defining a condition of moral, lawful constraint. "Do unto others" asks that we see each person as a person like ourselves and that we respect each in the same way that we would judge it appropriate that we be treated in that situation.

Thus respect for each implies that we be able to generalize each judgment; it requires that we treat similar cases similarly—the various traditions hold that the Rule is the sum of the law. In fact, it implies our concept of law—of treating similar cases similarly—as a necessary condition of its fulfillment. The fact that the notion of governing by law seems to be a universally held norm speaks in support of the view that the Rule, the concept of law, and the belief in generalizing moral judgments go together in that they are universally acknowledged and appealed to (if not always acted on). The idea of generalizing moral judgments calls to mind again the ideas of a community of moral reasoners and the respect that is due its members.

Marcus Singer, one of the few current theorists who have shown much interest in the Rule,[6] focuses just on its connection with generalizing in his *Generalization in Ethics*. Of the connection between it and generalizing judgments, he writes that, "stated precisely, the Golden Rule would be an immediate consequence of the Generalization Principle"; Singer's Principle, "What is right for one person must be right for any similar person in similar circumstances," is also phrased as "What is right (wrong) for one person must be right (wrong) for any similar person under similar circumstances."

Singer also quotes and approves Sidgwick's judgment that Samuel Clarke's "rule of equity ('Whatever I judge reasonable or unreasonable that another should do for me; that by the same judgment I declare reasonable that I should in the like case do for him') is 'the Golden Rule precisely stated.' '"[7] But, in spite of the fact that we find Singer and Sidgwick in agreement here, something is amiss in their conclusion: it is doubtful that the Rule of Equity or the Generalization Principle, as they are stated here, can be treated as implying or as being equivalent to all that is intended by the Rule—though the Rule implies the Generalization Principle, as we have just seen. The Rule's emphasis is on concern for, and empathizing with, others, while treating them equitably; the Generalization Principle as stated settles for treating others consistently, something one could achieve simply by treating everyone alike—say with equal disdain, though that was certainly not the intent of Singer or Sidgwick.

Singer, in his major theoretical work, gives no attention to the affective or emotional components of moral decision: compassion, sentiment, and concern for others are not mentioned.[8]

In a later essay by Singer, "Defense of the Golden Rule," he, in effect, acknowledges that the affective life must play a role in moral judgments. There, he holds that consideration of others' wishes and desires are necessary to moral reasoning.[9]

It does not require great philosophical subtlety to see that Jesus' intent in offering the Rule—an intent that is sustained by his emphasis on concern for others and by many of his stories and parables—was to insure that we get out of the egocentric bind and that we consider the consequences of our action from the point of view of those affected. Wherever a version of the Rule asks us to consider how our action will be taken from the point of view of those affected, it gets us away from reciprocating egoism and gets us focused on the particulars of the other's situation. The Rule offers a method (or an approach) that can be described as the "law and the prophets" because, when taken with its altruistic emphasis and with the attention to situation of Jesus' parables, the Rule gets us away from egocentric or unfeeling rule following and into moral reasoning as it must occur in a community of responsible persons. The point of many of his stories is to get us to enter into the life and perspective of those affected by the action contemplated. By telling the story he evokes the immediate sense of mutual awareness that we need in reasoning about ordinary moral situations—a sense and understanding that, as the already-cited treatises on the conditions of responsibility suggest, lie at the heart of ordinary concrete moral reasoning.

When we are brought into such concrete situations whose details are familiar to us (such as we encounter in daily tasks of moral reasoning), often we do not require further instruction as to what the other must feel and want. As Butler reminds us and as we have seen in considering such cases, we easily reach an agreement about what can be said and what should be done. When we reflect on ordinary judgments, such as those about our acquaintance George, or about some of Jesus' parables (such as the Good Samaritan story), we see that we make our generalizations and form our descriptions, faulting the priest and the Levite (and your acquaintance George) for failing to act out of concern. Thus, if Singer's account of generalization is to be defended as the logic of ethics, he, along with whoever defends a good reasons theory, must bring caring into it; he must speak of what reasons informed and concerned persons could adopt consistently with their concern for themselves and others.

That the Rule must be applied by taking into account how others could be affected by one's actions and that it involves taking others' perspectives into account leads us to set aside some of the objections that have been brought against the Rule by critics such as Shaw and Kant.

George Bernard Shaw suggests in *Maxims for Revolutionists* that we use his revised version of the Rule: "Do not do unto others as you would they should do unto you. Their tastes may not be the same." Shaw ignores the whole point behind Jesus' emphasis and use of stories in his teaching—namely, to bring one to an awareness of the others' perspective and situation and to act in the light of it. Our tastes and interests vary enormously, and so our obligation must be determined by projecting ourselves into the position of the other. Jesus' original Rule in fact seeks what Shaw wants: to get us to consider and respond in the light of the other's perceptions and tastes.

In considering these perceptions we can, nonetheless, make a judgment because there are features of personhood that are the same for all. It would not be important to take the other's tastes into account if we could not assume a common personhood to which the individualized tastes are attached—if we did not know that any person would be hurt by insult, resent willful injury, feel frustration at being thwarted, and so on. It is the sense of common personhood that must undergird our ascription of motives and personal predicates; it is the same sense of personhood that must be assumed in moral reasoning. To know how to act in the light of what the other is interested in and perceives, we must have some sense of what it means to be a person interested and perceiving. But in order to know the specific interests of a particular person, we must project ourselves into that person's place. Without doing so, we could not know what act of ours might lead that person to feel frustrated, insulted, or resentful.

Kant dismisses the Rule as "trivial" in a footnote:

> Let it not be thought that the trivial *quod tibi non vis fieris* etc. [Do not to others what you do not want done to yourself] can here serve as a standard or principle. For it is merely derived from our principle, although with several limitations. It cannot be a universal law, for it contains the ground neither of duties to oneself nor of duties of love toward others (for many a man would gladly consent that others should not benefit him, if only he might be excused from benefiting them). Nor, finally, does it contain the ground of strict duties toward others, for the criminal would on this ground be able to dispute with the judges who punish him; and so on.[10]

By arguments such as these, Kant and others suggest that the Rule would directly authorize acts we'd regard as morally wrong.

But Kant's judge would not be bound in the way that the supposed criminal argued, because, while regarding what the prisoner wants, the judge is to act as a generally concerned and informed person: as such he or she is equally bound to consider the concerns of all others and the effects that freeing the criminal would have on them. Although one can understand how Kant's denial of the relevance of specific conditions of action led him to overlook such effects, those effects are equally part of the "doing" under consideration, and those others affected would not welcome them (unless some strong justifying reason could be found). Thus, the effects on persons generally should be included in the description of the action and should be taken when considering whether to universalize the maxim of one's action. (The problem of including such details in a "maxim" is a point to be considered in the next chapter.) Since the effects on all others would always be equally a part of what is to be considered in our doing, our regarding the situation and reasonings of those others would prevent us from doing what was commonly regarded as harmful to them. The wants and concerns that can be granted are the wants and concerns that will not harm others; so, our duty to the other will be determined by what an informed and concerned person in the other's situation could ask for or accept. Our choice in such circumstances will be a choice with which immoral persons may not agree until they have changed their expectations or interests. The change we'd hope for and need in the criminal's case would be a change in heart, since concern for others is a necessary element in moral reasoning.

In such situations we still feel morally constrained to act in ways that are universalizable; but in universalizing we cannot give equal weight to everyone's expressed interests, nor can we wait to achieve agreement on acceptable reasons for our actions—a point to which we shall later revert. Rather, our acts are universalizable insofar as we act in a way that an informed, understanding, and concerned person would act and could agree to our supporting reasons. In such situations when applying the Rule, we seek to take the other's place and take account of the other's interests. We must finally decide to do what we take it that the other would want *as* a concerned person acquainted with that situation.

Part of the logical force of the point that concern is a prerequisite to moral reasoning is that moral reasons must always be construed as the reasons of concerned persons. Thus, for any action that affects other persons, we are morally required to act on their wishes only so long as those wishes can be made consistent with moral concern. We consider the wishes of all, even, for example, Nazis, but we are obliged to reject their genocidal proposals.

Kant might equally well have attempted to show that the Rule directly authorized wrongdoing by arguing that one totally ignorant of the situation or the consequences of a line of action—say a young child—might oblige a person (the child's parent, perhaps) to do something the parent knew would be harmful. But, of course, the Rule would no more authorize such action on the part of the parent than it would have authorized the judge's pardoning the criminal. For the act must be universalized by those who both are informed and understand the situation and are prepared to act out of concern for persons generally.

The fact that we do take an interest in others morally Kant takes to be the *result* of moral reasoning: our interest in treating others in accord with the moral law is derived from reason alone, independently of all inclination. But, as we have seen (in chapter 6), much moral feeling is not the effect of moral reasoning; rather it is the concern that makes moral reasoning possible. That same concern cannot be its effect, though we may come to have a richer appreciation of principle or law as a result of our reasoning.

Derek Parfit might be counted as another critic of the Rule, since he argues against the view that an appeal to moral agreement is part of the process by which we justify actions. He writes that "we must reject the view that for an act to be open to moral objection, there must be some complainant," for, Parfit reasons, "unfortunately when we choose a policy like Greater Depletion, there will be no complainants. If we believe this makes a difference, since the objection to our choice is just as strong, we believe that it is irrelevant that there will be complainants."[11] But, one wants to say, whoever can offer those strong objections would thereby become a complainant to the choice. One wants to add that there could not be a moral objection unless there were moral objectors or complainants. We would have to have reasons agreed upon *by some objectors*—Parfit has appealed to *our* agreement—in order to be able to call anything wrong; we could not take the objector seriously unless he or she could offer reasons others judged to be relevant. Moreover, we would have to feel that our action was secure from legitimate objections before believing it to be right: moral judgments can only be made by people. Thus, it seems that he must appeal to an actual or possible moral agreement to justify actions. In looking for possible objectors we must begin with the actual community of reasoners that we know. Hence, it will not be irrelevant if we find that the actual community presents no complainants to our proposal, though, of course, actual members of our community might miss some relevant reasons.

CARING UNCHECKED BY REASON
MAY BE DESTRUCTIVE

A number of recent writers have concentrated on the importance of caring and responding to a web of personal relationships in making a moral judgment.[12] Believing that moral judgments should take account of the importance of feelings and the need for sensitivity to particular involvements in moral decisions, some have been led to suppose that instructions for moral judgments can be summarized by "Be a caring person" or "Be compassionate" or "Follow your heart." There is a parallel kind of emphasis among current ethical writers to the effect that the only requirement for an act to have moral worth is that it be a "direct response to the good of another person'' and that ''[T]here is not the further requirement that the action be, or be regarded as, universalizable.''[13]

Whereas one can agree that concern is fundamental, it seems doubtful that there is not the further requirement that it be universalizable. It seems doubtful that we would want to describe all concerned actions as having worth. By that formulation, one's actions could be so described if one was genuinely concerned, no matter how partial or narrow one was in one's concern. Surely this is not intended: a Hitler, impelled by his warm feelings for the brave Aryans, would win moral praise for working in their behalf, so long as he described the action to himself in ways that focused just on the benefits he hoped to bring to his Aryan friends. He need not give a thought about what he might be doing to others.

By contrast, the Rule makes it clear that one must be *universal* in one's concern. We get clearer about who might be adversely affected by our act by asking if we could universalize the action. We need to ask if anyone could have reasons for not generalizing our concerned act. By asking ''Is it permissible?'' we get to the morally relevant description of the proposed act. Until we get such a description, we might praise the motive but not be clear about what was involved in what we were about to do.

Lawrence Blum agrees with a number of writers who have denied that ''all morally good action within personal relationships does in fact involve application of universal principle . . . one can certainly imagine individually worthy actions of friendship or parenthood which are animated not by a sense of applying principle but by a direct care for the friend or child.''[14] But, in caring for a friend or child in a morally acceptable way, one must also care for much besides them; for those other cares one must apply universal principle.

One can agree with Blum's supporting premise that not all acts are *animated* by a sense of applying principle, but that premise will not support the conclusion that universal principle is not applicable—that is, should be applied in assessing the rightness of the action taken. In caring for a child in the privacy of his or her home, a parent may have no *sense* of applying a principle (and certainly not be animated by it), but that is because in many contexts it is obvious that the care given does not violate anyone else's claims. We are often in an isolated situation where we obviously do not need to be worried about being partial in our caring, but to note the fact that we need not worry is itself to make use of the principle of impartiality. So long as we hold that caring acts are subject to appraisal and blame, we are saying that for anyone in the carer's situation, the act was right or wrong. In saying that, do we not universalize?

The just-be-compassionate view cannot stand alone even if one is universal in one's concern: a good will is *not* good without qualification. It may be admirable for one to have benevolent concern, but that does not mean that there are no qualifying factors. One cannot evaluate concern apart from considering the kind of action and world to which it might contribute. (It would not make sense to ask, Is it, is anything we evaluate, good just in itself?) To take the view that a good will is good without qualification is to assume that, if one has such concern, one will automatically choose the right thing to do— without bothering oneself about fact finding, imagining alternatives, or checking on points of law. But a person of uninformed good will could never know what would count as acting for another's well-being. Such a person could never know, for example, by what roles the other conceived of him- or herself and what was essential to those roles.

Against my view, someone may say that we never catch Jesus (a primary model for Rule application) in a fact-finding mood, thus, fact finding must be irrelevant to his version of the Rule. Jesus, the objector might continue, tells a story and asks us to decide from the heart. But we must remember that in inquiring what is the right thing to be done, he *tells us the story*, a story which we are to assume includes all the relevant details. And we must remember the Golden Rule explicitly tells us to put ourselves in the place of those affected by our action—a universalizing operation that could not be completed until we had become familiar with the other's place.

METHOD – NOT RECIPES – IN MORAL REASONING

Some have suggested that we must reject the Rule's method (and universalizing) as vague and imprecise. Alasdair MacIntyre (in *After Virtue*), rejected it for its failure to provide specific guidance. One can sympathize; precision would be welcome. The Rule is said to be imprecise and unscientific because it does not give us a specific directive for action that would apply in all cases; instead it asks us to consider others' subjective wants and perceptions that are not available for direct inspection.

It is true that we cannot directly inspect how others perceive themselves or their situation, nor can we directly see what they hope for. But we are often in a position to read the interests of those we care for just because we have cared for them and they are open with us—and this special relationship confers a special obligation upon us. At times we are able to help others become clearer about their situation and purposes. To gain a handle on such matters, we are (or should be) sensitive to a variety of factors that are expressive of their view of their situation: facial expression, nuances of phrase and inflection, persistent associations, and so on. I can say and so on because readers are familiar with the kind of thing that we could look for as relevant to discovering what a person would take his or her situation to be, which signifies that we would know how to inquire into purposes and intentions in specific cases. MacIntyre's mistake seems to lie in assuming that there is some rule which would—like a Kantian universal law of nature—tell each of us what to do on all occasions.

But the fact that we can learn how to read others' situations (to some degree) does not mean that there is or could be a precise rule stating what procedures we could always follow to determine what another took his or her situation to be. There is no such rule and there could *be* none. Any method of reaching decisions affecting specific individuals must be tentative if it is to be true to our freedom in the moral situation.

The salient characteristic of moral situations in a free society is their indeterminacy. They are indeterminate because they result from the voluntary actions of free persons, any one of whose decisions is continually open to reinterpretation or reconsideration. Individuals involved can, within limits, change the order of options they wish to pursue, their conception of themselves, or the plan of life they intend to follow. As my associates change their goals and interests, they will change—sometimes subtly, sometimes profoundly—what I am obliged to take note of in considering my obligation to them: if my student decides to drop out of school and marry his girlfriend, that alters what I must attend to. So long as we have the capacity for controlled, voluntary action—so long as we can be said to be persons in the full sense of the term—we must remain alert to each other's shifts in interest to know what we can do or are obliged to do for the other. Thus, moral reasoning turns on being sensitive and responsive to shifting relationships. This indeterminacy makes it imperative that one follow the method enjoined by the Rule—namely, that of putting oneself in the other's place—with all of the limitations that goes with this method.

We are morally required to put ourselves in the place of those whom our actions might affect and to consult their reasons about our actions. But that fact does not mean that their reasons are always infallible or that consulting them will always enable us to reach agreement with them. Because it is sometimes true that in using the Rule, we encounter unresolvable conflicts with others and uncertainties as to how we should act, some have concluded that the Rule should be replaced by some clearer and surer moral rule. But there can *be* no precise and definite rule for deciding about all of the indeterminate futures with which we have to deal. But others have rejected the Rule for reasons similar to MacIntyre's; one adopted what he terms *moral skepticism* for similar reasons.

John Mackie's *Ethics: Inventing Right and Wrong* is the influential case in point. Mackie claims to adopt moral skepticism as a result of his observations (1) that we may be biased in applying the Rule and (2) that the Rule will not always enable us to reach a definite decision. Yet, as I hope to show, it is misleading to speak of Mackie's position as one of moral skepticism, and none of his objections provides ground for rejecting or denying the Rule as a standard. To make these points, we first need to look at his observations.

Mackie first addresses the issue of the Rule as it is related to universalizability, which in its first and simplest form holds only that "purely numerical differences and proper name constants be treated as irrelevant"[15] to making moral distinctions. But, he says, this simplest form of universalizing would not suffice; since "no generic qualitative differences have been ruled irrelevant in principle, our so far merely formal constraints allow a moral system to discriminate between people for reasons that we would judge in practice to be unfair. . . . It is unfair in almost all instances to discriminate between people on grounds of colour" (*M*:89). Since by this kind of universalizing we might unfairly discriminate on the basis of gender or race, Mackie says we must move to a second stage of universalizing in which we exclude such qualitative differences as irrelevant. At this point Mackie turns to the Rule as the standard of what is fair: "To decide whether some maxim is really universalizable, imagine yourself in the other man's place and ask whether you can then accept it as a directive guiding behaviour" (*M*:32). He finds that "differences can be fairly regarded as relevant if they look relevant from whichever side you consider them" (*M*:90). Thus, Mackie uses the Rule as a criterion of what will "plainly be fairer," but he holds that in applying it "one may take unfair account of one's own distinctive tastes, ideals and so on"; one imagines oneself in the other's place "but still with one's own present tastes, preferences, ideals and values" (*M*:92).

In this final stage one tries to look at "things both from one's own and the other(s)' point of view" (*M*:92) to discover how one should act. Where many conflicting demands are to be met, he finds that we shall probably have to look for solutions that "represent an acceptable compromise" but that will "not yield completely definite answers to practical questions" (*M*:93–94).

What kind of compromise? Mackie ponders the question of whether we should try "to take not just some account but equal account of all actual interests" (*M*:93) including those interests which conflict with our own values. Mackie asks us to imagine a debate between one who applies the Rule and a Nazi. We are to imagine that the Nazi is a fanatic who would want himself and his family exterminated "if it turns out that they are Jews by descent" (*M*:94). The Nazi would "give no weight to interests which are incompatible with that ideal" (*M*:93). The question is: If our Rule-user were to confront such a Nazi, could our Rule-user weight "all ideals equally"?—including his own of treating all equally. Mackie concludes that if the Rule-user looks "upon himself *qua* participant as one among many," he "does not give equal weight to all actually held ideals" (*M*:94–95).

Oddly, Mackie says that the Rule-user "does not" rather than "could not": I say "oddly" because the Rule-user would be logically bound to disregard interests (like the Nazi's) that deny the possibility of applying the Rule; as Rule-user, one must consider the effects of the policy on all others, including the Jews whom the Nazi would exterminate. Here our response must be the same as it was to Kant's judge: our acts will be universalizable if we act in a way that an informed and concerned person could agree to act. Mackie here attempts to treat the Rule for evaluating interests as just one interest among all the interests it is to evaluate. But that's a *logical* impossibility: it can't be a rule for evaluating interests if it can be trumped by the interests it is to evaluate. The Rule-user who says "treat all equally" may address, but must rule out of consideration, policies that require us to treat others unequally.

What Mackie has done in this passage is to *use* the Rule as the criterion of what will "plainly be fairer" within ordinary moral reasoning but then to reject the Rule because it would not be compatible with others' (such as the Nazi's) desire to give unfair treatment. But Mackie can't reject his own acknowledged standard of fairness on the gound that, in application, it would not be unfair. Mackie's contradiction here—the Rule gives the standard of fairness; the Rule does not—seems to derive from the fact that he confuses the Rule for evaluating interests with one of the interests to be evaluated by it. And there could, of course, be no rule that would survive such a test. Yet it is this confusion (and contradiction) that leads Mackie to declare that universalizing (and Rule using) fails: he finds that "the third stage only approximates to the giving of equal weight to all interests" (*M*:92–95).

Mackie opens his criticism with two objections to the Rule: that we may exercise biases in applying it (considered above) and that the Rule will at times not "yield completely definite answers to practical questions." It is not much of an objection to its validity as a standard to say that it does not always yield definite answers to moral questions: as we've shown, the fact that we will often be unable to tell how a course of action would affect all concerned was a basis for the indeterminacy of many answers. The fact that we will not always—indeed, often we could not—be in possession of all relevant information does not mean that we have no reason for asking for the information. Mackie has used the Rule to determine what kind of information would be relevant; it seems that Mackie admits as much in calling the Rule the fairer way.

Psychologically, Mackie's move may arise from focusing on the wrong kind of case, possibly because these are the ones that require our careful attention and because these are the ones that we are most likely to refer to as moral issues. If we focus on the (many) problems that we seem to be incapable of resolving, we may feel that there is no possibility of using the Rule to judge any issue. Looking only at these cases, we may find it pointless to invoke a community of reasoners using such a standard: we may want to say that if they can't always reach agreement by using that standard, there's never much point in invoking it.

But this is to overlook the fact that Mackie has referred to the Rule as the fairer way and to overlook the many commonplace cases where we apply it and reach agreement through doing so. These are cases where we do not hesitate to make a judgment using it and have no doubt that others will agree with us. We are in no doubt that your acquaintance George was remiss in the cases cited (in chapter 2); we confidently say that anyone who behaved as he did would be remiss because he was unconcerned, failing to put himself in the other's place. And it is an important fact about moral reasoning and our use of the Rule that any of us could propose a number of ways that each case might be altered so that George would be excused (by users of the Rule); as we have noted, a responsible adult could normally pose an indefinite number of changes that would lead competent moral reasoners to withdraw their blame from George. Thus, it is apparent that Rule-use often leads us to clear judgments on which we are confident of agreement.

There are hard judgments and easy judgments, and it may be helpful to try to show some of the reasons why one kind is hard and the other is easy. We note that Mackie frequently points to public policy cases when he wants to illustrate the point that we frequently can't agree on a conclusion. As we noted in chapter 2, public policy decisions are likely to be difficult because they involve many people's future desires and plans—all of which are shrouded in uncertainty (for themselves as well as for others). By contrast we have the ordinary cases where we have to do with one or two individuals (as illustrated by our relation with our acquaintance, George, in chapter 2). We may also note that promoting the well-being or development of others can quickly lead us onto problematic ground, whereas we feel relatively secure about judgments that require us to avoid harming or injuring another person. Because what we'd call harms or injuries are often relative to another's already chosen line of development (and thus, are less likely to introduce the complicating factor of what they would want), we are likely to feel surer about judging what interferes with (rather than what would help them) to form or pursue their purposes.

Clearly, the same Rule applies in the hard cases and the easy cases; the harder cases are not harder because we are not agreed that we should consider the effects of our acts on others, but they are harder because it is difficult to consider those effects in cases surrounded by uncertainties. The difficulty and uncertainty is not in the Rule but in the facts that we would need to complete our decision. If the principle to be applied were not known—if it were merely subjective, to use Mackie's term—it would be equally arbitrary in the easy cases, and we should be prepared to consider willfully cruel acts as unwelcome, perhaps, but not known to be wrong.

Therefore, Mackie and MacIntyre don't seem to have much of an objection to the Rule when they say that it can't claim to provide a determinate answer for all problems, for we would have to reject any rule that claimed to be always able to provide such answers. Mackie's first objection—that we may misapply the Rule, exercising biases—seemed weaker still: it would not make sense to speak of misapplying it or of biased application unless we knew what it was to apply it in an appropriate and unbiased way. With these two arguments gone, Mackie's objections against the Rule really fall along with the others.

His description of his position as that of a skeptic is as misleading as his dubbing Rule-use a subjective approach. Since he appeals to and argues from common agreement on the Rule as the criterion of fairness, he's not a skeptic in any ordinary sense of the term. As we noted in chapter 3, Mackie's claim to skepticism and claim to find all moral language and reasoning "in error" cannot be sustained so long as he makes moral proposals and judgments about what is fairer.

NO MORALITY WITHOUT SELF-CONTROL

I've argued that ordinary moral reasoning and philosophical analyses of the conditions of responsiblity support the notion that the Rule indicates the motives and methods that are essential to moral reasoning about cases *between* individuals. As we shall note (chapter 8) there are morally significant decisions that individuals have to make for themselves that do not involve this method.[16]

However, our reasoning and analysis of this method will not support all that is suggested by all versions of the Rule; it will not support those passages or versions that advocate self-denial or selflessness. If the Rule is to require that we place ourselves in the other's situation and do what an informed and concerned person would do in that situation, it cannot require that we cooperate in or acquiesce to any proposed criminal or destructive scheme. Our acting with informed and imaginative concern requires that we keep a sense of self and maintain *self-control*: it does not permit acquiescence with what will destroy us, nor is it compatible with selflessness. It requires that we continue to have access to information and to some means of acting. The biblical "Love thy neighbor as thyself" takes regard for oneself as natural and appropriate; here and elsewhere, Jesus appeals to what one wants, or what one could want for oneself as a person, and uses this appeal as the criterion for judgment. One cannot give up that capacity to function as a person and continue to function as a moral individual. However, this conclusion seems to be at odds with those passages where we are enjoined to "take no thought" for our future needs; to "go the second mile"; to "turn the other cheek"; and to "forgive seventy times seven times."

Moral reasoning cannot use the criterion of putting oneself in the place of the other unless it proceeds by maintaining a sense of self as well as a sense of the other. It must alternate between both poles: self and other. Responsible moral action must proceed from maintaining control over what is required for one to take action. Thus, one is brought back to Hobbes's point that one's willingness to enter into moral reasoning must be conditional on others' willingness to restrict their liberties and respect the well-being of their fellow citizens—or conditional on the reasonable hope that they will do so. Moral reasoning, finally, must be the activity of a community of mutual concern, within which members must reserve the freedoms required to maintain a sense of self and some control over their ability to act.

Thus, we find points to reject in some versions of the Rule. But our philosophical analyses of the conditions of responsibility as well as our moral vocabulary and reasoning support the claim for universality of the common requirement of all versions: that we, as reflective, self-controlled agents, consider our actions from the perspective of those affected and respond with concern to meet each other's needs.

As we've noted, this is not to say that the Rule is the only moral principle we use—we cannot use it in decisions where we deal with masses of people. Nor is it to maintain that we will never have difficulties in applying it; again, indeterminacy in moral judgments is inevitable in a free community of moral reasoners: the flexibility and open-endedness of the statement of the Rule are part of its strength.

WHY SHOULD THE RULE BE
SO WIDELY ACKNOWLEDGED?

Given that the Rule has the strength, one may still want to ask: How does it happen that the Rule is applied so widely (or acknowledged so widely)? Why should the concept of law (of treating similar cases similarly) be universally acknowledged as a norm? Why, despite its critics, should there happen to be this common element of the Rule that is so widely acknowledged? The answer seems to lie partly in what we saw to be the fact that the Rule, the concept of law, and the giving of reasons are all expressions of the idea of treating individuals respectfully, as persons among persons.

I suggest, however, that it also lies in the point that for all languages, a necessary condition of coming to form a conception of oneself through language is that we must conceive of persons as alike; hence, we must conceive of others as persons like ourselves. If we know how to apply any descriptive predicate to ourselves, we must know how it applies to others; in knowing what it means for us, we must know what it means for others. Our linguistic conception of ourselves must come to us through seeing its terms in application to others. Thus, for all linguistic communities, our self-conception must arise from each seeing ourselves as a person among persons.

Therefore, *if we are considering moral reasoning and action, we are to respect others; if we respect them we must treat them as persons, and, (from the preceding reasoning), if we conceive of persons clearly, we conceive of them as persons like ourselves. It follows that: we must treat them as persons like ourselves. If so, we should treat them as we conceive it would be appropriate that we be treated under circumstances similar to their own. Hence, the Rule (as modified) is fundamental to acting with moral concern.* It seems inevitable that people widely acknowledge a principle so necessarily connected with how we conceive of ourselves and of moral action.

8 / Persons and Particulars

We've argued that one of the strengths of the Rule is that it leads us toward being sensitive and responsive to the demands of shifting and volatile situations. Its use is grounded in the nature of persons and how we must form our conception of them: we must conceive of persons by considering what we have in common, seeing others as like ourselves in fundamental capacities to respond. We use that conception by putting ourselves into their situation to respond morally to them. The moral appropriateness of the Rule response is tied to the fact that it leads us to take in universal relevance while considering persons' lives as built around their individual interests and associations.

What this adds up to is that we reach tenable moral decisions by informing ourselves about, and bearing in mind, particular projects, interests, and involvements of others and by considering the universal consequences of meeting their demands.

If we follow this procedure, and we judge an act to be right for a particular individual, we can say it would be right for any relevantly similar person in relevantly similar circumstances. That is, we can give the judgment a universal form because we do not ignore the relevant particulars around which the other's life is built: our judgment will not be coherent as moral reasoning unless it takes in such particular concerns.

In this chapter, I want to argue that without focusing on such particular concerns, we will not be able to make sense of either our judgments and reasoning about our projects or our pursuit of moral excellences. As we are beings-in-relationship whose development and fulfilment takes form through individualized engagements, if we exclude particulars in considering either our own or another's claims, we exclude what must be at the center of our moral life.

More specifically I will argue: (1) that the quest for universally applicable rules obscures the process of judging by starting us to look for general rules instead of the relevant information; (2) judgment is based on particular connections, not on the numbers of people involved; (3) in our personal dealings, we must be prepared to respond to persons in their particularity; (4) a person's achievement of a virtue is through particular abilities and opportunities; (5) as a consequence of the above, we will often be unable to prescribe for or respond to free persons with whom we are unfamiliar; and (6) it is a mistake to ask for a rule that would tell us exactly what our obligations would be for all individuals.

Many may question[1] that we can defend both that claim and any belief in universalizability. I want to argue that the force of particularized judgments derives from our understanding of a relationship. My reasons will repeatedly cut to the nature of our moral anatomy and the point that a life and a self are built around particular projects and concerns: that we are *essentially*, not contingently, beings who can develop fully only through particular involvements.

Yet, there are elements of moral reasoning that may tug us toward what has been called "strict universalizability," according to which a valid moral judgment must be valid for all alike, independently of our unique abilities or particular situation. These elements center around the point that in moral reasoning we work from and respond to a conception of our *common* moral anatomy. We have noted how we hold people responsible and praise or blame them with reference to what persons generally are and what one can legitimately demand or expect of them; moral assessments are possible because we respond to persons *as* persons. Our language and the notions of fairness and impartiality are possible because we treat each other as persons among persons; we could not articulate a conception of ourselves that did not make use of the idea that we are, and must be treated as, the same in many ways. Thus, when we consider possible universally applicable principles for moral judgment, some have felt that we could have coherent judgments only by requiring a strict Kantian kind of universalizability and (thus) by ignoring or minimizing the importance of our points of difference.

STRICT UNIVERSALIZABILITY

If we look at some of Kant's applications of the idea of strict universality, I think we will see how the insistence on it leads us away from clarity in judgment and away from our standard approach to moral reasoning.

Kant, concerned to preserve the strict universality of the moral law, was led to avoid all that was particular and contingent and focus on what he considered the essential feature of the moral agent, pure rationality: "The universality with which [moral laws] should hold for all rational beings . . . is lost when their foundation is taken from the *particular constitution of human nature*, or the accidental circumstances in which it is placed."[2] This reflects his belief in the need for strictly universal law and in considering our essential moral nature to be abstracted from all particular circumstances (as well as from our feelings). Our essential moral nature is rational since: "Pure reason is practical of itself alone, and it gives [to man] a universal law which we call the *moral law*."[3] Thus, moral law is said to be possible only because it derives from what we have in common and is based on the rational form of law. We can create the law to which we subject ourselves. In doing so we meet the "condition under which alone something can be an end in itself . . . [and have] intrinsic worth, i.e., *dignity*."[4] We possess moral worth, for Kant, because we are, and we consider each other, as rational creators and subjects of the law. We can attain virtue[5] in the same way—namely by approximating the purity of a will in conformity with the moral law.

Significantly, the moral worth and the virtue of the individual is not attained by attending to anything that is unique to an individual, a point that might give us pause and that I shall later challenge.

Another point that gives us pause is Kant's account of moral decision as a matter of framing and following rules that are universally applicable. The strict universality of Kant's development of his categorical imperative is reflected, among other places, in his reference to "the maxim" (*Maxime* in German) that one could will to become a "universal law" of a "system of nature." Here again we see the notion that if a moral judgment is valid, it is valid because it holds for a "system of nature"—for all people. These laws derive from the "fundamental law." In *The Critique of Practical Reason* we read: "So act that the maxim of your will could always hold at the same time as a principle establishing universal law."[6] We read that "pure reason is practical of itself alone and it gives a universal law."[7] By such rationally determined universal law we arrive at a "system of nature which is subject to a will."[8] Again, in *The Foundations of the*

Metaphysics of Morals, we see "there is only one categorical imperative. It is: Act only according to that maxim by which you can at the same time will that it should become a universal law."[9] And alternatively: "Act as though the maxim of your action were by your will to become a universal law of nature."[10]

Maxims that can become universal laws are connected with the belief that valid judgments must involve, be equally applicable, to all people—humanity in general. It is morally odd—false—to claim that to find what is obligatory or permissible for oneself, one must always look for a *maxim* for one's action that can become a universal law of nature.

The problem begins with the notion of maxims. Maxims are ordinarily considered to be moral rules; a maxim is, according to the OED (Oxford English Dictionary): "A rule or principle of conduct; also a precept of morality." The OED adds that, etymologically, it derives from the Latin, *maximus*, which refers to what is most used and useful to guide the actions of people generally. Maxims are terse, pithy sayings telling us how we ought to act. They are packed into single sentences such as: "Honesty is the best policy," and "A fool and his gold are soon parted." In a footnote Kant explains his notion of a maxim, saying that it is a "subjective principle," that it "contains the practical rule which reason determines according to the conditions of the subject (often its ignorance or inclinations) and is thus the principle according to which the subject acts."[11] For Kant, then, a maxim is to be understood as containing a description of the agent's intention or plan of action that is rationally grounded in an account of what the agent wants and of the conditions under which the agent acts. That is a lot to pack into a saying, however pithy it may be.

Here Kant appears to assume: (a) that we will always be acting from a maxim; (b) that we could find one that would include the relevant circumstances to guide us through the contemplated action; and (c) that it could serve as a universal law of nature. Kant seems mistaken on all three counts. We do not always have—nor do we want to have—a maxim or rule before us to guide our action; if we did, we would rarely be able to include all the relevant detail; and if we did have a maxim and could include what is relevant, the maxim could not be made into anything like a law applying universally to human nature.

But we need to expand on these points. His speaking of our acting from a "maxim" that refers to the description of our intention and conditions of our acting is odd. It suggests he believes that we act from rules and that the rules are or can be morally sufficient. If such rules could serve us, that would mean that there is not much particular detail that we need to include in considering what we must do on each specific occasion; that all of our accounts of justifying reasons could easily be cast into short and, therefore, fairly simple molds. Moreover, what would serve one as the guide to action would have to serve all, if we were to have maxims that could become universal laws of a system of nature. But all of these assumptions seem to be false.

Maxims Not Always Used

Kant's examples of maxim applications do not allay our misgivings. Consider the first one he mentions: "A man who is reduced to despair by a series of evils feels a weariness with life but is still in possession of his reason sufficiently to ask whether it would not be contrary to his duty to himself to take his own life. Now he asks whether the maxim of his action could become a universal law of nature. His maxim, however, is: For love of myself, I make it my principle to shorten my life when by a longer duration it threatens more evil than satisfaction."[12] Notice that in moving from the original description of his situation to the maxim, Kant has stripped away some of the specific details of his condition: he moves from one "reduced to despair by a series of evils" and feeling "a weariness" with his life to the not so desperate fellow who, out "love of myself," wants to settle it by cost-benefit calculation. It doesn't really sound like the same fellow or the same situation.

Kant settles the case, saying that the man would see that his suicide out of love of himself would not be consistent with a system of nature in which the "special office" of love of oneself is "to impel the improvement of life"; (supposedly) he would thus find that the act is not permissible, and so he must abandon the suicide plan. But, of course, the reader knows that many responsible moral agents do not have—and do not need—a list of such "principles."

General Rules Cannot Include Needed Detail

Moreover, if anyone were to attempt to apply a list of principles in this case, it could not have the scope to produce a decision because we need to have additional information about a lot of particular details: How many evils is the man suffering from? What kind of evils? Terminal cancer? Paralysis? Are any or all of his capacities to act or his plans for living destroyed? Will any of his associates' lives or life-prospects be destroyed by his continuing to live or by his dying? Patently, we will arrive at a range of *different individual* decisions, and the decisions will depend on the answers about these particular details. We have to know what specific evils are involved and how they bear on the specific individual involved. (The loss of the use of their hands would be more critical for some—artists and musicians, for example—whereas for others the loss of their eyes and voice might prove more important for their work and associations.) The moral weight of the specific evils is bound to vary with the individual case, so that we have no reason to believe that we would be able to arrive at a universally applicable maxim regardless of the individual circumstances. We might well have difficulty reaching agreement about what was appropriate for specific cases, but the point is that we need to understand the specific details of the cases before we can begin to consider the matter.

Thus, the suggestion that our effort should be toward finding a maxim of this sort is a morally misleading one. It *invites* us to *under*-describe or misdescribe—just as Kant underdescribes and then misdescribes—the situation about which we are to make a decision. In Kant's move from the description to the maxim, we see the distorting effects of attempting to strip away specific details and to compress into a generally applicable rule.

Similar problems accompany Kant's second case. There he considers: "Another man finds himself forced by need to borrow money. He well knows that he will not be able to repay it, but he also sees that nothing will be loaned him if he does not firmly promise to repay it at a certain time. He desires to make such a promise but has enough conscience to ask himself whether it is not improper and opposed to duty to relieve his distress in such a way. Now assuming he does decide to do so, the maxim of his action would be as follows: When I believe myself to be in need of money, I will borrow money and promise to repay it, although I know I shall never do so."[13] We see that Kant moves from the description of one who is in "distress" and "finds himself forced by need to borrow money" to that of a person who (in his maxim) is considering what to do when he "believes himself to be in need." Again, we see a shift.

While we do not advocate borrowing without intending to repay, we still find that, again, we do not have nearly enough information to be clear about the decision (that is supposedly to become a law of nature). What kind of distress is involved? Who else is involved? Is someone's life at stake here? Is a life crucially dependent on our man's loan? Are we to erect a general rule to the effect that nonrepayment of debt is so important that avoiding it should always prevent people from relieving all distresses—including the saving of lives? Could a person in need ever borrow money that he believed he could not repay? Clearly, the answer to the question and the duties of the individuals involved will vary according to the particular circumstances.

Again, we might have difficulty in reaching a decision in such cases, but we would need a great deal more information than Kant provides to begin making our decision. But more to the point, we see that Kant, in formulating a maxim for the case, *excludes* information and stretches its application so that he does not even include the highly relevant, though vaguely described, circumstance that we are concerned to relieve someone in distress.

Thus, the quest for laws and maxims that are applicable to people in general leads Kant to attempt to cast us all into the same vaguely described, amorphous classes so that we can plausibly be seen as having the same duties, and this leads him to ignore the circumstances that are actually relevant in judging individual actions.

What Is Appropriate for One
May Not Be Appropriate for All

Clear and tenable decisions require that our situations not be vaguely described. For clear moral judgments, we must consider carefully and describe accurately exactly those things that Kant prohibited our inquiring into—namely, "circumstances in which [the agent] . . . is placed." For, as Marcus Singer notes, "it is almost axiomatic that 'the character of every act depends on the circumstances in which it is done.' "[14] The nature and quality of the act can only be described by considering those circumstances: whether my swinging of my golf club will count as a good drive or a murderous, lethal blow will be determined by attending to the circumstances in which I swing it. Obviously, it follows that whether or not it will count as my performance of my duty will be dependent on those circumstances.

In actions, taken generally, as we noted in chapter 4, one aims to bring about a specific outcome by a specific set of moves. What moves are permissible or obligatory must be dependent on, among other things, what one can do and with whom one is associated. As we come in all shapes and sizes, all kinds of abilities and commitments, and all kinds of situations, we cannot all have the same obligations. And so, we cannot operate by common rules for each of our specific situations, and we should not attempt to find a "maxim" for each situation. What could not be a duty for a paraplegic might well be a duty for a strong athlete. What will be obligatory for the parent of a paraplegic child will not be a duty for another parent or for a stranger.

UNIVERSALIZING AND PARTICULARIZING

We saw that the impulse to sameness of duty arose from the desire to have a universalizable judgment, and it led to vague and inappropriately worded maxims that neither applied to the cases described nor permitted one to have a clear basis for judgment. It becomes obvious that if one has a clear basis for a universalizable judgment, it must be because one has a grasp of relevant specific circumstances. Therefore, the universalizing judgment must be particularized by adding qualifiers to the classes of persons and circumstances adjudged.

We must move from "What's right (or wrong) for one person must be right (or wrong) for all" to the particularized "What's right (or wrong) for one person must be right (or wrong) for any relevantly similar person in relevantly similar circumstances."[15] By focusing on the relevantly similar character of the persons and circumstances we will be able to show how the judgment is justified. But as some of the above examples suggest, there may be very few, if any, others who are relevantly similar in their persons and circumstances and, thus, relatively few to whom the judgment would apply. This may lead one to ask: If there could be no other relevantly similar person or circumstances, does it make any sense to speak of the judgments as universalizable?

In answering the question, we should begin by noting that moral judgments commonly guide us concerning a particular action and that we defend the judgment that the act is right by reasons—that is, generally acceptable reasons—to show that *acts of this kind* are right. Note that we are not saying that acts of this kind are right because we know of an actual group of persons—large or small—who meet the qualifications of the reasons. We do not intend to say that the act is right because there is a *specific group of people* who are exactly similar and in exactly similar circumstances. We do not look for an actual group in the world for whom this can be a law. Rather, we isolate and choose to make our judgments, generalizing about the connections between persons with those relevant characteristics. The actual existence of a group of such persons is logically irrelevant to the rightness of a specific act. If I am seated alone on a pier in front of my lakeside cottage when a toddler falls into the water in front of me, my obligation to the toddler is unaffected by the question of whether there is an actual group of other persons in relevantly similar circumstances. In saying that anyone in a situation relevantly similar to my own should have rescued the toddler, we do not assume that there is such a group on, say, Lakes Champlain, Winnebago, and Windermere.

Rather, we look to the relevant particular circumstances to define what makes the act the right one. Its rightness is dependent on the toddler's inability to swim and my ability to help it. The validity of the reasoning in support of the particular judgment—its universalizability—depends on our ability to fasten on the universal connection between the relevant factors in the particular situation.

PARTICULARITY IN THE SELF

Moreover, as F. H. Bradley argued, to realize what is purely rational is impossible: our identity is always particular and takes shape from living in a specific social context with the obligations and claims that grow out of it.[16] We find support for his claim in the point that in each action we must aim to bring about specific consequences in relation to specific conditions.

Milton Mayeroff's recent study, *On Caring*, explores the way in which one's life takes on meaning to oneself through individual projects appropriate to one's specific abilities.[17] In developing individual projects one gains a sense of the value of one's activity and life: one sees that one contributes effectively to the growth of something of value.[18] Our sense of self, worth, and place are ordinarily shaped by these particular involvements, whether or not we are ideally suited to them. This comes across vividly in the salty responses of a Brooklyn fireman to Studs Terkel's questions about his work: "The firemen, you actually see them produce. You see them put out a fire. You see them come out with babies in their hands. You see them give mouth-to-mouth when a guy's dying. You can't get around that shit. That's real. To me, that's what I want to be . . . I can look back and say, 'I helped put out a fire. I helped save somebody.' It shows I did something on this earth.'"[19] To the extent that we reflect on what we have actually done, we will consider our lives as constituted by the actual projects to which we have committed. As Terkel's other interviews show, those who find themselves in jobs that are not well fitted to their talents will speak of themselves and their lives as centering around these dominant activities. They see themselves as teachers, nurses, or writers, as well as parents and friends, and they order their activities accordingly.

The ordering must always be in relation to particulars. One can only be the parent of particular children. Friendships are formed through particular associations and persons. In one's work one attends to and exploits specific abilities: teachers, for example, must use specific aptitudes and opportunities to teach specific students with particular abilities, concerns, and projects of their own. In monitoring our performance and choosing what we are to do, we typically find that we are building toward a particular kind of development or growth, taking note of specific potentialities, planning, and watching for the opportune moment. If we considered development in general or potentialities in general, we would accomplish nothing. Rather we must be knowledgeable, attentive, and observant of the interrelation of specific abilities, giving ourselves over to such projects for an extended time. We may well find that there is a specific, uniquely right move for us to make at a given time, rather than a right move for persons generally. In seizing the right moment, we often see a need to extend our involvement, thereby reshaping our life activity.

Such projects lie at the center of the life of one who finds such appropriateness, and, we hope, at the center of the lives of those whom we care for. Our choices may well have a profound effect on the quality of life for both ourselves and those around whom our projects are built. Moreover, deliberation about these choices brings one's own life into clearer focus and thereby enhances one's ability to order and clarify other decisions. Although one can only be engaged in a limited number of such significant projects (for each calls for one's time, knowledge, and attention), those projects move to the center of one's world.

William Carlos Williams, in his *Autobiography*, explains how his attentive care for specific patients in his work as a physician has touched his own identity. He speaks of losing himself "in the very properties of their minds. . . . [F]or me the practice of medicine has become the pursuit of a rare element which may appear at any time, at any place at a glance. . . . Mutual recognition is likely to flare up at a moment's notice. The relationship between physician and patient, if it were literally followed, would give us a world of extraordinary fertility. . . . There's no use trying to multiply cases, it is there, it is magnificent, it fills my thoughts, it reaches to the farthest limits of our lives." Out of their mutual involvement and attention to the detail of the patient's life comes new communication. "The physician enjoys a wonderful opportunity to witness the words being born. Their actual colors and shapes are laid before him carrying their tiny burdens which he is privileged to take into his care with their unspoiled newness. No one else is present but the speaker and ourselves, we have been the words' very parents. Nothing is more moving." He is aiming not merely for medical diagnosis but for the discovery of a human relationship and a direction. They must be found in "the peculiar, actual conformations in which its life is hid. Humbly he presents himself before it and by long practice he strives as best he can to interpret the manner of its speech. In that the secret lies."[20] The richness and intensity of the experience and the clarity of direction comes from attending to the peculiar, actual conformations—by contrast with the method of strict universalizability.

Some might want to argue that, as the decision to become involved in such friendships and projects is a purely personal one and one for which there is no absolute necessity, one could not claim that such projects should figure in everyone's moral reasoning. In responding, one must acknowledge that it's not a necessary truth that every human life is centered on involvements, and it's true that there may be people who have no such involvement with other persons and projects. But it's also true that those who have no continuing involvement with others are exceptional cases whom we ordinarily describe in terms that indicate disorder; we say of them that theirs are lives without focus or order: "rootless," "adrift," or "empty."

Studs Terkel interviewed a prostitute who describes how desolation followed from her lack of attention to, and involvement with, her customers: "In order to continue I had to turn myself off. I had to dissassociate who I was from what I was doing. It's a process of numbing yourself. . . . I found I couldn't turn myself back on when I finished working. When I turned myself off, I was emotionally, sexually numb." The result: "The work becomes boring because you're not part of the life. You're the part that's always hidden. The doormen smirk when you come in, because they know what's going on. . . . You leave there and go back—to what? Really to what? To an emptiness."[21] Of people who are totally void of all such involvements we may even use pathological terms to describe them, speaking of them as "asocial," or "social isolates," or even as "sociopaths."

If we are talking about morally responsible people whose lives have a center, there is a logical necessity that they be involved with persons and projects in continuing engagements. To have a center for one's life is to have engagements about which one cares and to which one is committed. To take a responsible role in the community is to *take a role and care about taking a role*: to take a role is to become involved in practices with other persons, practices in which one seeks to fulfill acknowledged obligations through particular activities with persons. We make our lives—we invent ourselves— through such involvements.

Masters of fiction are, of course, sensitive to the way obligations emerge from, and identities rest on, attention to particular commitments and goals. We see Dostoyevsky's awareness of this in his treatment of the relation between the brothers, Alyosha and Ivan, following the Grand Inquisitor scene in *The Brothers Karamazov*. Alyosha, sensing Ivan's depression and fear of rejection, kisses Ivan, restoring his spirits: " 'Listen, Alyosha,' Ivan began in a resolute voice, 'if I am really able to care for the sticky little leaves I shall only love them, remembering you. It's enough for me that you are somewhere here, and I shan't lose my desire for life yet.' " As they linger over their parting, Ivan, attentive to Alyosha's religious commitment and his devotion to Father Zossima, remarks: "Come, go now to your Pater Seraphicus, he is dying. If he dies without you, you will be angry with me for having kept you. Good-bye. Kiss me once more; that's right, now go.''²² Their goals and their sense of self are chosen and worked out through a web of such relationships. Strict universalizability leads us away from seeing their importance.

Others might feel that because these choices are related to one's job, one's family or other *personal* projects, they have no bearing on one's moral obligations generally. But this is mistaken, for we are dealing here with how people generally define themselves as persons. Everyone's choices and preferences are related to his or her particular projects, and I must thus take note of that particularity in considering what will hurt or hinder each of the people whose lives I affect. Of equal moral importance, perhaps, one also defines and fulfils oneself by one's successive choices in such projects. In choosing, one is meeting others' moral claims as well as one's obligation to oneself.

The projects in which one builds relationships with others cannot be fenced off from moral assessment. We are blamed for our failures to meet our obligations as parents or as teachers; such blame is apparent in the fact that our performance can be described as negligent, inattentive, perfunctory, slipshod, or careless—all terms that carry moral force.

Whereas I have chosen the examples of a teacher and a doctor to illustrate how we might be involved in projects, in other projects we also become involved with particular persons and things. Our success depends on our deliberations about our abilities in relation to those particulars and our successive moves with them; we come to view new conditions as possibilities or challenges for the project. Thus, our sense of self and of the world arise from monitoring and deliberating about those particular involvements and our own individual abilities—our individual nature.

This is not to say that contemporary society presents no obstacles to one's attaining a sense of one's identity through one's involvements in job and community. The technology that urbanized us and presented us with laborsaving devices also keeps most young people outside the involvements and satisfactions of the work experience until they are past adolescence: they are effectively excluded from the working world. Those in the working world often cannot find a sense of identity in contributing to their particular community since they have no particular community, owing to the fact that their jobs require them to move frequently from community to community. Nor can they always find a secure sense of place or identity within the firms they serve, since many firms are likely to be swallowed up or eliminated through a takeover by distant economic entities. Obviously, this makes those involved less sure of their places and possibilities within such an economy. But that does not alter the conceptual point that as persons we find our roots, our sense of structure, and moral worth in using our specific abilities in involvements with specific other persons.

PARTICULARITY IN PURSUING A VIRTUE

Our particular abilities also become the materials for our moral self-definition through our pursuit of specific moral virtues, such as impartiality, courage, or loyalty. Their very names indicate their moral status and indicate that they must be taken into account in any tenable view of moral reasoning. Here one aims not simply to do something but to become a sort of person, one not merely morally acceptable, but especially laudable. One aims to achieve a particular kind of moral excellence, and this will take on a unique form; pursuing such a virtue involves one in a project dealing with unique particulars: one must deliberate about how one can use one's abilities in one's chosen projects to become the person one aspires to be.

Once again, if we attain such excellence, it is not all at once through a single decision or resolution, and it is not a matter for purely abstract reasoning. Rather, as in most significant achievements, we build toward it, through specific sequential and concrete, preparatory activities in which we discover how to use our abilities in specific kinds of engagements. To begin the first move of the sequence, we must choose from among the available alternatives the specific ones that are appropriate to us. Subsequently we build on that start to move toward what we hope to become. Aristotle says one becomes brave by doing brave deeds. By doing brave deeds in limited engagements we see how we can make use of the strengths and opportunities that we have, and we are thus prepared to move on from there to a wider arena. (It is not that we merely repeat the same choice until we have formed a habit.) In successive moments within those projects we learn what we are capable of as individuals and how to use our abilities and our past achievements to approach our goal. Margaret Urban Walker captures this point admirably; she speaks of such pursuits as *undertakings*, "because the strong moral self-definition these judgments embody is progressive and prospective. Every valid particular judgment and the action which fulfills it strengthens the moral persona from which it proceeds, and creates a stronger claim on the agent to apply certain particulars henceforward."[23]

It may be felt that the pursuit of virtue is irrelevant to the study of moral reasoning, since we are not *obliged* to pursue special excellences. It is true that we may not be blamed for failing to achieve some heroic excellence,[24] but its attainment involves us in reasoning and action in pursuit of what is morally praised and valued. It is also true that we will have different obligations toward others who pursue specific virtues because of their pursuits: we will be obliged to attend to the specifics of their situation to know what will help or hinder them in their pursuit.

In becoming the sort of person who can be, for example, brave in all one's engagements, one will have become a person of a particular *kind* (and so will be open to judgments about classes of people). But one will have embodied this virtue through employing one's own specific combinations of abilities to become a *particular* admirable person. As Walker observes in "Moral Particularity," one thus comes to have "an individuated moral identity," one whose attainment is not interchangeable with the processes others might employ; one's choices were rooted in one's specific situation and abilities, and one could not universalize each of them, "legislating one particular moral identity for everyone." We are not looking for anything that could become a universal law of nature. If we, following strict universalizability, seek to find our sense of worth or moral virtue by following a universally applicable rule, we shall miss our mark.

Rush Rhees's recorded memories of Wittgenstein's comments on writing biography are illuminating on this point:

Wittgenstein speaks of the different "natures" of different people: the difference between the nature which I may come to recognize in myself . . . and the nature I may come to recognize in someone else. . . . These differences in nature belong to what are given for the soul's choice, as do the time and the place, the historical and material circumstances in which we are born. . . . When I recognize my nature instead of attending to a touched up photograph, I shall recognize certain 'possibilities': what traits of character I may try to develop, and others which I cannot treat as possible for me without becoming false.[25]

Rhees recalls Wittgenstein's expansion of the point that choice must grow out of deliberation about one's own abilities (one's "nature") and one's situation, an expansion in which Wittgenstein (in effect) scores off strict universalism: "Wittgenstein would emphasize that one man's nature and another's are not the same, and that what is right (or imperative) for one man may not be right for another. So that in the case of certain questions it would be wrong to think of examples in the lives of other people and put trust in their solutions, or to ask what someone whom I admire would have done in a situation like this: 'Don't take the example of others as your guide but nature.'"[26] Wittgenstein's project toward excellence was grounded in his reflections on his particular abilities and situation; for one to avoid focusing on just one's own particular abilities and situation (as the strict universalist must) would, for Wittgenstein, be to "lead a life of self-deception."[27]

The last observation points up the way in which one's sense of oneself is bound up with one's close scrutiny of, and one's reflections about, one's particular engagements. Mayeroff remarked in *On Caring* that, apart from our involvement in caring for such projects, we lose a sense of ourselves and may feel like leaves caught in the wind. In the same recollection of Wittgenstein we find an echo of Mayeroff's point about our conception of ourself, when Rhees recalls a comment attributed to Otto Weininger: "A gifted human being does not recall the single incidents of his life as so many discrete images of situations which come to his mind. . . . He understands them together, in some way. . . . And this continuity in them is the only thing that can assure him that he is living, that he is in the world."[28]

But it should not be imagined that these considerations apply only to people with the talents of the order of Wittgenstein's. We commonly will ask a child what it is going to *do* or going to *be* when it grows up; these are questions that are usually intended to lead it into deliberation about its specific abilities and projects and their import for the person he or she is to become. When considering an adult's problems or prospects, one wants to know the specific interests and abilities he or she might employ to contribute to the world's work.

That one's sense of self arises out of exercising one's abilities in concrete engagements with particular others raises questions about how we can reach tenable moral judgments. If a sense of self can only be attained by pursuing and reflecting on highly specific involvements with persons, that should also profoundly affect both our reasoning about moral obligations and our confidence in the range of our judgments. Our moral concern and our means of conceiving of ourselves lead us to the Rule as moral principle; the Rule, applied by one who is mindful of the human situation, leads us to consider the particular abilities and involvements. Accordingly, one who has thought through his or her relations with another must often say: "It's all right for me; I can't speak for another."

PARTICULARITY AND INDETERMINACY

We will often be unable to make a judgment about the consequences of making a move under circumstances that are unfamiliar to us, for we will not understand what the move amounts to. For example, if we have not suffered extended severe pain, we might want to say that we could not make a judgment about what could be undertaken by a person who had been in continuous severe pain for several months. We might also want to excuse ourselves from making a judgment about an individual who had been reduced to despair by a series of evils. We (very properly) excuse ourselves from making judgments about such issues and situations.

When we are not dealing with processes that would not be interchangeable in the lives of other persons, we may feel like asking how the agent can decide that a given course of action is right or possible for him or her. If there are not groups of observable processes like this, how could the protagonist of our tale make the judgment? How could she or he know what we cannot know? To find the answer, we must remember that he or she is working from stage to stage of his or her own development or project. One can ordinarily know what one will be able to do because of what one has already done in some past engagement; one knows how to use one's abilities to go on from there, though there may be no one else who has gone just that route. One can know for oneself and may at times be able to point out possibilities for others, as we do in teaching or caring for a child—at least up to adolescence. But we are often unable to know about such possibilities for others, and so, we are unable to judge, or advise about, their moves.

This must be our response to many of the moves made by individuals, particularly those with special gifts and opportunities, such as Wittgenstein. Recall his judgments that "it would be wrong" to "ask what someone whom I admire would have done in a situation like this." It would be equally wrong for us to try to advise such individuals because so much of their situation must remain hidden from us that we cannot know what their possibilities are.

Indeed, we are also unable to advise or make judgments about many of the personal choices and commitments of more ordinary mortals, unless we are intimately acquainted with the personal involvements in their lives. Clearly, moral action and moral judgment depend on our having some understanding of others' abilities and needs: I cannot help—or avoid harming—you unless I know something of what you need and would want; I cannot blame or praise you unless I know something of what you could do in your situation. But it's equally clear that I cannot be knowledgeable about the promises, commitments, and mutual expectations of many of the people with whom I must deal. Obviously, these are factors that lie at the center of their decisions, factors with which one may be familiar for a few intimates, yet they are features of others' lives about which one is ordinarily ignorant.[29] It should be added that, in the ordinary course of affairs, one must *remain* ignorant of these personal involvements.

It follows that we will be incapable of making a reasoned moral judgment about a great many of the world's personal decisions and choices. We have spoken of the 'Indeterminacy Principle' in moral judgment (in chapter 7), noting the necessary limits of making judgments that concern others' future choices (as we often need to do in making policy decisions). Now, we are reminded of another reason why their choices will be hard to evaluate as well as hard to predict: choices are bound up with unique sets of private involvements. We see, therefore, that the 'Indeterminacy Principle' must be extended because of our necessary ignorance of these critical factors affecting the mass of personal decisions. We frequently must excuse ourselves from judging—"Who's to judge?" we ask—not because we lack an understanding of the principle by which one might fairly judge, but because in the ordinary course of events one lacks information by which a judgment might coherently be made. The problem is not such as might be resolved by some future psychological finding. Em-

pirical study will not eliminate the problem, for it turns on our ignorance of changing personal situations arising from people's free
choices of commitments and engagements with other persons.

CONCRETE INVOLVEMENTS AND OBLIGATIONS

Our understanding that our lives are built around concrete involvements profoundly affects our reasoning about our own and others'
obligations. For it means that in applying the Rule, one considers
both oneself and the other as persons whose identities and wants are
defined by a history with a network of particular relationships. One
looks at *people* with histories, with families, jobs, lovers or spouses,
and perhaps, special causes, rather than looking at individuals who
are thought of as being free of any essential, particular involvement
or concern. One's concern is to provide for individuals and their
needs rather than for a rule that will tell us precisely what to do for
each individual and all occasions.

The latter kind of mistake, perhaps a reflection of individualist
metaphysics, seems to prey on the minds of those who question the
Rule's emphasis on acting with concern; it seems at work in those
who ask: Exactly what does the injunction to respond with *concern*
add? What will its addition bring to "Do unto others as you would
have them do unto you"? What does it mean to say that we should
act with concern? How *much* concern? To expand the questioner's
point: if we are expected to show different kinds of concern in different situations, it seems that the injunction to show concern is pointless unless we can state just how much is appropriate for each kind.
The questioner might press the point to ask: If one cannot specify
the amount of concern that is appropriate for specific situations,
isn't the claim that we should show concern essentially meaningless?

In answer, one must acknowledge the point that the injunction is
vague, but add that it takes on more definite meaning when one re-
members that one applies it *as a person* and to other persons (and
persons live by their particular involvements in the world); moreover, the amount or kind of concern is often going to be dependent
on the particular relationship that one has.

The critic might be unimpressed by (or miss the point of) this response. He might say: "Look here, how does your 'Rule' of 'concern,' to do unto others as you would have others do unto you, tell you to *whom* you should 'do'? And for how much? How does it tell you whether you should spend your money and efforts to bring medical care to your crippled child or spend them for famine relief for millions in Third World countries?[30] If each person is to count as one, how could your Rule justify devoting your attention to your child rather than doing what you could for all those millions? If it can't answer that question, of what use is it?"

The answer goes back to the point that one applies it as a person and to others as persons. We might expand that answer by noting that the Rule is considered as a rule of ordinary moral reasoning and by noting that we are ordinarily obliged to respond with concern to other persons *with whom we have to do*; that is, those with whom we come in contact in the course of our continuing involvements. We can be held responsible for what we could understand and control, and this must be limited to what we have some contact with.[31] We are not, and could not be, obliged to prevent all evil, of course. We are not placed under obligation to come to the assistance of all people throughout the world who do not enter into our activities and of whose involvements and customs we are ignorant. Clearly, moral judgment is passed on our treatment of others with whom we must deal in our pursuit of our own concerns (and with whose situation we are consequently somewhat familiar). As we've seen, ordinary moral judgment condemns our failure to be responsive to them and to those immediately around us.

It may be urged that to relate our obligations to our associations in this way is outdated, inasmuch as modern technology continually extends what is "immediately" around us: today we can have a better opportunity to observe those on the far side of the world than our ancestors had for observing those a few miles away. One might also urge that such technology continually extends what we may control: witness micromanipulation techniques, remote control devices, robotics, and so on. Accordingly, a critic might continue, our primary obligations cannot be confined to a small number of persons whom we can see with the naked eye and touch by reaching out with our hands.

The point about technology is well taken and illustrates an important point about defining the limits of our responsibility. We can be held responsible for what we can understand and control; we are expected to respond to those persons with whom we come into contact. But because of expanding technology we find our ways of contacting, seeing, understanding, and controlling are changing. Accordingly, we cannot lay a fixed, unwavering line on what we can be held responsible for: we come back to the importance of the flexible Rule response. Because our concepts (of seeing, controlling, contacting, and so on) are subject to change with changing technology, it is a *mistake to try* to give a fixed, precise definition to what we can be held responsible for or should direct our concern toward. It follows that it is also a mistake to ask for a rule to provide such definition. Certainly, our responsibility cannot be confined to those we can see with our naked eye or touch with our outstretched hands.

But it is nonetheless true that we can have only a limited number of primary obligations. We could not attend to more than a limited number of projects; we certainly could not attend to all individual persons who might be in need. One must focus on a limited number of objectives to deal responsibly with *any* project or obligation: one must limit oneself to being one person. In order to be able to act responsibly, one must be allowed to pursue a limited number of concerns: that is fundamental to being a responsible person. As one expands the number cared for, one necessarily reduces the time and quality of one's own attention to each.[32] If one were to attempt to carry out obligations to every individual in the world, one would be incapable of taking any action at all.

The critic rests his or her argument on the point that each one counts for one. But in agreeing that each person counts for one, we do not mean that we can or should accord exactly the same kind of treatment to each one of them. We cannot be a parent to a child unless we treat the child as special to us; to fail to provide such special treatment is to fail as a parent. Similar considerations apply to our other personal engagements. This is apparent in the emotional freight carried by, and the expectations aroused by, such titles as *Friend, Brother, Sister,* or *Lover.* When one assesses one's obligation to another, one must look to the character of the shared involvements as well as to that of the other involvements that define one's situation as a person; one's own involvement with another must be considered in the light of others who are significant in both lives.

Obviously, parents, by their history and involvement, are ordinarily in a position to provide nurture that is crucially needed and that no one else would or could provide in the ordinary course of events.

Thus, the reason that children ordinarily have strong rights claims and parents are under the strongest obligation to provide care for their own children—and under far weaker obligations to the millions of children with whom they are unconnected—goes back to the nature of persons and the demands of responsible action. As persons, parents are to be responsive to those with whom they have to do while in controlled pursuit of their own concerns. As persons, they ordinarily care for and build their lives around involvements with other persons, and especially with their children, who are critically dependent on them. To fulfill obligations arising from such involvements, they must be able to center on and maintain control of their actions; such centering and control can occur only if they are *primarily* obligated in a limited number of particular involvements and concerns.

To say that we as persons have primary obligations to other persons (such as our children) is not to say that we have no obligations to contribute to famine relief and to assist others remote from us who are destitute. Nor is it to deny that our response to persons remote from us should sometimes lead us to postpone or set aside requests from our children. On the pretext of caring for our commitments, we cannot exhaust the planet's limited resources on our own or our children's wasteful self-indulgences while millions go unhoused, unclothed, and unfed. It will be part of our caring for our children to encourage them in caring for others. We cannot do so unless we discourage them from self-indulgence and from being insensitive to others' needs. A most important part of such discouragement will be for us to involve them in assisting some of those who are destitute.

That does not give us an answer to questions about just how much aid and to how many destitute persons. In reaching a decision about how much one can afford to give and to whom, one moves away from ordinary moral responsiveness and toward a situation in which one tries to calculate what will provide the maximum benefits to the maximum number of people. Despite the ways in which technology has extended our information and opportunities, such calculations are clouded over by lack of information and lack of control over the use of one's resources. Under those circumstances, one will be involved in guesswork in deciding which plea to respond to. As we move beyond the arena where we can act with control, we move away from strict accountability for our moves; we will rarely be open to blame for not responding to a specific plea.

Whatever ways one decides to respond to such appeals, one will still have primary obligations to one's child and to other persons with whom one has become involved. Friends, lovers, and others with whom one is intimate have been given one's trust and thus have privileged information about one's plans and abilities. In the case of friends, for example, they have been given to understand that theirs is a special relationship, and they have thus come to expect one's assistance. Conversely, in our times of confusion or need, we have reason to expect that they will be there for us, if they can manage it. We understand that we have a stronger claim for their help than does the ordinary person, and that, if they fail us without showing some overriding claim, something has gone wrong with our friendship.

In saying that a primary obligation may be overridden, we show that the appeal to persons' particular involvements does not remove moral conflicts or make them easy to resolve. If my student is despondent and asks to confer with me at a time when I have promised my friend I would help him, I *may* be able to resolve the problem by determining whose need is the more severe. But, as noted in chapter 7, we often must take action before we can inquire into such points, and so we take action on the basis of our best guess. It should be added that, even if we had leisure to investigate such cases thoroughly, we couldn't guarantee that the claims would not turn out to be equally strong. Thus, the conflict and the moral problem may remain.

But we should not be put off by the fact that we are led into unresolvable conflicts by appealing to persons as defined by particular involvements. As we've noted, indeterminacy is an inevitable feature of moral reasoning among free people. Although we do not commonly hear the Indeterminacy Principle explicitly invoked in ordinary moral reasoning, it's apparent that we ordinarily make no assumption that all moral problems are resolvable. We have the language ready to hand, when we refer to bewildering moral dilemmas, or perhaps describe our deliberations as soul-searching. Moreover, it is a commonplace that no one is to be blamed for moves in cases on whose interpretations reasonable people could disagree.

By bearing in mind these features of the nature of persons and their involvements, we have an immediate line of inquiry for investigating what we are obliged or required to do. Within the limits of specific engagements, one can often come to agreement on what the relationship requires and what one is capable of doing. When I say, "Helen was a young mother of four, recently widowed, unemployed and unskilled, and Sarah was her only friend in the city," I say something about Sarah's obligation to Helen. Without considering such particular relationships—and considering what was specially owed because of them—one could not make a judgment of what was morally required of one. The Rule's emphasis on persons and particulars is not misplaced.

We see further support for this point in the fact that we use others' ability to grasp and interpret particular facts as a basis for holding them accountable. As Bishop Butler notes,[33] we agree to hold people responsible in proportion to their abilities. The critical ability here is cognitive: we expect more from those who are experienced, educated, and literate; we hold even very young children responsible for dealings in situations and relationships familiar to them;[34] and we are prepared to excuse moral lapses in those from a sheltered and limited background.

I have argued that the Rule is shown to be an appropriate as a method moral reasoning because tenable—that is, generalizable— moral judgments can come about only by attending with concern to one's own and the other's particular abilities and involvements with persons.

We were led to this conclusion because:

1. We saw that to achieve strict universalizability we had to ignore the particulars of action and search for commonly applicable rules, leading us to vague, underdescribed accounts of the action situation and vaguely stated rules, neither of which could provide us with the specific kind of information needed for tenable moral judgment.

2. Judgments are binding and universalizable if they are supported by tenable reasons; they are tenable if the connection between the specified features of the situation and the agent always holds. The objectivity of the judgment depends on our being able to inquire into and agree on the description and on the moral connection between it and the act contemplated. The fact that we use counterfactuals and the subjunctive mood to express the connection illustrates the point

that the moral constraining power of the judgment does not depend on the number of people to whom it applies, but on the connection between the specific circumstances cited in the reasons.

3. Whereas Kantian univeralizability holds that we all attain moral worth and virtue by aiming toward what is universally applicable, in fact, we must always act, build projects, pursue vocations, and form associations in relation to particular conditions and persons: we are beings-in-particularized-relationships, and our concerns and identities revolve about them. As a consequence we must look to those (in making our moral judgments about obligations) to determine what would help or hinder another.

4. We are also obliged to consider the particular by the fact that any person, in working toward any virtue, must move toward its achievement, building on individual abilities and opportunities toward a unique moral persona.

5. Because moral claims may conflict and because many personal relationships are private, we may lack the information needed to assess many claims; thus, indeterminacy must remain a permanent feature of moral reasoning so long as we are dealing with free persons who can choose their own projects.

6. Since our primary obligations grow out of the individual pattern of relationships that each person chooses to develop, it will always be a mistake to ask for a rule that will dictate precisely what our obligation must be for persons generally.

Whereas a judgment affirms a universally valid point about a person's situation, the judgment can only be made by focusing on particular points in the person's situation. Thus, we go back to the point about the nature of persons: one's development is always a concrete process growing out of particular associations and conditions. To reaffirm this point is to bring forward with special urgency some of the claims of relativism, claims to be explored in chapter 9.

9 / Universal Moral Principle: Critically Relativized Judgments

The force of our argument in support of a universal moral principle requires that we recognize many moral judgments to be dependent on and relative to specific codes and practices. For, if we exercise moral concern, we must direct it toward others whom we must conceive of as like ourselves. In so directing it, we must project ourselves into the particular involvements of the other's situation and honor such involvements—unless we would harm others by doing so. Thus the Rule or reversibility oftens leads us to moral judgments grounded in, and relative to, concrete involvements and local custom. Yet many argue that to ground moral judgments by appeal to relative customs is to deny the importance or the reality of any universal moral principle.

That point may help to account for the perplexity and moral passion which reverberates through discussions of moral relativism. The discussions often seem motivated by moral concern, yet discussants feel themselves being led to relativism, to denying the reality of any moral principle that could justify a moral stance. As Martin Hollis and Steven Lukes remarked, "The road to relativism is paved with plausible contentions."[1]

In countering moral relativism, I oppose the species of moral relativism that denies the reality or importance of any universal norms and the version of cognitive relativism used in its support. I focus on this species (and ignore the other species of moral and cognitive relativism that have emerged in recent literature) because it is commonest[2] and because it gives rise to confusion and conflict. In its simplest form, this species of moral relativism denies the reality of any universal moral norm and condemns (morally condemns) any cross-cultural moral judgment. Its more sophisticated philosophical cousin, "romantic relativism," is also self-contradictory (as we shall see): it denies the importance of any universal moral norm while insisting on the moral importance of judging by means of relative codes and practices. The contradiction of the simpler form is well brought out by Bernard Williams's account: in it, " 'right' means (can only be coherently understood as meaning) 'right for a given society'; that 'right for a given society' is to be given a functionalist sense; and that (therefore) it is wrong for people in one society to condemn, interfere with, etc. the values of another society."[3] As Williams and others have observed,[4] the position is inconsistent because, in judging interference to be wrong, it uses a nonrelative sense of "wrong" not allowable by its definition. Relativists, whether the simpler or the "romantic," are also inconsistent in judging it to be right that one confine oneself to the practices within a given society, for they thereby use "right" in a nonrelative way. Once stated, the point is obvious. But one sees how relativists might have been led into such contradiction.

As we have noted, it is moral principle and the facts of our moral anatomy and situation that lead us to say of specific judgments that they are "right for a given society" and that judgments of what is right can only be made in relation to the person's specific situation. But as decent and humane people, relativizing anthropologists and sociologists will, as a matter of course, insist on the dignity of each human being; their intelligence and their discipline make them mindful of our moral situation, and so, they, as moral people, are led to insist that we deal with every individual by means of the cultural situation of each. In brief, as intelligent, decent human beings, they are Rule-users in their moral reasoning: they insist that we respond to a person's needs and wants by addressing the person's involvement in specific institutions and practices in the community. Those practices and institutions, in the words of anthropologist Richard Shweder, are "where the action is" in moral reasoning.

At the same time, anthropologists have focused on the diversity of moral codes and practices. Moreover, they show that, not only do the practices and codes vary with the culture, but also that they are important to the internal integrity of each culture: the responses appropriate to the practices and codes of one culture would not be appropriate to those of another. Therefore, many anthropologists have claimed that there are no, or no significant, universal moral standards. As self-respecting and sensitive people, they are Rule-users; as anthropologists observing the diversity of moral codes ("where the action is''), they deny the reality or importance of any moral standard. In saying we *ought* to pattern our actions after specific cultural codes, they must contradict their general denial of moral norms.

How can one avoid it? Logically, how can one accept the diversity of moral codes (for which we have long had evidence), yet argue for universality of a moral standard or principle? The question itself may give us a clue. It suggests that relativists have conflated moral *code* and moral *standard* and that they believe there is no difference between the two: if there is a difference, there is no logical problem in arguing for a universal standard while acknowledging a diversity of moral codes. (And there is no occasion for raising the question.)

That there *is* a difference between codes (or practices) and standards might be guessed from the fact that the anthropologists' injunction, ''One ought to pattern one's actions after specific cultural practices,'' does not seem to be a self-contradictory statement: the ''ought'' is the expression of the universal standard: the contradiction enters when one at the same time denies the existence of a universal standard. By the universal standard, one ought to respect the individual in his or her specific situation, the specific involvements and obligations of which are defined by the diverse codes (or practices). It is, as we have noted, the Rule or universal standard that dictates that particular codes and practices be considered.

As Williams's account of the simpler relativism might indicate, relativistic anthropologists have long insisted on treating ethical codes and practices as if they were equivalent to principles or norms.[5] But they are not alone in conflating the two; in the philosophical literature, one often finds references to codes and standards which suggest that there is no difference between the two. This seems to be the case when Jack Meiland and Michael Krausz characterize modern moral relativism as the view that holds an action is ''morally right only relative to a particular moral code or set of principles,''[6] and when Philippa Foot refers to relativism arising from the diversity of practices, codes and standards, and the fact ''that no one set of . . . opinions appears to have any more claim to truth than any other.''[7] Both Foot and the Meiland and Krausz studies speak as if it made no difference whether one spoke of ''codes,'' or of ''standards'' or ''principles''; both codes and principles were aspects of a culture's ''set of moral beliefs'' or ''set of moral concepts.'' A similar conflating of concrete rules and principles is found when Bernard Gert (as we have seen) treats all moral principles as if they could be summed up in his coda to *The Moral Rules*.[8] Nor is this melding merely a recent phenomenon; one finds it in the discussion of ethical relativity in so venerable a treatise as Walter Stace's *The Concept of Morals* (1937).

To the extent that these writers suggest that there is no important difference between rules and principles (including them both in the same global set of moral concepts or beliefs) and that they acknowledge (what is incontrovertible) that there is within that global set a diversity of moral *codes and practices*, they set up the philosophical problem. They evoke the question, raised by Meiland and Krausz: "How is the use of a particular set of concepts to be justified? There seems to be no higher standard to which to appeal in order to provide such justification."⁹ Once one assumes that one need not differentiate between principle and code, lumping them all together as an indivisible set of concepts or beliefs, one is ready for the features of the problem as characterized by Philippa Foot and endorsed by Meiland and Krausz: "(1) There are wide variations in moral judgments between different cultures and different generations. (2) No one set of these opinions appears to have any more claim to truth than any other. (3) The concepts of 'objectivity' and 'truth' apply to moral judgments only within a community of shared relations."¹⁰

But once one divides the set, treating the Rule or reversibility as a separate principle, it is obvious that the above statements are misleading. For we have seen that whereas there are variations in the expression of the Rule, we have also seen—against (1) in the above quotation—that there are elements common to them all. Moreover, against (2), we have explored extensive philosophical reasons that give these elements a claim to truth independent of their being commonly held. Finally, against (3), we've seen that the judgment of the truth of these elements is not confined to any specific culture.

Using that distinction between the Rule and specific codes and practices, I want, first, to review some of the points that have been made against the older relativism, and then to focus on the difficulties underlying more recent versions of relativism (among them, that of the "Romantics"), and finally, examine their philosophical opposition to cultural criticism.

OLDER RELATIVISM

Engaging in cultural criticism and working for reforms are practices that could have no justification according to the older relativism. In holding that "right" or "wrong" must mean in accord with, or in opposition to, the accepted practices of one's culture, the proponents of the older relativism hold that the whole notion of ethical evaluation of practices is an outmoded one. It becomes a tautology to say that whatever is done in accord with those practices is morally right. But, as Carl Wellman[11] and others have observed, it is no tautology; if it were, it would be a self-contradiction to say that some acts that are in accord with one's culture's practices are morally wrong. But that is no self-contradiction. Rather, it is a statement we take to be obviously true—consider cultures afflicted with slavery, apartheid, or the purdah.

The stand that a society's ethical practices define what it means to be right also leads us to the position that virtually every educated person (woolly-headed absolutists would be an exception) should be aware that what is called "right" is only what is locally called right; there would be no such thing as what is really right. Relativists have held that this view will lead one to ethical tolerance; Melville Herskovits, for example, finds that "in practice the philosophy of relativism is a philosophy of tolerance [and] that a larger measure of tolerance is needed in this conflict-worn world needs no arguing."[12] But it needs arguing for relativists. For, as many have asked, Would relativists (having no overriding principle), have any good reason for believing that tolerance (or ridding ourselves of conflict) is a good thing? When or how are we to be tolerant? Are we to be tolerant of widow burning and slavery? If we (as relativists) are to believe that there really is no principle of what is generally right, why should we believe that it is right to tolerate practices which differ from our own?

PROBLEMS OF 'ROMANTIC' RELATIVISM

A number of contemporary anthropologists are prepared to grant that certain universal ethical principles, such as fairness or generalizability do indeed exist cross-culturally but hold that these "formal principles that define morality do not contribute any content to a moral code."[13] They, unlike the older relativists, contrast the content of the moral code or practice with the formal criteria of fairness and generalizability; they find that the practice or code determines what is of value or importance whereas the formal principles are essentially empty.

Such a relativist position is outlined and supported by anthropologist Richard Shweder. He and other anthropologists hold: that moral codes rest upon ultimate declarations of what is of importance and value; that such declarations cannot be given any further warrant or rational defense; and that such "judgments about what is of importance are cross-culturally variable (and) charged with symbolic value."[14]

Finding that the "formal criteria (fairness and generalizability) and content are unrelated," these anthropologists hold that the formal criteria do seem to be reflected universally in societies' universal use of reasons in moral judgments and in the universal appeal to considerations in support of moral judgments. But Shweder and others find that such criteria are open to the objections raised by H. L. A. Hart about the insights to be afforded by the principle of justice. They quote approvingly Hart's comment (in *The Concept of Law*) that justice "cannot afford any determinate guide to conduct . . . 'Treat like cases alike and different cases differently' is the central element in the idea of justice [but] it is by itself incomplete. . . . This is because any set of human beings will resemble each other in some respects and differ from each other in others and, until it is established what resemblances and differences are relevant, 'Treat like cases alike' must remain an empty form."[15] This is an important passage for Shweder's thinking: it occurs at the beginning of two of his passages in which he argues for skeptical-relativist conclusions. By this argument one can establish that the principle of justice alone cannot lead us to a conclusion; Shweder and his associates take it to mean that it (and generalizability) have no importance at all in our reasoning, that justice and generalizability have nothing to say about what should be valued or what is to be regarded as having importance. With this view of what is universal in our moral reasoning and what the moral reasoning process consists in, it is not remarkable that Shweder and his associates should conclude that the universal element and method of reasoning is of no great moral importance.

So long as anthropologists take this view of the criteria of moral reasoning—and it is a view they would find supported in much Kantian moral theory—moral reasoning would have very little to do with the content of moral judgments; "Be consistent" and "Treat like cases alike'' will give one no clue as to how one is to treat anyone. A machine will respond consistently, but it will scarcely be a moral judge. As we have seen, asking if we can consistently universalize a judgment tells us nothing by itself: for our universalizing to bear freight we must universalize in a way that is consistent with our commitment to persons and with the facts of our moral anatomy and the moral reasoning process.

Romantics and ''Ultimate Beliefs''

But Shweder and his associates hold that, ultimately, it is one's culture's ultimate declarations of value or its beliefs about what is of importance and to be valued that determine how we shall apply the fairness criterion and how we shall consider people to be relevantly similar:

> For example, given our culture's belief that there are relevant differences between an adolescent and an adult in the capacity for responsible judgment, there is nothing unjust or unfair about refusing a thirteen-year-old the right to vote or enter into a contract. To be just, fair, equitable or impartial is not necessarily to treat all sentient beings in identical fashion. Quite the contrary. It is out of respect for the principle that relevant differences between people must make a difference for how they are to be treated.[16]

Such ultimate beliefs provide the underpinning for the cultural practices around which people organize their lives. The beliefs are ultimate, in the view of these anthropologists, in the sense that they provide a general framework on which a culture's practices are based and ultimate in the sense that they are beyond logical and empirical support.

''Where the Action Is''

Whatever one's view of such ultimates, Shweder's account of moral reasoning has the merit of taking us to the realities of individuals' lives—to ''where the action is,'' in his phrase. For (as we argued in chapter 8) actions typically cannot be either planned or described without referring to the practices in which those acting are involved. Shweder's account shows that, in this sense, cultural relativity is ineluctable: if one is to act in relation to a person of another culture, one must enter into and consider the practices in which that person is involved. Culturally unique practices related to, for example, earning a living, mating, or dress, will help to determine a person's role and how that person views his or her situation. Thus, cultural practices will determine what would count as treating a person with respect and concern. If one treats another with respect and concern, one must put oneself "in the other's shoes"; one must consider the institutions and practices around which that person has built a life and expectations. One's life plan and, hence, most of what each person must consider as needs must be built into such a context of cultural practices.

I am speaking here about what is obligatory and not simply about what etiquette would dictate. I cannot cooperate with a person from another culture and ignore his or her ways of earning a living. Similarly, the person from another culture cannot cooperate with me in my culture and ignore our practices, such as property rights. If he or she pretends to cooperate and knows about such rights, yet fails to honor them, it would not sit easily with us.

Suppose that you have become acquainted with a person from another culture; let's say he's named Cary. Cary has pleaded with you to loan him enough money to give his daughter the medical care he says she desperately needs. You tell him that if you do loan him the money, you must turn down your daughter's request for the new braces she's been counting on. But Cary responds convincingly that his daughter's need is greater than your daughter's—that his might die without assistance, whereas yours wants only to have her teeth straightened. And he promises to repay the money as soon as he can. So you relent and loan him the money. Suppose that subsequently, when you note that he is spending large sums of money freely, you broach the subject of his repaying the loan. In response, he laughs and says, "Loan? I don't have any money for you and I'm not worried about getting it." "What do you mean, 'not worried about getting it?'" you reply. "I need that money and you promised to repay it as soon as you could. I only loaned it to you because your daughter so desparately needed the medical care." Cary then grins and says, "Yeah, that was a pretty good story wasn't it?" "Story!!" you shout. "Look, you promised. I want my money. And now!!" "Promises and borrowing are your little practices," Cary replies. "They don't mean anything to me."

All of us would resent such treatment. The fact that Cary came from another culture would not be seen as excusing his actions, for clearly he understood the practices and your situation well enough to exploit them—and you. By ignoring the requirements of these practices (and the code of rules normally associated with them) he knowingly treated you like trash.

In giving reasons for our judgment against Cary, we note that we appeal to the relation between the choices and the practices involved. Thus, using Shweder's terms, "form" and "content," we see that form and content *interact* in our making the judgment. In judging that anyone who would treat another person in the way Cary did is a rotter, we generalize, offering reasons which we are clear that others will recognize. To do so, we must give reasons that note the inappropriateness and Cary's *awareness* of the inappropriateness of his act to the practices involved, especially those of borrowing and promising.

But if we reflect on this example we see that the anthropologist's claim that "formal principles do not contribute any content to a moral code" is misleading in two ways: It overlooks the importance of principle in determining specific moral choice; and it fails to note the values and the understanding of the moral anatomy implicit in the reasoning process itself, as well as the other values that flow from the reasoning process.

Principled Moral Reasoning Determines Choices. We have noted earlier that reasoning could not count as moral reasoning unless it reflected concern for members of the community. To serve as any kind of basis for choice (as Shweder and Hart agree) generalization must be coupled with some value concern; it cannot be called moral generalization until it reflects concern for persons. Once it is coupled with such valuing, it is no longer empty of content. It directs us to "treat like cases alike" in such a way that we can care for the persons affected. In order to care for persons we must attend to their roles in practices (as Shweder insists).

But we must reason in order to decide how we ought to respond. For example, consider another acquaintance's repayment of a debt. We note that we could not describe his act or my request without reference to such codes and practices. But clearly, the fact of the institution of money and of borrowing and the fact that my friend has borrowed money from me do not by themselves determine whether it would be right or wrong for my friend to defer payment. Other factors may give one reason to defer payment or limit my claim against him: he may have been beaten up and robbed or his house may have burned to the ground during the night. If so, I may still have a claim against him for immediate repayment, though it will be a relatively weak one under such disastrous circumstances. But the point is that the cultural institutions or practices will not of themselves determine what I or my friend should do. For there is no umbrella institution or rule that includes all the relevant factors and that dictates standard obligations and expectations to cover every eventuality: there is no rule covering repayment-of-debts-to-friends-when-one's-house-has-just-burned-to-the-ground, nor are there rules or institutions for the other disastrous scenarios we might encounter or imagine. There could *be* no custom or practice corresponding to each of the combination of circumstances in which we find ourselves when we face decisions; each action may well involve us in a set of practices unique to that action; which of these practices is to have the dominant claim on us cannot be determined by referring to the content of any one practice or rule. As we saw, in discussing Bernard Gert's Rules in chapter 6, the same holds true of *any* code of rules that attempts to dictate specific responses; in considering each response we will always have to consider the possibility that the present case is an exception to that rule. Nor is it the case that all of an individual's involvements or all of a community's customs must be honored and preserved. Clearly, we must refuse to uphold racist and sexist institutions in our own society and do so because they violate principle.

We must go to the practices to go where the action is, to define the situation of the persons involved, but we must use principled and informed concern to assess the relative claims of the different practices. To decide, for example, if it would be permissible or preferable for my friend to defer payment we would have to consider whether anyone would be hurt or consider what course of action would cause the least harm to those involved. Thus, it is our principled review of the situation and not just our referring to practices or rules that is to determine the specific content of the action that we take; it is principled concern that determines the sequence of the actions and the priority of the claims of the various practices. It is principled concern—or the moral reasoning process—that *makes it possible to apply* cultures' practices and codes. Thus, the content of acceptable moral behavior turns on both principled concern and the specific practices.

Values Are Implicit in the Reasoning Process. This duality of content is, in fact, apparent in the observation by Shweder and other anthropologists that people in all societies give reasons and appeal to specific cultural practices in support of their judgments. That observation shows how one's reasons in support of moral judgment are justified by appeal to a community of moral reasoners (with their beliefs and culturally relative practices). It confirms the points that moral reasoning involves the use of reasons that are acceptable to others; that the others are givers and takers of reasons, persons who must be reciprocally aware and mutually concerned to reach agreement with each other.

Its members must also be informed about, and have an understanding of, the practices and situations in which they are to act: for each must know how a choice will affect those involved (if the choices are ever to be generally acceptable and agreed upon). To be able to assess or give reasons in a situation one must be able to say what an informed, understanding, and concerned person would do in that situation.

Thus, a precondition for making responsible moral choices in all societies (as well as a precondition for taking responsible action) is that one have access to information and discussion about the situations where one is to act. Thus, contrary to the group of relativist anthropologists, the conditions for moral reasoning show that persons who are held morally responsible have a rights claim to what we call First Amendment freedoms, such as access to information and discussion. It is the *form* of moral reasoning that dictates that these rights are important for societies where reasons are to be given and people are to be held responsible. By the Romantic relativists' own description of the structure of cultures, that means for all societies.

Our giving such claims for First Amendment rights does not seal them into locally specific social practices (as Alasdair MacIntyre would seem to require for a rights claim),[17] nor does it give them the protection of law. Our giving of this claim is not to guarantee that it will not be overridden by other values—we sometimes see it fall before relatively weak claims in our own society. But neither is it empty of moral importance. As access to information and discussion is integral to all (reason-giving, reason-assessing) responsible action in a community, the claim must command respect in all cultures and provides continuously relevant reasons for reforming any practices that conflict with it.

PHILOSOPHICAL OPPOSITION
TO CRITICAL ANALYSIS

Anthropologists Richard Shweder, Elliot Turiel, and Nancy Much claim that "moral codes rest upon declarations of what is of importance, value and significance, declarations that cannot themselves be justified and are matters of preference that have neither a deductive nor an inductive warrant."[18] Shweder, representing the views of a bloc of contemporary anthropologists, explains their notion of ultimate declarations of preference in his "Anthropology's Romantic Rebellion against the Enlightenment," subtitled "or there's more to thinking than reason and evidence." Representing this "relativist-romanticist" view, he writes that many "ideas and practices fall beyond the scope of deductive and inductive reason, that [such] ideas and practices are neither rational nor irrational but rather *nonra-tional*."[19] Their importance lies in the fact that they support, and, hence, lead us to focus on, the specific and arbitrary contents of an actual cultural system: "From the romanticist tenet flows the concept of arbitrariness and culture . . . the celebration of local context, the idea of paradigm, cultural frames and constitutive presuppositions. . . . According to the romanticist account, a social order is a self-contained 'framework' for understanding experience . . . a self-sufficient 'design for living.' . . . Governed by their own rules, different frameworks do not lend themselves to comparative-normative evaluation." (S:28).

As nonrational notions, ideas are part of a total system and are not open to comparison or evaluation. Shweder sees them as having their significance in the concrete practices that they undergird. He holds them to be akin to Thomas Kuhn's idea of a paradigm (S:40). Explaining that these conceptual underpinnings are ultimately nonrational, he holds that they provide the support for practices that constitute the only basis on which members of societies can organize a life together.

Speaking on behalf of those whom he regards as on the leading edge of anthropological theory, he writes that "a good deal follows from the idea of the 'arbitrary' or 'nonrational.' To be a romantic is to be anti-normative. . . . That's not to say the romantic is an anarchist—clearly there are rules to any game, and any 'frame' has its own 'internal' standards" (S:47). To live in a society one must become "skillful at functioning with (its) rules of the game." Thus, for Shweder (and for others) it's a case of "When in Rome, do as the Romans do," for he adds, "The romantic's anti-normative point is that there are no standards worthy of universal respect dictating what to think or how to act" (S:47). To speak of the internality of standards is another way of speaking of their relativity to a specific system, for there *are* no universal standards: "To ask what is the proper way to design a society and so on, is like asking what is the proper food of man or what is the best language to speak" (S:47–48). We note, once again, that the support of relativism is based on treating standards as inseparable from a total belief system, as if one could never reform a system by parts.

The relativism is reflected in Shweder's habit of putting scare quotes around such terms as "right" and "rights." Thus, when he has (they have) occasion to speak of rights, he writes (on their behalf): "To whom shall 'rights' be granted?" (S:47–48). He thinks that one can use such terms without scare quotes only if one specifies the cultural frame within which one speaks: "For a romantic it is meaningless to ask, for example, 'Is abortion right or wrong?' The meaningful question is 'Within what frame is abortion wrong?'" (S:45).

Criticizing Cultural "Frames"

What are some examples of some of those ultimate frames which undergird cultural practices? As an example of such a frame, Shweder, Turiel, and Much cite "our culture's belief that there are relevant differences between an adolescent and an adult in capacity for responsible judgment." Given that belief, however, they hold that "there is nothing unfair or unjust about denying a thirteen-year-old the right to vote or enter into a contract."[20]

But surely we would want to say that this belief about adolescents' responsibility is not an ultimate and arbitrary declaration of preference, for it has both inductive and deductive support, some of it from the Romantics' own work. This is seen in the fact that in order for one to be held responsible, one must be informed about, and be understanding of, the cultural practices one is involved in; in

Shweder's phrase, one must become "skillful" in them. Given the complexities of our cultural practices, a thirteen-year-old could not have the required information and understanding of our cultural practices generally (though clearly he or she could manage some of them). Hence, a thirteen-year-old could not be skillful enough to be held responsible for dealing with those practices generally. Therefore, this "frame" about adolescent responsibility is not immune from empirical and rational support; rather, it seems to be made necessary by what we know of our social situation.

When Shweder offers his examples of "frames" to emphasize that they can be neither confirmed nor refuted, he writes: "The litmus test of a frame is that no evidence or experience can possibly count as disproof" (S:40). Now, this notion of the litmus test raises questions of its own—to that we shall later return—but the examples of frames that Shweder gives do not seem to pass this test, or at least not equally well. He lists as other examples of frames: "Fetuses have souls possessed of infinite value"; "God blesses men in the sign of their prosperity"; and "Man's only motive is to maximize pleasure and minimize pain" (S:40). The first of these assertions might pass the litmus test, but if it passes, it passes because one does not know what would count as being "possessed of infinite value": because it has indeterminate meaning, nothing could count as disproof.

But here we come to a more fundamental difficulty with the litmus test (and consequently the whole conception of frames and the Romanticism they are alleged to support). If the frames are to provide *conceptual* underpinning for a set of practices in the social order, they must have a determinate meaning for someone. If a frame has explanatory value for anyone, then it must have a sufficiently determinate meaning to imply that some state of affairs is the case. For concepts support others by explaining why or how they are true. A concept can explain another only by implying that some state of affairs related to the other is true. Thus, if it explains in a way that makes sense to anyone, it must directly or indirectly imply that some states of affairs do obtain and others do not. If it does not imply or explain any events, it is hard to see how we could call it either a conceptual framework or a paradigm.

Accordingly, one must say that the litmus test that excludes the relevance of any evidence also excludes the possibility of its having any bite, or relevance to our experience. If a concept is compatible with *any* state of affairs, then it could not require or imply any of those practices that are to provide us with a design for living. In order for a concept to be able to provide support for the appropriateness of a practice, it must be made definite enough to imply the existence of a definite state of affairs—in which case evidence will count for or against it. If it *could* pass the (defining) litmus test of being uncriticizable, it could *not* serve as a conceptual frame.

The other examples Shweder lists confirm one in the judgment that frames must be subject to support or criticism. Thus, the second one, "God blesses men in the sign of their prosperity," is also vague, but we are familiar with similar assertions and the sense in which they are standardly taken. If we give it the standard reading, that the virtuous or godly are always blessed with prosperity, we find that evidence does bear on that statement. As Voltaire notes, in *Candide*, such a view is called into serious question by tidal waves and earthquakes that wipe out whole cities by "acts of God," destroying the pious along with the rest of the population. Similar considerations apply to the third frame offered: "Man's only motive is to minimize pain." It, too, is vague as it stands. But it seems to be a variant on the view that one enters into any action only because one thinks it will maximize one's own pleasure. The latter proposition has not only long been disputed and challenged by counterevidence, it was, as we have seen,[21] long ago effectively refuted by Joseph Butler.

If we wish these assertions to be immune from empirical or rational criticism we must make them so indeterminate in meaning that they are compatible with every proposition and observation— but that will mean that they will imply nothing determinate and, therefore, cannot serve as explanatory frames. If we endow them with a determinate meaning so that they can serve as part of a conceptual framework, then they could not be beyond rational and empirical support or criticism. As Shweder explains them, the statements are to provide logical import for a frame, but it seems that they conveniently lose logical import when critical questions arise.

Robert Fogelin refers to such vague global assertions as self-sealers,[22] that is, as explanations that seal themselves off from evidence. As he notes, a time-honored mode of defending self-sealers from logical or empirical criticism is to shift back and forth between determinate and indeterminate meanings: indeterminate for immunity from criticism, determinate for explanatory force. But if we *consciously* seek to use such a method it is to no avail: we are onto the trick. We could no longer deceive ourselves by the "sealers" nor could we be reassured by them.

At one point Shweder speaks of these framing declarations as paradigms similar to those presented by Kuhn (in *Structure of Scientific Revolutions*). They are said to be like Kuhn's paradigms in that they determine how members of the community experience, explain, and describe their world. One of Kuhn's central points was that such theoretical terms were resistant to refutation and were not open to the kind of falsification by single observed counterexamples that some students of science had previously thought possible.[23]

But we should note that Kuhn's "resistant to criticism" is not to be confused with Shweder's "beyond criticism." Kuhn does not take paradigms to be nonrational; he sees them as having a history in which they are open to refutation—for which logical and empirical evidence is relevant. Theoretical paradigms (according to Kuhn's account) have been abandoned in the history of science because they have fallen before the weight of evidence and argument.[24] If frames are like paradigms, they are resistant to, but not beyond, logical and empirical argument.

At bottom, cultural frames seem to be a good bit like philosophical presuppositions: they are not always clearly stated; they are not brought out for inspection or refutation; they are not to be refuted by single counterexamples; and the evidence or argument that bears on them is sometimes ignored or kicked under the rug. But, like philosophical presuppositions, cultural frames have a history in which their hold on the community is either strengthened or weakened by argument and evidence.

We have not found it impossible to revise or reject paradigms or fundamental assumptions of our culture. Are we to believe that it will not be possible for members of other cultures? We have not found it impossible to separate these frames, considering them apart from our total view. Are we to believe that other peoples are somehow less able to do so? That they can only consider their views as a total set? No doubt framing concepts of person and social relationships help to define the moral codes of cultures to which they are indigenous. Also, there is no question that holders of such beliefs will resist criticism of those beliefs. All of us resist, in varying degrees, attempts to change our lifestyles and fundamental beliefs. However, the difficulty with the anthropologists' "Romantic rebellion" is that they hold that any attempt to examine such cultural frames reflects conceptual befuddlement rather than intellectual and moral vigor.

But the charge of befuddlement fades because the romanticists have no case. Their claim that such framing concepts are beyond logical and empirical support is incoherent. Their notion that such frames and the practices they imply provide a culture's only concept of person and values ignores the concept of value and person that is implicit in the moral reasoning process, a process that, by their account, is present in all cultures. They fail to note that cultural practices would be as mute in giving moral guidance as "treat like cases alike" without the ordering and selecting done by moral reasoners.

We also have factual evidence that other cultures do subject their practices and beliefs to criticism by rational standards. Amartya Sen and Martha Nussbaum note that the assumption of internal harmony of the elements of a culture is to be challenged; they cite the example of India's culture, noting that the internal conflict provides occasion for Indians to employ rational standards to criticize other values and elements of their culture.[25]

Romantic relativists do not escape the contradiction and nihilism that threatened earlier relativists. The recent group claims that there are no universal moral norms, yet holds that what is morally important for everyone to attend to is specific practices. If it is always important to attend to specific practices, then there must be universal norms—without them nothing could be taken to be *generally* of moral import.

Romanticists can avoid this impasse at the same time that they go where the action is—to specific practices—if they remember that only concerned and informed moral reasoners could apply the practices in the selective, ordered way that we require. Their remembering that will lead them to see something of the concept of person involved in the moral reasoning process and to see the values and importance of the form of reasoning. That might also lead them to abandon some of their Romantic "rebellion against enlightenment" and to criticize the practice of self-sealing because of its conflict with the values of moral reasoning. But their rebellion has also been given support by supposedly "higher" philosophical ground.

Are There Any Universal Logical Norms?

The "Romantics" invoke the later Wittgenstein as supporting their rebellion, and some of the followers of Wittgenstein do reject the possibility of any external criticism of cultural practices. The one providing the support closest to the Romantic position is also the most familiar—namely Peter Winch. In his *Idea of a Social Science*, he argues against logical and empirical criticism of cultural concepts and practices by appealing to a kind of cultural relativism, supposedly one that is essential to an understanding of the way in which ordinary language functions in any society. We should review some central points of his position.

Winch supports important broad features of the Romantic position in arguing that if one is to describe accurately the actions of the members of a society, one must describe them as the members would describe it to themselves. As their thought about actions are tied to their language and as their language takes on meaning in relation to actions in their community, their purposes and reasons for action must be described by using that language, with its built-in connections to the practices of their culture. The nature and quality of the actions are determined by those practices and their interconnections. Of the language's meaning, he writes: "Our language and our social relations are just two sides of the same coin. To give an account of the meaning of a word is to describe how it is used. And to describe how it is used is to describe the social intercourse into which it enters."[26] Thus, as an outsider one cannot describe in one's own terms what the members do, for they always aim to accomplish something in relation to their own practices, and those practices are described in their own terms. Those practices are where the action is. The life of the terms is in their use by the members of the community: "it is only from their roots in the actual flesh-and-blood intercourse that . . . formal systems draw such life as they have" (W:126).

Winch takes a critical step when he describes the role of logic in such systems. Logical forms could only have meaning through being used by members of a community, "for the whole idea of a logical relation is only possible by virtue of the sort of agreement between men and their actions" (W:126). Thus, Winch leads us to the point that to apply any norm we must agree on how to apply it—that is, by a mutual awareness and recognition of its appropriateness. It is a function of life in a community.

From the point that logical relations could only have meaning among members of a community, Winch evidently concludes that we could not find the same logical forms used in different language communities. From what he says, it seems he believes that logic, too, must be wholly contextual and relative: "Criteria of logic are not a direct gift of

God, but arise out of, and are only intelligible in the context of ways of living or modes of social life" (W:100). The idea is that they are tied to the specific modes of social life from which they emerge; there could be no universal basis from which one could criticize all modes: "It follows that one cannot apply criteria of logic to modes of social life as such. For instance, science is one such mode, and religion is another; and each has criteria of intelligibility to itself" (W:103).

From Winch's point of view there could be no logical and empirical basis for the criticism of cultural practices; thus he provides philosophical ground for the relativist notion that cultural practices, being "internal" to the cultural frame, are thereby immune to any rational criticism. Winch holds: "It is not its [philosophy's] business to advocate any *Weltanschauung*" (W:103). And so he can support Wittgenstein's dictum: "Philosophy leaves everything as it was."

Winch's conclusion certainly makes us wonder about his argument. The claim that philosophy leaves everything as it was seems to ignore the fact that in the practice of philosophy since Socrates, philosophers have not left everything as it was. They have made it their business to criticize cultural practices internal and external to their own culture and, in doing so, have advocated new weltanschauungen.

Winch, like Shweder, believes he has found a more adequate view of man in society, one that is universally valid and one that he aims to get us to adopt. (*He* advocates.) For his account to make sense or for any philosophical overview to make sense, it must be possible to break the bounds of cultural relativism, because such accounts presuppose some universally applicable norms: in making universal claims and in advocating changes in others' views.

Winch's argument centers on the point that meaning and description are functions of life in a community and, more particularly, on the point that for us to apply norms of reasoning, there must be agreement among persons in a community on the appropriateness of its application. These are points one must endorse: no application of reasons without a community of reasoners who agree on the validity of the form. But it is a fallacy to conclude from the above that there are no universal norms of logical inference that are acknowledged and applied by all members of the human community. All that is required by Winch's argument is that *people* have to agree on the application of a norm of inference; patently, people can agree on the application of norms of inference without being from the same culture. Hence, it is a fallacy to conclude that norms of inference emerge only within the context of specific modes of social life.

One may readily grant that each culture has its distinctive style of reasoning and that there will be informal inferences that one can make only in particular areas because they tie onto local practices. But that will not support the philosophical conclusion that there are no valid forms of reasoning that apply across cultural lines, or that our forms of reasoning are peculiar to Western technological society. Are we to believe that members of nontechnological cultures see no need to avoid contradiction in what they say or that they do not seek evidence to support observational generalizations? Such a conclusion is hard to accept and anthropologists are among those that caution against such a view. Evans-Pritchard argued that primitive peoples, living close to the harsh realities of nature as they do, could not afford to be illogical children of fantasy.[27] Another anthropologist observed, "No society would survive for any length of time without basing a large part of its daily activities on beliefs derived from evidence. You cannot farm without some rationally based knowledge of soils, seeds, and climate; and no society can achieve any reasonable degree of harmony in human relations without the basic ability to assess claims and allegations by the method of objective investigation."[28]

Indeed, it seems that one must argue that sharing certain modes of inference is the necessary *precondition* for modes of social life to emerge. For, by Winch's argument (and the romantics' assent), forms of social life only emerge through language—they are "two sides of the same coin." We must communicate about the activities that we share and communicate about them to agree to the appropriateness of any description. But to agree to the appropriateness of another's description, one must know what state of affairs the other intends to refer to. To know that, one must know that the other does not intend to refer to the reverse of that description, and one must be able to derive *further inferences* from that knowledge. Understanding our daily actions and ordinary practices depends on our ability to describe and to infer from such descriptions. To take a well-worn example, to be able to understand another's assertion, "The cow is in the corn," one must know that it is not the case that the cow is not in the corn. One must understand that this entails that the cow is not in the living room. It appears that one must *bring* certain norms of inference—minimally, noncontradiction and *modus ponens*—to the acquisition and application of language. It seems indisputable that the use of such norms of inference is integral to the forming and following of rules, as studied in prelingual infants and as discussed in chapter 4; as noted there, such rule following is necessary for one to learn the language. If these points are valid, then certain forms of logic must be direct "gifts of God," contrary to Winch's claim.

A number of philosophers—Max Black, Richard Grandy, and Donald Davidson—have made a similar point,[29] but Martin Hollis has developed it in its connection with the anthropologist's problems of translation and the study of cultures.[30] As Hollis observes, users of all languages and members of all cultures must be able to communicate facts and give explanatory reasons. Unless we could communicate information or give explanations, we could not share a common way of life or know what its coherence consisted in. We could not act as responsible people, for we could not give passable descriptions of our actions or give reasons relating our choices to the relevant practices. But, as the "cow is in the corn" example shows, these functions would be impossible unless all humans shared at least some logical norms. We could not communicate any fact—and this is an achievement on which the description of practices is dependent—unless others knew that, when we gave a descriptive assertion such as "the cow is in the corn," other facts would follow from it. We must share some logical norms for any language, understanding of behavior, or social practices to emerge. Note, too, that canons of logic are applied to individual sentences, showing that they can be considered and assessed without considering their possible place within a total system. This shows that, for investigator and native speaker alike, descriptions of cultural beliefs need not be considered to be parts of an indivisible "set of beliefs."

Sociologist Steven Lukes argues (in a way parallel to arguments by Davidson) that the relativizing anthropologist must assume that the peoples he or she studies are persons like him- or herself, who have beliefs and desires and want to act in the world to attain their ends. Such students of alien cultures could not get evidence to support their relativizing claims without assuming a logic that is not relative:

> In the very identification of beliefs and *a fortiori* of belief systems we must presuppose commonly shared standards of truth and inference and . . . we must further presuppose a commonly shared core of beliefs whose content or meaning is fixed by application of the standards. Neither the evidence of cross-cultural variation in schemes of classification nor that of radically divergent theoretical schemes or styles of reasoning, nor arguments for the possible ap-

plicability of alternative logics undermine this position, which must, indeed, be accepted before the problem of relativism can be set up in the first place.[31]

Invoking one of Strawson's conclusions (from *Individuals*)—that there must be "a massive central core of human thinking which has no history"[32]—Lukes finds support in, among others, Richard Grandy, who argues that, as investigators, we must have a "model of the agent" to "assist us in making a prediction," and that we use ourselves in order to arrive at it: "We consider what we should do if we had the relevant beliefs and desires."[33]

Drawing support from Jurgen Habermas as well as from Grandy's point, Lukes concludes: "The necessary model of the agent appears to require at least that those whose beliefs are to be identified are in general behaviourally rational in their actions and that they are, in general, sensitive to deductive argument and inductive evidence (though the degree to which these propensities are developed will depend on situation and opportunities). It will also involve the assumption that they have at least two fundamental cognitive interests: in explaining, predicting and controlling their environment and in achieving mutual understanding."[34] Thus, the anthropologist who denies that our common logical tools of analysis and self-criticism are available to all cultures must do so in contradiction of his or her own assumptions as a working anthropologist.

Winch's suggestion that logic is *purely* contextual gets some credibility from the fact that it is *partly* so. We are aware that we can often infer more from an assertion if we know the details of the situation in which it is uttered. And the same assertion, uttered under different circumstances, will have different implications. Shweder invokes this point in support of his notion of nonrational ideas: "All real-world communications have an explicit or tacit illocutionary force; thus, 'Go to your room,' uttered under the 'right' circumstances, communicates and permits the explicit expansion 'I "order" you to go to your room'" (*S*:42). Agreed: there can be no doubt that many of our inferences are tied to our knowledge of the context. We could not know all that the other wanted to do or say without an awareness of the other's situation.

But the fact that there are culturally specific modes or styles of inference does nothing to deny that there are universal modes of inference. We cannot know about or communicate about the context and its interconnections—we could not talk about there being a room of yours—

without first employing the principles of noncontradiction and *modus ponens*. If any sentence we want to communicate has a determinate meaning, it is not compatible with its own denial: noncontradiction is packed into the possibility of our understanding of descriptions of facts (and, among the facts, of plans of action).

The case here is parallel with our remarks about the use of universal norms of moral reasoning. Context is important in determining what can be judged to be true or right, but context can tell us nothing without the application of universal norms: contextual logic cannot serve us without universal norms of inference, just as specific moral practices cannot guide us without the use of principled moral reasoning. We must apply universal norms of inference to *begin* communicating about the contextual modes of life—to get to where the action is—just as we must use principled concern to get a morally acceptable application of specific cultural practices. If universal forms of inference are preconditions for any communication, and modes of communication are essential to forms of social life, then there are universal norms of inference that can be applied for criticism of any form of social life.

To say that seems to remove romanticists' chief remaining philosophical ground for refusing to subject cultural practices to criticism.

Harmony among Indigenous Practices?

But some Romantics will resist any such criticism on the ground that whoever criticizes cultural practices will interfere with what is indigenous to a system—with a "self-sufficient 'design for living'."[35] This is a design that is supported by an entire value system and is composed of cultural practices that have evolved together over time. As such, it is held, these cultural practices will be found to be mutually compatible, parts of a total system with which one cannot meddle—the global system syndrome again.

It is not just the global system syndrome that makes this strategy of resistance seem a bit too romantic. For, whereas one must agree that the practices of a culture have evolved historically, are mutually related, and are to be understood in their inter-relatedness, the strategy will *not* show that the practices are accepted by its members as mutually compatible or uniformly fair. We've noted how Amartya Sen and Martha Nussbaum are, like Shweder, students of the culture of India; Sen and Nussbaum have described how Indians opposed and criticized Indian practices and have used rational methods in their criticism. Sen and

Nussbaum, like others, have noted that a culture is part of a world culture that contributes to the evolution of traditions and values around the globe:

> Contributions in philosophy and logic belong at least as much to Indian intellectual history as do popular myths about the earth. . . .
>
> Similarly, the achievements of Indian mathematics—neither particularly spiritual nor especially mystical—were substantial enough to rival Indian contributions to the world of religion and spirituality. In particular, the development of the decimal system (and the related numerical representation) in India had a major impact on the flourishing Arab civilization in the Middle Ages and through the Arabs reached Europe early in this millenium.[36]

The suggestion that we would find no real conflict within cultures and find indigenous practices to be fair (did we but understand them) does not tally with what we see and read about conflict and abuses around the world. We certainly find conflict and contradiction between practices in our own history and culture and in other cultures' history. Why should we assume, against evidence to the contrary, that we should consider other cultures to be immune from such conflict?

Nor does the fact of mutual relatedness of practices within a "design for living" show that it would be ruinous to subject to scrutiny those practices that seem unfair. We certainly find that some cultural practices of our own culture and some of other cultures have been subjected to steady criticism, and some have been changed in response to criticism. Why should we believe that the same cannot be done again?

When we look at cultures with indigenous racist and sexist discriminatory practices, we have good reason to believe that *no* global set of values could consistently support such practices. For we have reason to believe that there will be an inevitable conflict between the unequal treatment accorded to the victims of such practices and the ways in which such victims, as members of a common language community, must be conceived as equal in the indigenous language. A language, in order to serve the purpose of communication between persons, must conceive of persons as alike: as we have just noted, it describes their behavior as intentional; as adapting means to ends; as developing purposes, and as pursuing life plans. The language must make use of the same predicates to ascribe motives and purposes to the victims that it uses to ascribe motives and purposes to others. To apply the language to the victims, users of the language must, on some level, see victims and oppressors as fundamentally alike.

Users of the language, observing the victims to be articulate speakers of the language, must see the victims as able to relate and compare their own intentions and goals to those of others around them in the *same way* that the dominant members of the culture do. Thus, the victims, as articulate language users, exhibit their full possession of the capacities fundamental to life in society: reciprocal reading and assessing of intentions; the ability to describe their moral situation and compare it with others; and the making of moral judgments in accord with permissible practices. In speaking and in social dealings with the victims, dominant members of the society are brought into intersubjective, reciprocating activity, activity in which they can only cooperate by mutual reading of intent and concern. As Frederick Olafson has noted, "if [one] . . . is asked why the same person to whom he has stood in a relation characterized by intersubjective reciprocity is for other purposes to be treated in accordance with the logic of egocentricity, he cannot very well deny that that person is *capable* of functioning as a partner in the kind of relationship from which he is now excluded."[37] If the fully privileged members of society must directly witness the victims employing the same capacities that they do—capacities that qualify them for full membership—can they *consistently* deny to victims the same status that they themselves enjoy? If they must see that the victims have all the capacities that enable one to be a normal and fully cooperating member of society, can they consistently deny them the rights that accrue to fully privileged members? Can a culture that harbors such discriminatory practices be free of conflict? Can we believe that everything is in order as it is in such a society?

If we are to avoid relativism's "whatever is, is right" stance, such practices and their cultural frames must not be regarded as being immune to criticism or regarded as part of an indivisible set. If we are to be responsive to the needs of persons, we must adapt our action to the realities of their lives, the specific practices around which their lives are built.

Since we must make our judgments by putting ourselves in another's place, we are obliged to attend to the specific, and often culturally relative practices around which the other's situation must be conceived of and acted on. It is the universal norm that signals the appropriateness of acting in accord with relative practices, out of concern for the interests of each individual. It is the same concern that justifies one in refusing to comply with, and in working toward the rejection or reform of, those practices that are cruel or unfair. Part of the process of working toward their rejection is to exhibit the empirical or logical incoherence of the practices and the cultural presuppositions that undergird them.

I have argued that to be responsive to others as persons one must attend to relative moral codes and that one can do so, yet avoid the relativists' conceptual muddle, by noting the following points:

1. One can (and should distinguish) between moral principles and the codes or practices of a specific culture.

2. Although our involvement in specific practices must be considered in making moral judgments, local practices and codes alone do not define what is right or wrong. The notion that the Rule is purely formal and empty is shown to be mistaken because it must be employed in order to apply the specific practices of any code. For, in specific actions, we will be involved in practices with conflicting claims; as a consequence, we could not reach a decision regarding such actions without employing a general norm to mediate between the claims of the practices in conflict. Thus, we see that local practices could not even be applied without using a general norm to order priorities and claims.

3. The ethical relativists of the "Romantic rebellion" hold that a mature culture's ethical codes and practices are immune from rational criticism because they are elements of (a) stable, (b) internally harmonious set of beliefs and traditions, and (c) are supported by logical norms deriving from their own context. Against these points, we see evidence that even the most ancient of cultures (a) continue to evolve and interact with traditions of other cultures; (b) exhibit internal conflict and critical discussion; and (c) do so employing "Western" norms of logic.

4. It is a logical contradiction for "Romantic" cognitive relativists to claim that cultural beliefs both serve as the framing explanation for cultural practices and are beyond logical and empirical support or criticism: they could not serve as explanatory concepts if they did not imply some empirical propositions related to the practices (and hence, derive some empirical support from them). Historically, we have seen that framing cultural beliefs have been, and are, resistant but not immune to criticism.

5. Nor can relativists claim that the operative forms of inference in a culture are authoritative and idiosyncratic to the context of that cul-

ture. For some universally employed logical norms (noncontradiction and *modus ponens*, for example) are preconditions for the use of any language by which a culture's members could describe and communicate facts to each other. It follows that the universal logical norms must be preconditions for the identification and description of cultural contexts, and hence, the use of the universal logical norm is a precondition for the use of norms arising out of those cultural contexts. This parallels the point that universal moral norms are required in order to apply the specific codes and practices of individual cultures (point 2 above).

If we are to apply the Rule out of concern for persons involved in cultural practices, this will entail, in addition to the points discussed in chapters 7 and 8, the following:

6. that in being morally animated by compassion, we work for the reform of those practices that discriminate against individuals and that we secure to members of the community of moral reasoners access to the information, discussion, and expression that is required for the giving and taking of moral reasons (rights such as are recognized under the First Amendment to the U.S. Constitution). We have reason to secure such freedoms because whoever is held responsible has a continual need to understand and communicate about the situation in which they find themselves, a need which could not be met without such freedoms.

Although remembering these points will give one a coherent basis for moral judgment and critical reform, in undertaking such reform, one will face conflict and resistance from those who will cling tenaciously to current practices and their framing concepts. In seeking to change such practices, one will place oneself and those involved in the practices in new and morally ambiguous situations. These will bring with them puzzling complexities to be worked through. There seems to be no responsible way of avoiding such complexities. Better to wrestle with them and initiate reconstruction than to pretend that everything is in order as it is.

10 / Moral Anatomy and Moral Reasoning: Summary and Support

We've argued that to understand moral reasoning we must understand our *moral anatomy*, an expression we've used to refer to the motives, reasons, and responsiveness that interplay in judging and acting. In judging about persons and their actions, we generalize, relying on our sense of what persons are: what they can do, what they should care about, and how these are related to their decisions and responses. Some sense of person, whether clearly formed and fully articulated or not, underlies every step of our moral reasoning, and so, an account of moral reasoning must focus on that sense and its operation.

Fundamental to our understanding of persons is our understanding of the process by which persons come to conceive of themselves and of persons generally. All coherent moral description and discussion turns on an understanding of the action of persons. To reach agreements on what is morally acceptable, we must employ a language to discuss and compare what persons generally are to do. This entails that we conceive of ourselves as persons, and this entails that we conceive of persons as fundamentally alike in the powers, motives, and abilities that they can exercise.

A moral life is possible only by means of a moral language. We can compare, assess, and come to agreement on plans and actions only by the descriptions and distinctions that the language permits. Accordingly, we get at the nature of moral reasoning and the moral community by studying the use of ordinary moral expressions and judgments and the situations to which they are an appropriate response. As John Austin remarks: "When we examine what we should say when, what words we should use in what situations, we are looking again not *merely* at words . . . but also the realities we use the words to talk about: we are using a sharpened awareness of words to sharpen our perception of phenomena.''[1]

The phenomena in question are those of our life in the moral community, with the standards for motive and reflection that are implied in the use of its terms. Forms of moral reasoning are forms of *life*. If we are to get clearer about what is possible or necessary in moral reasoning, we must first attend to the web of attitudes and responses of our actual community; we must look to the expression (with the implied judgment) of people who stand in physiological and emotional relationships to each other—and not to merely abstract models of rationality.

It is as *members* of a moral community that we make our judgments: our judgments are responses to others who are also responsive to others as members. To see others as members is to see them as committed to moral norms that one shares. Moral intelligence exists through that reciprocating awareness and concern of persons who are bound together in a community of concern: it cannot be understood as the work of individuals who calculate or reason in isolation.

Children's entry into the moral community and their exercise of moral judgments can be observed in their use of moral language and in the motives that underlie its application. By observing infants acquiring and using moral language, we can observe, in primitive form, the basic elements of moral intelligence and motivation.

In our observations, we see once again that moral reasoning must begin with interdependent attitudes, with concern for others, as well as with concern for what is acceptable to a community of reasoners. We see that we proceed from a number of motives as well as from a number of cognitive foci. As Frederic Olafson notes, ''Reciprocity is something more than an appendage to an already constituted self . . . [it] governs the relationship of one consciousness to another.''[2] Cognitively, we alternate, in making judgments, between a consideration of our own and others' situation; affectively, we proceed from a concern for others and for ourselves as well as from a regard for what a community of informed and concerned reasoners find acceptable.

These elements of our anatomy are brought together in the principle of moral reasoning that we have described as ''the Rule,'' the injunction that reflective, self-controlled agents are to consider their actions from the perspective of those affected and are to respond with concern to meet each others' needs. Judgments and actions can then be found to be acceptable on objective ground: they are to proceed from an investigation of what those acts would mean to those affected by them and from a concern for their well-being.

To reach a judgment about how an act would affect another (and thereby reach a conclusion about what acts are acceptable), we must reason from our understanding of our particular differences and individual situations as well as from our awareness of our common abilities and concerns. While our reasoning must be based on our awareness of some common features of our moral anatomy, (such as motive, reasoning ability, and use of information), it must also take note of our particular (and possibly unique) abilities and situation. Universal principle requires that we respect each individual, but we are beings of such a kind that we can only do so by seeing and reasoning about individuals in their particular relationships and involvements.

Attending to individuals' situation must include respecting their involvement with local customs and cultural practices, around which their habits and expectations are built. One's moral choices will often be shaped by those particular practices and customs. While one must honor those cultural involvements, one must often reject and work to modify or reform those customs that deny individuals' rights.

The two questions we began the book with were: How do we come to want to do what is morally demanded of us? and How does our being moral relate to what we are and to how we are related to each other? We have concluded that when we believe that what is generally approvable defines what is moral, if we act out of feeling for others and a regard for their opinion of us, we will be led to take what is generally approvable as authoritative. In this way our feelings for others and our desire to be worthy of their approval provide a constraining motive for moral choice: other desires are to be constrained so as to be in accord with the desire to have our actions approvable by informed and concerned persons. Thus, the answers to the two questions come together: It is because of our relationship to each other that we can come to want to do what is morally acceptable and demanded.

If we adhere to acceptable behavior we will act in a way that a person in the situation of those affected could approve. Thus, we arrive at a variation of the Golden Rule, a version of which is held to be a universal standard by the major world religions. That it is to be re-

garded as a universal principle follows from the standard meaning of
"moral" and from our answer to the second question as to how we
are to conceive of persons:

> If we're moral, we treat others with respect;
> to do so, we must treat them as persons.
> Persons must be conceived as like ourselves.
> Thus, to treat others as persons we must treat them as we would
> want or expect to be treated in like circumstances.

In framing moral judgments, we must take persons as beings-in-rela-
tionships, as embedded in and defined by their circumstances and
their relationships with others. Thus, when the Rule is applied as a
universal standard, it yields judgments that are based on the particular abilities, expectations, and relationships of individuals—not
statements that are meant to function as universally applicable laws
of nature.

Notes

CHAPTER ONE. RESPONSIVENESS AND
RESPONSIBILITY

1. Immanuel Kant had provided one source of the puzzle by saying: "How reason can be practical—to explain this all human reason is wholly incompetent and all pain and work of seeking an explanation are wasted" (Immanuel Kant, *Critique of Practical Reason and Other Writings in Moral Philosophy* [New York:Garland, 1976], translated and edited by Lewis White Beck, p. 115). The passage cited is from *Foundations of the Metaphysics of Morals* [1785]. Kant reached this conclusion after having determined that moral agents choose "only that which reason independently of all inclination recognizes to be practically necessary" (ibid., p. 72). If impartial reason must operate independently of all inclination (to use Kant's term), how or why could we have any inclination to direct our practices in a moral way? If we cannot be moral when acting on our inclination, how or why do we ever want to act morally?

Although Kant had special epistemological reasons for denying that we could explain moral motives, he was not the only philosopher who had difficulty reconciling moral standards with the motive to act. Others who sought to base standards of evaluation on inclinations (instead of excluding them as Kant did) faced difficulty in showing their standard able to account for moral claims or community moral standards.

For example, in the *Nicomachean Ethics*, Aristotle proposed as the standard of the Good (by which all acts are to be evaluated) the attainment of one's own *eudaimonia* (or well-being)—an end everyone would surely be inclined to seek. Taking this well-being to be attainable only through one's own excellence of function, he held that an act is morally choiceworthy if it contributes to one's vigorous and healthy function. (One of his definitions of excellence or virtue is "what makes a man good and enables him to do his work well.") He thus provides a unifying criterion of evaluation. But, in approving or condemning acts solely on the basis of whether they contribute to his own vigorous function, he seems, as Bernard Williams observes, "disquietingly concerned with himself" (*Ethics and the Limits of Philosophy*, (Cambridge, Mass.: Harvard University Press, 1985). By his criterion we would judge the rightness of our acts to be relative to the extent they served our own well-being (or were perceived to do so). Aristotle, of course, was not so self-obsessed as the standard would suggest: adultery and murder (and other acts interfering with others' rights) he condemned categorically—and not just to the extent that they impeded one's function. Moreover, he found that the friendships that were essential to our well-being were those in which we valued the friends for their own sake (see opening bk. 8) and not because they served our own well-being. But these are points that are not easy to reconcile with the motivation implicit in his standard of the Good.

A similar difficulty faces John Stuart Mill's attempt (in *Utilitarianism*) to tie the morally desirable to one's inclination toward happiness (described via pleasure and pain): "pleasure and freedom from pain are the only things desirable as ends" (*Utilitarianism and Other Essays* [New York: Penguin, 1987] p. 278). Although Mill wrote that we would be happier if we were unselfish and sought the happiness of people generally, he had problems explaining why it should be so: "No reason can be given why the general happiness is desirable except that each person, so far as he believes it to be attainable, desires his own happiness" (ibid., p. 307). (From one's desire for one's own happiness, it does not follow that one has any desire at all for the general happiness.) We might suppose that by saying this is the *only* reason for desiring the general happiness, he was thinking of it as a centrally important reason, to be coupled, perhaps, with our concern for other people. Even so, the resulting position, taking pleasure and freedom from pain for people in general as "the only things desirable as ends," would seem to be at odds with Mill's acknowledgment that " . . . the mind is not in a right state . . . unless it does love virtue . . . as a thing desirable in itself" (ibid., p. 308).

2. *An Enquiry Concerning the Principles of Morals* (1751; Indianapolis: Hackett, 1983), pp. 74–75.

3. It may be helpful to indicate briefly how this notion bears on the senses of "responsible," as "agent of change" and as "held to account." To be responsible we must be agents of change: as agents we qualify as the answers to the question, Who brought about the change? (Who's responsible for it?) If we ask more pointedly, as in, Who's responsible for this broken window? the notion of community of judgment is implied in the notion of "held to account." As the one who is responsible for (is the cause of) change one may also be held to account; as such, one must be able to give an account of one's actions and one's reasons for acting to a community of persons who can assess them; one's reasons must count as reasons acceptable to a community. Other senses—legal and financial responsibility—spin off of these, but the point to note here is that in acting in a morally responsible way, one is responsive to a community and the kinds of reasons its members can accept.

Often members of the community will disagree about the appropriateness of particular acts (though it is important to realize that often they will not), but one's reasons will be morally motivated insofar as one aims to find reasons on which others agree or should be able to agree. It is not that reasons will be moral insofar as one aims to conform to opinions and practices that one knows others endorse; rather one is responsible in one's reasoning (and one's reasons are morally motivated), if one aims to act in ways that others could endorse if they were given adequate information and similar motivation. Being responsible turns on motive. One does not aim to adopt the opinion that others happen to have: rather moral aim is aiming to achieve mutually acceptable reasons and choices. To be morally responsible in one's motives and reasoning is to want to be able to base one's actions on reasons which others, similarly motivated, could accept, were they given the relevant information and the opportunity to think it through. One's moral responsibility is reflected in showing respect for the reasoning and interests of others and in one's willingness to work out an agreement by reasoning together.

4. In *The Theory of the Moral Sentiments*, sec. 3, chap. 2, par. 7. (1759). In *Adam Smith's Moral and Political Philosophy*, ed. H. Schneider (New York: Hafner, 1948).

5. I argue this case in "Who's in Control Here?" *Philosophy* No. 51, (1976): 421–30.

6. The fact that we must conceive of persons as alike in order to use a language does not mean, alas, that we must be consistent in how we think of them. All too often we see people make reasoned demands on others and then speak of them as if they were subhuman (or perhaps submasculine). That doesn't mean we should not point out the incoherence of their doing so.

7. Speaking of this account in both descriptive and normative terms (as I have) may seem to be a willful attempt to confuse the two. But I do so because it's important to be clear that our understanding of the terms is grounded in observing them to work in an actual community making moral judgments—it's grounded in seeing what one would or could say about those situations. The moral normative terms are like the norms of formal logic in this respect: we need to be able to see them put to work to get the point. They are like logical norms in another respect: we see that people do not always live up to what either logical or moral norms require. If people did, we would have no occasion to employ the terms either for pointing out fallacies or for placing judgments of moral blame. That we commit logical blunders and sometimes argue poorly does not mean that we do not or cannot acknowledge or understand logical norms. Neither does it mean that the norms have no validity for the remainder of the community. Similarly, the fact that we commit moral blunders and sometimes deceive ourselves about the moral appropriateness of an action does not mean that we do not acknowledge or cannot understand moral norms. Nor does it mean that moral norms therefore have no validity for the remainder of the community.

8. Bk. 4, chap. 10 (1776) [emphasis added].

9. Bk. 4, chap. 2.

10. Pt. I, sec. 1, chap. 4, par. 4.

11. Anthropologist Richard Shweder holds that one of our fundamental and irrefutable beliefs is that "Man's only motive is to maximize pleasure and minimize pain." It is so fundamental as to provide a "frame" for Western culture. See his "Anthropology's Rebellion against the Enlightenment" in *Culture Theory: Essays on Mind, Self and Emotion*, ed. Richard Shweder and R. A. Levine (New York: Cambridge University Press, 1984), p. 40.

12. *Butler's Works* 1726, ed. W. E. Gladstone (Oxford: Oxford University Press, 1897), p. 159.

13. Ibid. p. 158.

14. Ibid. p. 160.

15. In *Morals by Agreement* (Oxford: Clarendon Press, 1986), p. 311.

CHAPTER TWO. FEELINGS, REASONS, AND
PERSONS

1. *Philosophical Papers* (Oxford: Clarendon Press, 1961), p. 130
2. In *Ethics, Inventing Right and Wrong* (New York: Penguin, 1977).
3. From "Freedom and Resentment" in *Studies in the Philosophy of Thought and Action*, edited by P. F. Strawson (New York: Oxford University Press, 1968), p. 76.
4. *Philosophical Papers*, p. 142.
5. *The Possibility of Altruism* (Oxford: Oxford University Press, 1970), pp. 3, 144. Not all neo-Kantians follow Nagel's approach, of course. Barbara Herman and Christine Korsgaard, for example, seek to develop Kantian argument so as to relate it to interests and feelings. On this issue, see my further comments on Kant, pp. 51ff. For another account which seeks to show that morality can't be based on a single principle, see Owen Flanagan's *Varieties of Moral Personality* (Cambridge, Mass.: Harvard University Press, 1990).
6. From *Genealogy of Morals* in *The Philosophy of Nietzsche* (New York: Modern Library, 1927), p. 651.

CHAPTER THREE. MUTUAL RESPONSES AND
OBJECTIVITY

1. From "Foundations of the Metaphysics of Morals" in *Critique of Practical Reason and Other Works in the Theory of Ethics*, ed. T. K. Abbott (London: Longmans, Green, 1959) p. 43.
2. *A History of Western Philosophy* (London: Penguin, 1987), p. 313.
3. See the introductory essay of *Morality and Universality*, ed. Nelson Potter and Mark Timmons (Dordrecht: Reidel, 1985) esp. p. xxvi. Others have suggested that a more sympathetic reading of Kant would focus on Kant's reasoning about moral imperatives that are applied to the world and hence must be tied to particular features of human nature. Even if one thought (as I do) that this reading simply excuses Kant's inconsistency in passages of *The Critique of Practical Reason* and in *The Foundations of the Metaphysics of Morals*, such a sympathetic reading would have the merit of showing how Kant's discussion of maxims-to-be-universalized relates to the actual role of reason in ordering our actual concerns. But once we (adopting the sympathetic reading) argued that maxims-to-be-universalized must be tied to particular features of human nature, we could no longer accept Kant's argument that moral judgments cannot be grounded in an understanding of the particular features of human nature.
4. *Ethics: Inventing Right from Wrong* (London: Penguin, 1977; 1979), pp. 35, 40.
5. In "Errors and the Phenomenology of Value" in *Morality and Objectivity*, ed. Ted Honderich (London: Routledge and Kegan Paul, 1985), p. 12.
6. Ibid., p. 6.

7. In "Rule-Following and Following a Rule" in Steven Holtzmann and Christopher Leich, eds., *Wittgenstein: To Follow a Rule* (Routledge and Kegan Paul, 1981), p. 186.

8. "Errors and the Phenomenology of Value," p. 16.

9. David Hume, *Enquiry Concerning the Principles of Morals* (Indianapolis: Hackett, 1983), pp. 23–24.

10. "Errors and the Phenomenology of Value," p. 8.

11. In "Values and Secondary Qualities" in *Morality and Objectivity*, ed. Ted Honderich (London: Routledge and Kegan Paul), p. 119.

12. In "Psychology as Philosophy" in *Essays in Action and Events* (Oxford: Clarendon Press, 1980), p. 237, n.5. Davidson emphasizes the objective conditions for judgments in "The Myth of the Subjective" in Michael Krausz's anthology, *Relativism: Interpretation and Confrontation* (Notre Dame, Ind.: University of Notre Dame Press, 1989).

13. *Philosophical Investigations*, I: 337.

14. From "Dissertation on the Nature of Virtue" in *Butler's Sermons and Dissertation on the Nature of Virtue*, ed. W. R. Matthews (London: Bell, 1958), p. 249–50.

15. In "Objectivity and Disagreement" in *Morality and Objectivity*, ed. Ted Honderich (London: Routledge and Kegan Paul, 1985), p. 82.

16. Sermon 5, par. 4 in *Fifteen Sermons*, ed. W. E. Gladstone (Oxford: Clarendon Press, 1897).

17. From pt. 3, chap. 1 of *The Theory of the Moral Sentiments* (1759), in *Adam Smith's Moral and Political Philosophy*, ed. H. Schneider (New York: Hafner, 1948) p. 144.

18. David Hume, *A Treatise of Human Nature* (Oxford: Oxford University Press, 1978), p. 582.

19. Hume, *Treatise of Human Nature*, p. 583. See Marcia Baron, "Morality as a Back-up System: Hume's View?" *Hume Studies* 14 (April 1988):25–52.

CHAPTER FOUR. MORAL REASONING AND
ACTION IN YOUNG CHILDREN

1. In "Conditions of Personhood" in *The Identities of Persons*, ed. Amelie Rorty (Berkeley: University of California Press, 1976), p. 191.

2. P. F. Strawson, *Individuals* (London: Methuen, 1959; 1979), p. 100.

3. The point is forcibly developed by Marcus Singer in *Generalization in Ethics* (New York: Alfred A. Knopf, 1961).

4. See comments by Richard Shweder, Elliot Turiel, and Nancy Much in "The Moral Intuitions of the Child" in *Social Cognitive Development*, ed. John Flavell and Lee Ross (Cambridge, Eng.: Cambridge University Press, 1981), pp. 288–306.

5. "Culture and the Construction of Values: A Comparative Ethnography of Moral Encounters in Two Cultural Settings" in *The Emergence of Morality in Young Children*, ed. J. Kagan and S. Lamb (Chicago: University of Chicago Press: 1987), p. 123.

6. In, e.g., Martin Hollis, "Reason and Ritual," *The Philosophy of Social Explanation*, ed. Alan Ryan (Oxford: Oxford University Press, 1973), pp. 33–50.

7. *Moral Life* (Totowa, N.J.: Rowman and Littlefield, 1978), p. 32.

8. Ibid., p. 109. "Meaning by it what they mean" requires the rejection of Nagel's "no feelings involved" stance, for as samples of reasoning and usage indicated (in my chapter 2), "they" mean to refer to our feelings of concern in making the judgments and in applying the terms. As we noted, "unfeeling," "callous," and the like are terms that apply blame for lack of feeling or compassion. So the terms cannot have the same motivational content unless feelings are involved.

9. "Talk of the Town," *New Yorker*, 9 March 1987, p. 26. The writer also effectively suggests the logical ultimacy of such attentive interest when he adds: "How could this be? Of all the possible objects of regard, what is so naturally compelling about two dark pools of returned attention? I could already imagine the scientific explanations—that the newborn infant displays a quantifiably verifiable predilection for certain facelike configurations, for example, or that this predisposition to gazing at eyes is instinctive, a sort of visual sucking reflex—but all such explanations beg the question. For I already *knew* that she had a predilection for facelike configurations, for dark dots ranged in pairs—the evidence was as obvious as the face before me— and the explanation for this predilection was equally obvious: because "facelike configurations" are *like* faces."

10. "Origins of Reciprocity" by T. Brazelton, B. Kosloski, and M. Main in *The Effects of the Infant on the Caregiver*, ed. M. Lewis and L. Rosenblum (New York: Wiley, 1974), p. 68.

11. Ibid., p. 74.

12. Ibid., p. 73.

13. Richard Q. Bell, "Contributions of Human Infants to Caregiving and Social Interactions," in Lewis and Rosenblum, *Effects of the Infant on the Caregiver*, p. 9.

14. Ibid.

15. Brazelton, Kosloski, and Main, "Origins of Reciprocity," p. 53.

16. Mary D. Ainsworth, *Patterns of Attachment* (Hillsdale, N.J: Erlbaum, 1978).

17. Ibid. and Mary Main and Donna Weston, "The Quality of the Toddler's Relationship to Mother and Father," *Child Development* 52 (1981): 932–40.

18. R. Arend, F. Gove and L. A. Sroufe, "Continuity of Individual Adaptation from Infancy to Kindergarten," *Child Development* 50 (1979): 950–59; Main and Weston, "Quality of the Toddler's Relationship."

19. Martin Hoffman, "Empathy, Role-Taking, Guilt and the Development of Altruistic Motives" in *Moral Development and Behavior: Theory, Research and Social Issues*, ed. T. Lickona (New York: Holt, Rinehart and Winston, 1976), pp. 124–44.

20. "The Beginnings of Moral Understanding" in *The Emergence of Morality in Young Children*, ed. Jerome Kagan and Sharon Lamb (Chicago: University of Chicago Press, 1987), pp. 91–112.

21. In "Particularity and Responsiveness" in Kagan and Lamb, *The Emergence of Morality*, pp. 306–38.

22. Mary Main and Donna Weston, "The Quality of the Toddler's Relationship to Mother and Father," *Child Development* 52 (1991): 932–40, and S. Londerville and M. Main, "Security, Attachment and Maternal Training

Methods in the Second Year of Life," *Developmental Psychology* 17 (1981): 289–300; and R., Arend, F. Gove, and L. A. Sroufe, "Continuity of Individual Adaptation from Infancy to Kindergarten," *Child Development* 50 (1979): 950–59.

23. Lawrence Kohlberg does not deny these abilities. However, Kohlberg elaborated Piaget's notion of stages of moral development, and Kohlberg's description of the motives and concerns of those in Kohlbergian Stage 1 and Stage 2 gives no indication of a role for concern for others and reasoning about others' intentions. Despite that, Kohlberg held that "psychologically, both welfare concerns (role-taking, empathy) and justice concerns are present at the birth of morality and at every succeeding stage." In "From Is to Ought" in *Cognitive Development and Epistemology*, ed. T. Mischel (New York: Academic Press, 1971), p. 220. He finds that it is only when one reaches moral maturity that one's judgments and actions are, in general, "motivated by awareness of the feelings and claims of the other people in the situation." (ibid., p. 231). But this is to say only that those at Kohlberg's highest stage are persons who have accepted responsibility for all their actions. This gives us no reason to deny that children may use the same *form* of moral reasoning as adults and act on the same concerns within their specific limited situations.

24. See *The Moral Judgment of the Child* (New York: Free Press, 1965), pp. 92–93; and *The Construction of Reality in the Child* (New York, Basic Books, 1954), pp. x–xi.

25. See Margaret Donaldson's *Children's Minds* (New York: W. W. Norton, 1979).

26. *A Theory of Justice* (Cambridge, Mass.: Belknap Press, 1971), p. 464 [emphasis added].

27. Ibid., p. 469.

28. See Sharon Nelson's "Factors Influencing Young Children's Use of Motives and Outcomes as Moral Criteria," *Child Development* 51, No. 3 (1980): 823–29.

29. Rawls, *Theory of Justice*, pp. 470, 471.

30. Ibid. [emphasis added].

31. *Dialectics of Action* (Chicago: University of Chicago Press, 1979), p. 24

32. In "Freedom and Resentment" in *Studies in the Philosophy of Thought and Action*, ed. P. F. Strawson (New York: Oxford University Press, 1968), p. 94.

CHAPTER FIVE. PHILOSOPHICAL EGOISM:
DENIAL OF THE SELF

1. *Problems of the Self* (Cambridge, Eng.: Cambridge University Press, 1973), pp. 251, 252. In Williams's later *Ethics and the Limits of Philosophy* (Cambridge, Mass.: Harvard University Press, 1985), he acknowledges that the egoist position is difficult to sustain as an ethical position (pp.12–13), since an ethical position ordinarily carries the notion of being good for everyone.

2. *Problems of the Self*, p. 251.

3. The point is developed in arguments in chapter 4.

4. Ibid. See also chapter 2.

5. See Nozick's *Philosophical Explanations* (Cambridge, Mass.: Belknap, 1981), p. 407.

6. As Michael Pritchard observes in his article, "Responsibility, Understanding and Psychopathology," *Monist* 58(October 1974): 630–45, it is instructive to compare the exclusive egoist position (described by Williams) with the attitudes and motivations of his flesh-and-blood cousin, the psychopath. It is a mark of the philosophical unattractiveness of the egoist position that we look to the psychopath's condition for its approximation. We note, however, that not even psychopaths are totally lacking in concern for others (though it may be fleeting). Thus, it seems that not even they provide an example corresponding to the strict egoist's total lack of concern.

CHAPTER SIX. GAUTHIER, GERT, HOBBES, AND HOBBESIANS

1. This study owes a great deal to Annette Baier's "Trust and Anti-Trust," *Ethics* 96 (1986): 231–60; Stephen J. Massey's "Is Self-Respect a Moral or Psychological Concept," *Ethics* 93 (1983): 246–61; and Rodger Beehler's *Moral Life* (Totowa, N.J.: Rowman and Littlefield, 1978).

2. *Leviathan*, ed. M. Oakeshott (Oxford: Blackwell, 1957).

3. Bernard Gert, *The Moral Rules* (New York: Harper and Row, 1973), p. 33.

4. That we blame on such a basis is apparent from our use of terms of judgment, already noted in chapter 2, such as "inconsiderate," "reckless," etc.

5. David Gauthier, *Morals by Agreement* (Oxford: Clarendon Press, 1986), p. 4.

6. Cited from his "Rationality and Affectivity," *Social Philosophy & Policy* 5 (1988): 154–72.

7. "Rationality and Affectivity," pp. 154–72.

8. Cited from "Morality, Rational Choice, and Semantic Representation, a Reply to My Critics," *Social Philosophy & Policy* 5 (1988): 173–221.

9. Ibid.

10. The method requires us to take the other's place so as to restrain ourselves from harming others. Accordingly, it comes as a surprise that Hobbes says it is equivalent to that Law of the Gospel (the Golden Rule) which demands more from us.

CHAPTER SEVEN. THE GOLDEN RULE: MOTIVE AND METHOD IN MORAL REASONING

1. Consider also the *Buddhist*: Hurt not others with that which pains yourself (*Udanavarga* 5.18; *Confucian*: Is there any one maxim which ought to be acted upon throughout one's life? Surely the maxim of loving kindness is such.—Do not unto others what you would not they should do unto you (*Analects* 15.23); *Muslim*: No one of you is a believer until he loves for his

brother what he loves for himself (*Traditions*); *Jainist*: In happiness and suffering, we should regard all creatures as we regard our own self, and should therefore refrain from inflicting upon others such injury as would appear undesirable to use if inflicted upon ourselves (*Yogahastra* 2.20); *Sikh*: As thou deemest thyself, so deem others. Then shalt thou become a partner in heaven (*Kabir*); *Taoist*: Regard your neighbour's gain as your gain: and regard your neighbour's loss as your own loss (*T'ai Shang Kan P'ien*); *Zoroastrian*: That nature only is good when it shall not do unto another whatever is not good for its own self (*Dadistan-i-dinik* 94.5). Quoted from S. G. Champion, *The World's Eleven Religions* (New York: Dutton, 1945), xviii. Cf. also Robert E. Hume, *The World's Living Religions* (New York: Scribners, 1924), pp. 265–67.

2. Consider, for example, the differences between the positive statement (Do unto others as you would have others do unto you) and the negative (as, e.g., the Hindu: "Do naught to others which if done to thee would cause thee pain"). This is a difference of content. The Christian version explicitly requires us us to do something—provide a benefit in some cases—whereas the negative versions require only that we avoid harming others. The Christian statement of the Rule would require action in some instances to prevent suffering or future injury, whereas the negatively phrased versions, as they are explicitly stated, would permit one to do nothing in these instances, since by one's inaction one would not oneself be causing the suffering or injury. Here the story of the Good Samaritan comes to mind. It seems that the priest and the Levite who did nothing for the half-dead man could be said to have lived up to the negative versions.

3. See chapter 3.

4. A readily accessible version is in Fogelin's *Understanding Arguments* (New York: Harcourt Brace Jovanovich, 1982).

5. See *Luke* 10:25–28 and elsewhere.

6. But see also R. M. Hare's treatment of it in *Freedom and Reason* (New York: Oxford University Press, 1963) and Alan Donagan's use of it as a fundamental of *The Theory of Morality* (Chicago: University of Chicago Press, 1979).

7. Marcus Singer, *Generalization in Ethics* (New York: Knopf, 1961), p. 16.

8. As Singer notes in *Generalization in Ethics*, pp. 63–65, generalization depends on our judgment of what is desirable or undesirable, but he provides no criterion for making that judgment.

9. *Morals and Values*, ed. Marcus Singer (New York: Scribners, 1977), p. 123.

10. From *Grounding of the Metaphysics of Morals* in *Immanuel Kant Ethical Philosophy*, trans. J. Ellington, ed. Warner Wick (Indianapolis: Hackett, 1983), n. 23, p. 37.

11. *Reasons and Persons* (Oxford: Clarendon Press, 1984), pp. 526, 523. In decisions affecting many people, we may be driven to use other procedures (see note 24), though it seems that we would often be driven to use the Rule's method as well. T. M. Scanlon, in "Contractualism and Utilitarianism," in *Utilitarianism and Beyond*, ed. A. K. Sen and B. Williams (Cambridge, Eng.: Cambridge University Press, 1982), takes the desire to act on reasonable agreement as a fundamental motive of morality and agrees that the idea of "changing places" provides a rough guide. He takes reasonableness to be the

decisive criterion. Observing that individual points of view may be simply irreconcilable in complex cases, he notes that " 'judgmental harmony' requires the construction of a genuinely impersonal form of justification which is nonetheless something which each individual could agree to" (p. 117). So he finds that the "fundamental question is what it would be unreasonable to reject as a basis for informed unforced agreement" (ibid.). Fair enough. But it seems that we could not hazard a guess as to what it would be reasonable for others to reject until we knew something of their specific situation—until we "changed places." Hence it seems that Scanlon is not removing the need to change places to acquire mutual awareness but rather extending it to more complex settings—those of constructing solutions together.

12. See, e.g., Owen Flanagan and Kathleen Jackson's "Justice, Care and Gender: The Kohlberg-Gilligan Debate Revisited" *Ethics* 97, no. 3 (1987): 622–37.

13. Lawrence Blum, *Friendship, Altruism and Morality* (Boston: Routledge and Kegan Paul, 1982), p. 89.

14. "Gilligan and Kohlberg: Implications for Moral Theory," *Ethics* 98, no. 3 (1988): 487.

15. John Mackie, *Ethics: Inventing Right and Wrong* (New York: Penguin, 1977; 1979) p. 88.

16. It should be acknowledged that the Rule is not applicable for decisions affecting masses of people. For such decisions scientific methods and decision procedures may be appropriate. In the (fairly rare) situations where we can make predictions about future choices of a portion of the population and can do so with a fair amount of accuracy, we can and should make policy decisions based on such predictions. Such predictions often have moral implications, and our choices must be based on the way the predicted consequences affect the well-being of the greatest number of persons. But it is important to note that these are methods that apply only to group behavior: they do not enable one to predict what specified members of the group will do. The original statistical description from which such predictions flow are not based on, nor do they predict, the behavior of specific members of the group. So long as this is true, the method of the Rule (and not a formula involving scientific predictions) must be used in judging cases involving specific free individuals.

There are tragic cases that we must decide in which the individuals involved are less than free. Although they may involve only a few individuals, we scarcely employ the changing places method, for we are unable to supply what anyone would want. When we must decide in a moment who is to be saved from a raging fire or a sinking ship, we are taken out of the situation of personal moral judgment and put into that of an administrator of benefits or of an avoider of harms. Fair treatment of all concerned may be out of the question: in these situations, the best we may be able to do is to minimize the harm (or maximize the gain). While it is true that in some cases we would be assisted in making these judgments by looking into the specific capacities and purposes of those involved, it is also true that in many cases it's not possible to do so. One may question whether these are to be called moral judgments, since they involve split-second and, perhaps, panicked responses. This point seems to be borne out by the fact that, ordinarily, we would be reluctant to assign moral blame to anyone for making an unsuitable decision in such situations. It seems more likely that, if we faulted them at all, we would fault them for defective judgment, and so on.

CHAPTER EIGHT. PERSONS AND PARTICULARS

1. See, e.g., Jonathan Dancy's "Ethical Particularism and Morally Relevant Properties," *Mind* 92 (1983): 530–47; and Lawrence Blum's *Friendship, Altruism and Morality* (London: Routledge and Kegan Paul, 1980).

2. "Foundations of the Metaphysics of Morals," in *Critique of Practical Reason and Other Works in the Theory of Ethics*, ed. T. K. Abbott (London: Longmans, Green, 1959), p. 61. [Kant's emphasis.]

3. *Critique of Practial Reason*, ed. Lewis White Beck (Indianapolis: Macmillan LLA, 1989), p. 32.

4. From "Foundations of the Metaphysics of Morals," in *Philosophical Writings*, ed. Volkmar Sander (New York: Continuum, 1986), p. 99.

5. Ibid.

6. Kant, *Critique of Practical Reason*, p. 30.

7. Ibid., p. 32.

8. Ibid., p. 45.

9. "Foundations of the Metaphysics of Morals," 86.

10. Ibid., p. 87.

11. Ibid., p. 86.

12. Ibid., p. 87.

13. Ibid., pp. 87–88.

14. *Generalization in Ethics* (New York: Alfred A. Knopf, 1961), p. 13. Singer here quotes Justice Holmes's statement from a Supreme Court case.

15. Singer, in his *Generalization in Ethics* , pp. 14–15. Singer also provides an illuminating discussion of the need and logical appropriateness of the particularized judgment.

16. *Ethical Studies* (Oxford: Clarendon Press, 1952), pp. 151–52.

17. Milton Mayeroff, *On Caring* (New York: Harper and Row, 1968).

18. In *Civilization and Its Discontents*, ed. James Strachey (New York: W. W. Norton, 1989), Freud makes this point. Marx makes a similar point in a number of his early writings. See, e.g., his " Feuerbachian Criticism of Hegel," in *Writings of the Young Marx*, ed. Easton and Guddat (Garden City, N.Y.: Doubleday Anchor Books, 1967), p. 281.

19. Studs Terkel, *Working* (New York: Avon, 1972), p. xxx. Terkel documents the point through interviews with a wide range of American workers, many of whom are alienated from their work experience.

20. In *The Doctor Stories* (New York: New Directions, 1984), pp. 119–25.

21. In *Working*, pp. 96–97.

22. Fyodor Dostoyevsky, *The Brothers Karamazov* (New York: Airmont, 1966), p. 239.

23. In "Moral Particularity," *Metaphilosophy* 18 (1987): 171–85.

24. See Michael Pritchard's "Self-Regard and the Super-Erogatory," in *Respect for Persons*, ed. O. H. Green (New Orleans: Tulane University Press, 1982).

25. *Recollections of Wittgenstein*, ed. Rush Rhees (Oxford: Oxford University Press, 1984), p. 185.

26. Ibid., p. 187.

27. Compare this with the swiftness of Kant's judgment about the man reduced to despair by "a series of evils."

28. *Recollections of Wittgenstein*, pp. 181-82

29. I refer to such promises and commitments as arise in the privacy of intimate relationships (such as those discussed by Carlos Williams) where volumes can be spoken by a smile or a lifted eyebrow; this point seems incontrovertible if one considers the well-known difficulty in defining the publicly observable conditions for making a promise. Thus, whereas the nature of persons and their personal involvements give us the line of inquiry to pursue in applying moral principle, the outcome of the inquiry will often be inconclusive or conceptually messy (or both).

30. The example was suggested to me by James Griffin.

31. This point was developed in chapter 4 under "Sketch of the Moral Anatomy."

32. Mayeroff, *On Caring*, develops this.

33. In "Dissertation on the Nature of Virtue" (in many editions).

34. As argued in chapter 4.

CHAPTER NINE. UNIVERSAL MORAL PRINCIPLE:
CRITICALLY RELATIVIZED MORAL JUDGMENTS

1. In the "Introduction" to *Rationality and Relativism*, ed. Martin Hollis and Steven Lukes (Oxford: Blackwell, 1985), p. 1.

2. See discussions by Bernard Williams ("An Inconsistent Form of Relativism") and David Lyons ("Ethical Relativism and the Problem of Incoherence") in *Relativism: Cognitive and Moral*, ed. Jack Meiland and Michael Krausz (Notre Dame, Ind.: University of Notre Dame Press, 1982).

3. Williams, p. 171.

4. Ibid. See also Walter Stace, "Ethical Relativity," in *The Concept of Morals* (New York: Macmillan, 1937).

5. See, e.g., Ruth Benedict, "Anthropology and the Abnormal," *Journal of General Psychology* 10 (January 1934).

6. In the introduction to the section "Moral Relativism" in *Relativism: Cognitive and Moral*, p. 8.

7. *Relativism: Cognitive and Moral*, p. 154.

8. See chapter 6.

9. *Relativism: Cognitive and Moral*, p. 8.

10. Philippa Foot, "Moral Relativism" in *Relativism: Cognitive and Moral*, pp. 152-67, and Meiland and Krausz's introduction to that chapter, p. 149.

11. In his "The Ethical Implications of Cultural Relativity," *Journal of Philosophy* 60, No. 7 (1963).

12. *Cultural Relativism* (New York: Random House, 1972), p. 31.

13. Cited by Richard Shweder, Elliot Turiel, and Nancy Much in "The Moral Intuitions of the Child," in *Social Cognitive Development*, ed. John

Flavell and Lee Ross (Cambridge, Eng.: Cambridge University Press, 1981), p. 301.

14. Ibid.

15. Ibid.

16. Ibid.

17. Alasdair MacIntyre suggests that only by being connected to actual and specific social practices does a rights claim become intelligible. MacIntyre, in setting aside recent attempts to provide objective bases for moral norms, comments: "One reason why claims about goods necessary for rational agency are so different from claims to the possession of rights is that the latter in fact presuppose, as the former do not, the existence of socially established sets of rules. Such sets of rules only come into existence at particular historical periods under particular social circumstances. They are in no way universal features of the human condition." After acknowledging that the existence of a term referring to rights is not a necessary condition for the embodiment of the concept of a right in forms of human behavior, he cautions that "those forms of human behaviour which presuppose notions of some ground of entitlement, such as the notion of a right, always have a highly specific and socially local character, and that the existence of particular types of social institution or practice is a necessary condition for the notion of a claim to the possession of a right being an intelligible type of human performance. (As a matter of historical fact such types of social institution or practice have not existed universally in human societies)" *After Virtue* [London: Duckworth, 1981], p. 65). What MacIntyre's discussion adds up to is that he thinks no rights claim is intelligible unless it is supported by a specific practice.

One should grant to MacIntyre that showing a good to be necessary to moral reasoning would not be intelligible as a rights claim in the sense that an individual could give such reasons and expect the right to be granted immediately to him or her. But it clearly is intelligible as a rights claim in the sense that we understand that members of the community have objective reasons for granting a condition to everyone as a right, if the condition is shown to be necessary for moral reasoning.

18. "Anthropology's Romantic Rebellion against the Enlightenment," in *Culture Theory: Essays on Mind, Self and Emotion*, ed. Richard Shweder and R. A. Levine (New York: Cambridge University Press, 1984), p. 28.

19. Ibid.

20. Shweder, Turiel, and Much, "Moral Intuitions," p. 301.

21. In his *Fifteen Sermons*, many editions, first published in 1726.

22. See Fogelin, *Understanding Arguments* (New York: Harcourt Brace Jovanovich, 1982), pp. 113–16.

23. Thomas Kuhn, *The Structure of Scientific Revolutions* (Chicago: University of Chicago Press, 1962), pp. 158–59.

24. Ibid.

25. "Internal Criticism and Indian Rationalist Tradition," in *Relativism*: *Confrontation and Interpretation*, ed. Michael Krausz (Notre Dame, Ind.: University of Notre Dame Press, 1989), pp. 299–326.

26. Peter Winch, *Idea of a Social Science* (London: Routledge and Kegan Paul, 1958), p. 123.

27. In *A History of Anthropological Thought*, ed. A. Singer (London: Faber, 1981), p. 128.

28. K. Wiredu, *Philosophy and an African Culture* (Cambridge, Eng.: Cambridge University Press, 1980), pp. 42–43.

29. See Max Black's "Reasoning with Loose Concepts," *Dialogue* 2: 1–12; Richard Grandy's "Reference, Meaning and Belief," *Journal of Philosophy* 70 (1973); and Donald Davidson's *Action and Events* (Oxford: Clarendon Press, 1980), pp. 238–39.

30. In "Reason and Ritual," in *Philosophy of Social Explanation*, ed. Alan Ryan (Oxford: Oxford University Press, 1973).

31. "Relativism in its Place," in *Rationality and Relativism*, ed. Martin Hollis and Steven Lukes (Oxford: Blackwell, 1985), pp. 261–306.

32. Ibid., p. 262.

33. Ibid., p. 265.

34. Ibid., referring to Habermas's *Knowledge and Human Interests* (London: Heinemann, 1972).

35. Shweder and Levine in *Culture Theory*, p. 28.

36. Sen and Nussbaum, "Internal Criticism and Indian Rationalist Tradition," pp. 304–5.

37. In "A Passage in Mill's Utilitarianism," in *Morality and Universality*, ed. Nelson Potter and Mark Timmons (Dordrecht: Reidel, 1985), p. 110.

CHAPTER TEN. MORAL ANATOMY AND MORAL REASONING: SUMMARY AND SUPPORT

1. In "A Plea for Excuses," *Philosophical Papers* (Oxford: Clarendon Press, 1961), p. 130.

2. *Dialectics of Action* (Chicago: University of Chicago Press, 1979), p. 24.

Index